The 91% Factor:

Why women initiate 91% of divorce, end most relationships, and what can be done about it.

The 91% Factor:

Why women initiate 91% of divorce, end most relationships, and what can be done about it.

By Edward Baiamonte

The American Political Press
215 Henry Street
Stamford, CT 06902
(203) 359-1186
BJE1000@AOL.COM

FIRST EDITION

- Library of Congress Cataloging-in-Publication Data

Baiamonte,Edward
   The 91% Factor: Why Women Initiate 91% of Divorce
Edward Baiamonte---- 1st ed.
      p. cm
   Includes bibliographical references and index
   ISBN 0-9631799-2-6
1. Divorced Women-United States-Case Studies 2.Love 3. Man-Woman

To all the women who so generously trusted me with stories
of the most intimate parts of their lives

Contents:

INTRODUCTION

Women should be ashamed of themselves for initiating 91% of breakups and divorce. Of course men are involved and they too should be ashamed, but apparently much less so than women. My thinking on this subject began a couple of years ago when a colleague mentioned to me that women initiate the vast majority of breakups and divorce. My first reaction was that this could not possibly be true. With all the talk about family values and divorce, it seemed that such a finding, if it were true, would have been widely circulated and that an acquisitive writer like myself would have heard it, remembered it, and wondered about why women are so much more inclined than men to end relationships.

If it were true that such a huge percentage of women all do the same thing, then it would probably also be true that they do it for the same or a similar reason. It would then only be necessary to discover that reason to know why women initiate 91% of divorce and, quite possibly, how divorce can be prevented. It seems obvious that if a man were going to marry a woman he should be informed, 1) that there is a 46% probability (assuming a 50% divorce rate) that his wife will want to divorce him, 2) why she will want to do it, and 3) what can be done to prevent it. Similarly, it seems obvious that if a woman were about to marry a man, she should be informed that there is a 46% probability that she will fall painfully out of love with and divorce her husband, why she will fall out of love, and what she can do to prevent it.

Sadly and pathetically, virtually all of today's polite and politically correct experts asseverate about divorce, and all failed sexual relationships, that they are merely disputes between two equal parties without drawing attention to the absolutely critical, gender based differences between the way men and women approach relationships and breakups. Despite some feminist willingness to blame men more than women we generally spare ourselves and the parties involved as much of the deathly pain associated with breakups and divorce as possible by pretending that both parties are equals even though nothing could be further from the truth. We react this way because we, 1) really don't know who to blame, 2) don't know even if one party or the other or both is to blame, 3) want to spare ourselves the pain of involvement, 4) want to spare the participants the pain and embarrassment of our involvement, 5) no longer have the values with which to determine blame, and, most importantly, 6) we increasingly live in a culture which wishes to see men and women as equal in all things even when the forces of evolution have created men and women specifically for their physical and behavioral differences. Accordingly, we have mistakenly begun to institutionalize the idea that we can have no-fault divorce, (as well as no fault crime, poverty, pregnancies, and school work) without encouraging more of exactly what it is that we want to discourage.

Men and women were created by evolution to be different and to behave differently in relationships. To say that both parties are equal parties to a divorce dispute is similar to saying that two child combatants on a playground, the United States and Japan in W.W.II, two neighbors with a zoning dispute, or two businessman with a disputed contract, are equal. Both parties to a dispute always have a story to tell, to be sure, but this does not mean both stories are equally legitimate or interchangeable.

If women are the ones whose family values overwhelmingly enable them to initiate divorce we ought to finally develop the courage and intellectual rigor to discover why this is so or why men provoke them to do it, or why men, if they are so provocatively anti-family, don't just end marriages themselves. If a pattern occurs 91% of the time we ought to learn about it despite our fears, manners, ignorance and/or laziness.

In fact, the more we are inclined to regard both parties to a relationship or divorce dispute as mere equals who are on some sort of legitimate quest for self development the more we lose our ability to shape and organize societal and individual behavior. This, we should be reminded, just is not consistent with civilization. In the case of divorce, our lack of understanding has naturally led to a great deal of divorce. Our children, for whom marriage is intended, have suffered the most and in unprecedented ways. Even if we don't wish to assign blame to women or men for the high rate at which they fail to honor their marital contracts we ought to at least identify and understand their specific behavior and how it may be encouraged or even provoked by the specific gender based behavior of the other party. In the end both sexes obviously have a responsibility to do the right thing before relationships can work but we simply cannot escape the idea that today's current psychological, cultural, and political environment has thoroughly confused men and women, and dramatically discouraged women from thoughtfully examining their marital sexual behavior in light of basic and inescapable biological realities. The most common explanation for divorce has become:

irreconcilable differences; this is exactly tantamount to: differences which we are too lazy or too cowardly to understand. But we must understand the differences and know how to reconcile them if we are to support relationships, marriages, families and children.

But, is the crucially important statistic true? Do women really initiate 91% of divorce? My first thought was to secure a court calendar, from the local courthouse, which contained a list of all the divorce cases which currently had a motion that was to be adjudicated before a divorce or family court judge. Having done that I found that there were several pages on the calendars which listed the Plaintiff and the Defendant in each case. The Plaintiff, for those who may not know, is the party who brings or initiates the legal action (in this case a divorce action) before the court. By counting masculine and feminine names I was able to determine that exactly 91 % of the Plaintiffs on that particular calendar were female. Other calendars at other times have turned up numbers down to a low of 80% but the average turned out to be 91%. This still wasn't proof, given the small numbers and limited geography involved, but it was getting close. Any reader who wants to see the actual court calendars can obtain copies from the publisher of this book or visit a local courthouse in her area to see how representative their immediate area is.

With a background that included some study of statistics (where you learn suspicion of statistics, if nothing else) I still was not really satisfied that women accounted for so much of divorce, but without the intention of using the information I let the matter drop. Then, I happened to be reading Shere Hite's popular book titled Woman And Love. On page 405 she said: "91% of divorces are initiated by women, according to this study-contrary to the popular stereotype that "men leave women." Ninety-one percent of women who have divorced say they made the decision to divorce, not their husbands. This is quite surprising, it so completely contradicts the popular view that it is the woman who is normally left, that women are more security-oriented than men, etc." Hite goes on as follows: "Most women say they tried for several years to improve their relationships before deciding to leave. And most ask for and receive divorces, not because the man is being unfaithful (even though he may be- also she may be), and not because of poor sex but because of loneliness and emotional isolation within the marriage." At that point I was convinced enough of the high bias toward women to begin thinking about why they would initiate 91% of divorce. Shere Hite's explanation that they were lonely and isolated merely described a overall negative condition that developed during the marriage, but the existence of such a condition prior to divorce was inherent. Who would expect women to report an overall positive condition prior to divorce? The real question had to do with whether there were common relationship dynamics that led to the development of the condition and whether couples can be made aware of that development dynamic in order to head it off.

Next, I began to thumb through books at my local book super store to see if the numbers were agreed upon and considered important by scholars and to see if the numbers had filtered down to those who write books for the very general audience that frequents such stores. It turned out that over several months of looking in various places I found only one more author who mentioned the numbers. While it seemed that she considered them important she was not able to explain why they were important or how important they were. This lone book, discovered after months of looking, was Ashton Applewhite's Cutting Loose-Why Women Who Divorce Do So Well. She got through the issue of women's proclivity to divorce very quickly and utterly without explanation by saying, "Well publicized figures showed a divorced man's income soaring while his ex-wife's took a nose dive, and until I read Susan Faludi's book Backlash, I believed them. If this was indeed what lay ahead, how come wives have always sought divorce in greater numbers than their spouses, two to one at the turn of the century, almost three out of four (71% in 1928, and 75% in the 1990's)?" Although the entire book does not go one tiny step deeper than saying, "my ex, who I mistakenly married, was really just a male chauvinist, let's pretend to ignore any excruciating agony that the divorce may have caused him, my new boyfriend delights in my independence and competence, and the kids are actually thriving, it does use the statistics about the high rate of female initiated divorce on the book jacket and on the second page as if to say: "the numbers are obviously important and very very compelling so I'm pointing them out to you, but I'm terribly sorry, I just don't know how to explain them or even what to say about them." She apparently wanted women to know the numbers and use them as sustenance toward their own divorces even though they represent a tragedy for husbands, children, and yes, wives too, something which she much later, grudgingly and contradictorily is forced to acknowledge.

Although Ms. Applewhite's numbers were somewhat lower than mine they did serve to confirm the basic notion that the vast majority of all divorce is initiated by women. Writing in The Journal Of Divorce, Antonette M. Zeiss, et., al, volume 4(2), winter 1980 confirms this by saying, "Thus, both men and women reported that it was the women who were more likely to initiate the separation in this sample." In another study Spanier and Casto found that 9 of 11 (82%) divorces are initiated by women. The remaining problem, then, to which the next 270 pages of this book is devoted, is to discover why women do what they do and what they or men can do about it. Please keep in mind that a marriage is a system created by a wife and husband. If we say we wish to identify and change the behavior of women we are not necessarily saying that their behavior is independent from their husband's behavior. As an intensely personal, often painful, and familiar topic, relationships and divorce, as a subject, leave the reader with infinite chances to withdraw from the intellectual arguments presented herein into evasive and comfortable, but mistaken, emotional or political assumptions. I can only beg the reader to resist these strong temptations and persevere to the end, with an open mind, before rendering a final judgement which, at that point, will at least be based on much new information about this very critical and rapidly developing subject. But first a thought on how such an important statistic (91%) managed to hide itself so well for so long from so many.

My first idea about this came from Dr. Gray who, when trying to explain the phenomenal success of his Men Are From Mars; Women Are From Venus book said, in effect, that due to the feminist movement whose credo was: men and women are the same, there was now a huge pent-up demand for the obviously true, but sequestered idea that men and women are actually different, or from Mars and Venus as he innocuously and defensively put it. We know that many women these days are too embarrassed to admit to being feminists for fear not only that it would label them but that it might also label them as shrill or even fanatical. Accordingly, it didn't seem that they exerted enough influence to hide such a crucial statistic, if indeed they cared about it at all.

But then I spoke with a veteran literary agent who gave me some insight about the way at least some of the world has begun to work over the last couple of decades. She said they had been talking about the statistic in her office with co-workers and they had agreed on the obvious answer to the question about why women initiate 91% of divorce. Their answer was: "because they're married to men." She then proceeded to describe her balding, lazy, paunchy husband to drive home the obviousness and universality of her point. Whether she was a feminist wife or maternal wife taking care of her wayward husband/child, or some other complex cultural/genetic derivative, I don't know, but it was very obvious that gender bigotry has become very natural for her, and probably for many in our society directly or perhaps indirectly through feminism. To this day Gloria Steinem is fond of militaristically stoking the fires by saying that not everybody can be your friend in a revolution. For feminists it is a revolution mostly against men; enemies are needed; often more than good ideas.

Perhaps, with the Louis Farrakhan and Promise Keeper's marches, during which men proclaimed to the heavens that they would re-assume their abandoned familial responsibilities, it is not surprising that so many women think as ill of men as many men apparently think of themselves. The above woman did, however, seem to confirm exactly what Dr. Grey was saying, i.e. there is pent-up demand for a more loving and balanced truth about men and women and marriage at a time when the truth has been hidden or shouted down by feminists (and others) whose influence seems to far exceed their numbers and whose political objectives are far more important to them than the personal marital consequences of those objectives on others.

Despite what they lack in number, feminism is very powerful in many of the most influential places. This is particularly true in New York City publishing, the Courts, Gov't agencies, the major news media, and in our Universities and Colleges. These are key and important places that provide the intellectual framework on which the rest of us unwittingly think and live. Feminists have found a home in those places; they don't need to be out among the general population to be very influential there. Feminists are as Christina Hoff Sommers said in her popular bestseller, Who Stole Feminism, "world class chatterboxes and great busy bodies" who exert influence way beyond what their numbers would suggest. In most universities, for example, there will be dozens of women's studies courses attended by only a handful of students while the practical career oriented courses that the vast majority of students must sign up for are actually fewer in number and often filled beyond capacity. Feminists are like intellectual guerilla soldiers or Green Berets. Everyone fears them. They are force multipliers who are expeit at multiplying their influence. Influence, they have taught us, has more to do with intensity, perseverance, and skill than with mere numbers, or rationality.

Since divorce has risen from 5% to 50% only in the last 30 years and since feminism has been influential only during that same period it does seem plausible that feminism may be responsible or at least a significant contributing factor to the high divorce rate and to the fact that we haven't as yet heard, understood, and dealt with what it is that finally makes women the gender that initiates 91% of divorce. Beyond feminists-lawyers, psychologists, and a "dumbed down" me first anti-authoritarian popular culture have all certainly contributed greatly to and profited from the rise in divorce. But perhaps most importantly, we have all contributed to divorce, by default, with our ignorance, disinterest and shyness. We're all shy about divorce, and heterosexual relationships in general. They are still relatively new topics to us despite the recent sexual and feminist revolutions. Feminists may not want us to know that men and women were created by nature or God to be different, and to relate differently to one another, and that women initiate 91% of divorce, but this is not to say that the rest of us would, if given the chance, regard this as a really engaging topic that we could comfortably embrace and study. We can talk about last night's dinner very easily but we can't talk about or learn about last night's sex nearly as easily. It is inherently a deeply private matter that, accordingly, we just don't know much about. Whether women divorce men because men are over-bearing male chauvinists or because men don't fulfill women's Barbie Doll fantasies or for some other reason, the subject is discomforting enough to be happily avoided by almost all of us all the time. Our broken homes, and children, serve as sad testimony to this.

Just this morning, for example, I heard a VISA credit card radio ad for consumer credit counseling. The ad started with the lie: "when Bill and I decided to divorce." Anyone who has looked at divorce at all knows that this is like saying: "when Japan and the United States decided to go to war." In fact there are no no-fault wars and there are no no-fault divorces. One party takes the step. They file the papers, commit adultery, abuse their spouse in some other way, and inevitably accuse their spouse of being the party at fault. With the now easy habit of acknowledging divorce and hiding the gender anomaly contained therein we're hiding the obvious pattern in divorce, and other broken sexual relationships, from each other. And, as importantly, we're hiding from the pain from which real knowledge and understanding can grow.

A woman doesn't want to tell her next lover that she divorced her husband lest he fear suffering the same fate at the hands of an unjust woman. A divorced man doesn't want to tell his next lover that he was the victim of divorce lest she too think him unworthy. In whatever circumstance or environment the subject of divorce and broken sexual relationships comes up it is most commonly characterized by our ability to develop new reasons to become comfortable with and accepting of the idea of gender free no-fault divorce, but until this book we have not been able to acknowledge and understand the critical gender differences which lie at the heart of the divorce/relationship revolution and, therefore, we have not been able to stem the tragic tide toward broken homes for ourselves and our children.

1.) THE SEX LIVES OF COUPLES IN TROUBLE

THE WOMAN WHO CONFUSES SEX AND LOVE

Relationships and diet are very similar. The more we discover about them the more certain we are that we should adhere to nature's biological model. It took us 10 million years to discover that nature's dietary model was better for us than our own ingenious corporate / chemical inventions, but we still are too buffeted by special interests and our own imperfect natures to have discovered that nature's sexual relationship model is far better for us than our own modern and whimsical inventions. Human culture may produce a thousand ways to view marriage and diet but in the end we are forced to acknowledge and act on the biological basis of them if we want to survive. In the end biology leaves us no choice but to do its bidding. Our tiny biological brains allow us to perceive and understand only the tiniest fraction of the universe and so our concerns and endeavors can in the end only be biology's concerns and endeavors.

Below are some examples of the complications that result from ignoring nature's relationship model. The first couple, sadly, is not happily married. The wife earns most of the money and does most of the house work and child rearing. She is an avid reader of romance novels (some would say: female pornography) with Fabio or his imitators on the cover. She constantly berates her husband and threatens him with divorce. The husband generally prefers to hang out with the guys, pretty much as he did when he was growing up. Both parents love and care for the kids, although certainly not with the same level of enthusiasm and attention.

Each parent is interested in the other sexually. The husband, typically, is much more frequently interested. His frequent sexual advances are often rejected by an angry, frustrated, and neglected wife. Considering the high probability of rejection his advances (always nonverbal) have become very tentative and always incorporate a dignified escape route. His interest is so strong and typically male, though, that if it is not satisfied romantically he just transforms it so that the emotional distance between them becomes the basis for his relentless sexual interest in his wife. If she won't be his lover, he'll settle for her as his whore or fantasy sexual object. Mystery, anger, distance, unavailability, and romance can easily stimulate sexual passion in men. In this case, emotional distance made the wife seem something like the alluring women in the strip clubs that he frequented.

This is not to say that he is turned off when they are emotionally close. On the contrary, like most men, he is just highly sexed; not good or evil, or consistent. He'll take it any way it comes, thank you. Nature has sent him on a mission and he is dutifully flexible about the context in which he carries out his mission of love.

If the wife in this family wanted to play the role of an alluring wife and mother or that of a tough, whip toting dominatrix, or anything in between, he, like most men, almost certainly would play along. When she asked, "does it hurt yet" he would say, "yes, but please go on." If she wanted to offer him her body in thanks for having spent a trying evening helping the kids with homework he, again, would almost certainly go along.

For love to exist it needs a context and women can easily provide that context for their very focused and goal oriented men. In fact, women always provide a context for love. The problem is that it is most often context by default rather then context by volition. Something must be on a woman's mind beyond raw sex when she makes love and it can be virtually anything she chooses. Beyond pure sexual pleasure a woman must know why she makes love. Is it because her lover goes out to get high with the guys or because he helps the kids with their homework? Is it because he cares about what a long day she has had or is it because he sat around all night watching television?

A woman can civilize a man; she can provide the right context for love by sexually insisting on the loving behavior that she was so easily able to encourage at the beginning of her relationship when her man was so eager to please in anticipation of their first sexual encounter. Even if loving behavior wasn't there in the beginning, there is nothing to prevent her from putting it there later. Men will often settle for their wives as detached lovers, and wives will often acquiesce under male pressure to being detached lovers but in the end this makes women far more uncomfortable than men. Women must learn that where there is sex there can also be love.

In this case, the wife's infrequent advances (always non-verbal too) typically consist of lingering naked a few seconds longer before bed, or wearing fewer clothes to bed, or simply not moving away from him as he cautiously slides closer to her. She can't simply tell him that she wants

1.) THE SEX LIVES OF COUPLES IN TROUBLE

him for three typically female reasons: 1) she fears rejection even though it is highly unlikely; almost an impossibility, 2) it is still in her biological nature to be coy, and most importantly, 3) she doesn't want to give him the idea that she approves of his generally unloving behavior.

Unfortunately, though, her sexual needs often get the best of her and he does get the idea that she does approve of him, at least enough to keep him somewhat satisfied sexually, and enough to keep the marriage intact and stumbling painfully forward. Even a psychologist, who might be tempted to offer years of expensive therapy to this couple, would probably feel despair at the thought of trying to help them overcome generations of poor habits on both sides of the marriage. Nature's biological model, however, offers inexpensive, quick, and real help.

The wife who so desperately longs for a loving marriage would have to accept the idea that her job as a wife requires her to manage her sex life; to just communicate and say, "no." "No, I won't make love to you until you give me half your pay check, or take me out to dinner, or brush my hair, or take the kids to the beach." This would admittedly be a big and difficult step for her, but it is a clear and obvious step. She and the rest of us, have all taken many big steps before. She got married, gave birth, went to job interviews, got fired, got sick, watched loved ones die, had fights with relatives, etc. The problem with relating to her husband arises not so much from the complex psychological difficulty of the task but rather from the simple failure to realize the appropriate context for marital sex. She, like all women, desperately wanted love, but she lacked a simple working definition of the very thing she wanted most.

How did she ever come to think that she could have a loving relationship with a husband to whom she could not deny sex? The answer is simple. In the beginning she played her biological role. She played coy; he eventually impressed her; then they made love and got married. Now she doesn't play coy, he doesn't impress her, and they don't make love very often. When they do it's certainly not with the Zen like harmony that truly joined lovers feel. Why should there be harmony? He wants sex and she wants a loving husband and father for her children. From her point of view the problem is simply that her husband has become an irresponsible insensitive bum; not that she too has become an irresponsible insensitive bum by letting him reap the sexual rewards of family life without paying

12

the same price she unconsciously made him pay in the beginning. She has given up the unconscious discipline of love that was so obvious and natural to her in the first few days and weeks of the relationship.

A husband who gets sex because he wants it is as contradictory as an employee who gets a paycheck because he wants it rather than because he earned it. When a couple's sex life is out of biological perspective this way, their marriage is out of perspective. If the man is getting sex, even infrequently, he will be happier and more content in the marriage. The woman in this typical situation will be far less happy. Deprived of the affection she so cherishes and clueless about what to do she will be more depressed than even single women and inclined to be among the 91% of women who initiate divorce.

In a similar vain, another man I knew ended his wife's second marriage (his first) by saying, "I'll never come back in this bed again." This is a real switch. In both of his wives' divorces the husbands took action because they were repelled by the pressure to satisfy a seemingly insatiable woman. It seemed that the second wife, a Ph.D. no less, liked the feeling of having her man constantly inside her even though it didn't often lead to an orgasm for her. Although this intense expression of female sexuality is somewhat unusual it is very consistent with what we constantly hear about women and what biologists tell us about them, namely, they value the feeling of closeness as much or more than a sweaty; often elusive orgasm. This is understandable to a biologist since the female orgasm is mostly irrelevant in the sense that it is not required for procreation (nature's primary purpose for breeding us) and may even impede it.

What makes this case very unusual is the degree to which this liberated woman pursued her own narcissistic and non-orgasmic sexual/closeness interests. Rather than use sex as an avenue to her husband's heart she aggressively used it to satisfy her own isolated sexual needs. She was much like a man in her drive to get what she personally wanted from sex, and in mistaking it for a complete relationship. Most women are forced to settle for the pretense of getting theirs during or before foreplay, while the man is actually impatiently waiting for intercourse, or immediately after the man has come but before he leaves or falls asleep. This woman insisted on exactly what she wanted, got it, and in so doing ruined two marriages. She had sex in a non-biological context.

She turned the basic biological model upside down, got divorced twice, and was deeply lonely despite ongoing psychological therapy. She quite mistakenly saw herself as the victim of her first husband's premature ejaculation and her second husband's lack of interest in family. The later argument was easy to make since the second husband had a horrible childhood and, as an adult, was very committed to a long term, promising, and high level cancer research project that conveniently left him with few other concerns or needs.

This was all very fertile and profitable ground for her therapist. He spent months exploring the abnormal or dysfunctional childhood that led the second husband to his final impotent pronouncement. Then they explored the first husband's premature ejaculation problem. When they finished, they could then start on her childhood, which featured two fathers, both of whom abandoned her (just like her husbands later did), and presumably caused her to so aggressively cling to and drain her poor husbands of all their sexual desire. Sorting through all of this history using the psychotherapeutic method in order to understand all the forces that shaped her life and personality would have been a monumental if not impossible task; something that only a "paid by the hour" therapist would love. A simple focus on her current sexual modus operandi really was all that was needed.

The woman above who was abandoned by both of her fathers and husbands might have followed a few simple guidelines based on biological common sense. These guidelines would have gotten either of her marriages closer to nature's model and probably would have been sufficient to save both of them. Those rules are 1) don't give your man too much sex; this is the opposite of what the pursuit oriented male was bred for by the forces of evolution. It is certain to kill his sexual interest in you; if not his entire interest in you and the outside world. We all remember the classic Gene Kelly movie: Singing In The Rain, which demonstrated how even a rainy day can seem wonderful to an amorous man. It reminds us that sexual energy charges a man's whole life; not just his sex life. Everything from a rain soaked street to the smart lines of a new car is little more than a prop in nature's testosterone laden sexual production. If a man has too much sex, much of his reason for being disappears, 2) if you insist on a lot of sex, learn to be more orgasmic so you too will have a resting phase that perhaps will coincide a little more with his, 3) learn how to masturbate or to have sex with him in different ways that do not always involve an orgasm for him. This will keep his interest high, but not satiated, the way it generally is from puberty to marriage, and the way it was during the long period when humans evolved without the benefit of constant marital sex; and most importantly, 4) remember that too much free sex is actually opposite to the expensive biological sex that men must purchase or earn with various kinds of good or impressive behavior.

When women stop playing the romantic role they were evolved to play their marriages often falter and they will then often initiate a divorce. They blame their husband for his new found insensitivity or overbearing nature. It often never occurs to them that they were equally or more responsible for what their marriage became. This process occurs because the side of them that is evolved to be maternal and nurturing, and to therefore look for nurturing from their mates, overrules their sexually powerful and selective side that at one time was used, albeit unconsciously, so skillfully to compel their mates to behave with affection and reciprocity. It seems so obvious to them that if they can be nurturing and affectionate, then their mates should be too. In reality this is no more obvious than a man feeling that if he can enjoy a football game his wife should be able to enjoy it too. Nature specifically and purposely bred men and women for different behaviors and did so for good reasons which should only be gently tampered with by those who thoroughly understand the complex ramifications of doing so.

Women who divorce mostly see themselves as innocent victims of their husband's new insensitivity or the old insensitivity which they never saw. But in the end they accomplish very little by responding through divorce. It leaves them alone, and still without a method to gain the connection and nurturing they seek, or, re-married with the probability of the second marriage being shorter than the first. When Samuel Johnson spoke of, "the triumph of hope over experience" he was actually addressing a statistical truth about second marriages, i.e., that they are shortened repeats of the first marriage.

Women who stay with their husbands after 20 years of physical abuse suffer from a similarly destructive, although exaggerated, mentality. They are excessively loyal, (as well as scared to leave the nest) which is an essential characteristic given a man's fluctuating fortunes as he does battle with the indomitable outside world, and their sense of sexual power has been so severely diminished for so long that assertive sexual self-defense or divorce does not even appear on their internal list of options. Rather than blame their aggressive husbands they make the easier feminine choice of blaming themselves. It seems to them like a far less dangerous approach. Unfortunately, weak women and weak people in general, often have a tendency to justify acquiescence to and acceptance of superior strength as a psychological trick to rationalize their fear and inability to resist it. This is an equally irrational manifestation of a lack of purposive sexual power. Deborah Tannen writes of this when she says: One time he beat her so badly that she was knocked unconscious. When she came to he said, "I guess it's over." She replied, "I still love you." What he saw as a blow so vicious that it would surely drive her away, she saw as a chance to prove once and for all that her love was truly unconditional. Even with such provocation, she did not consider defiance or challenge to be an available response." If she could love him more he would beat her less, she thought, when in reality it is always the purposive application of female sexual power that creates love; where it does not exist neither does love.

1.) THE SEX LIVES OF COUPLES IN TROUBLE

A FANTASY ABOUT ANIMALS

Allison was a proud, authoritative, and gorgeous airline stewardess, certainly the kind of woman that many a dreary businessman must have dreamed about. In her late thirties she was finally seduced into marriage by a wealthy businessman whose limousines often picked her up at exotic international airports. After two years and one beautiful child Allison was divorced and without the job or husband on which her self-esteem had come to be derived. When asked why she was divorced she explained that her husband fell out of love when it seemed to him that she was no longer the beautiful and elusive stewardess with whom he had fallen in love.

In reality, she had become a mother/housewife who offered free sex to the man who had often traveled half way around the world for it. From Allison's point of view the mileage change had changed the context of her relationship and there was nothing she could do to maintain the sexual unavailability and attractiveness that her career had given her.

After the divorce she was in a bad state. When asked for a date Allison's psychological state quickly became apparent. She would actually warn prospective suitors that she was just a sales clerk at Lord & Taylor and therefore perhaps not very suitable as a date. But she had a saving grace. She was beautiful and she loved sex almost as purely as a man. She even noted that masturbation was the escape that got her through her divorce. This encouraged her to take an occasional date and the men to happily overlook her circumstantial career deficit. The relationships quickly became sexual prompting one date to say, at the most obvious moment, "Allison I love you." Allison, having realized that her date had stopped taking her out after the first two dates and now seemed to prefer sex exclusively, compassionately replied, "don't fall for me, you love this (the sex); not me." She broke off the affair that night, despite her sexual interest, having concluded that he did not really love her.

For her date, the inclination to find a larger value in sex; to connect sex with love, was a given, but for her there was absolutely no larger value to sex although it provided her with a great deal of pleasurable distraction. If her date had said, "I love the way your vagina feels on my penis" it would have made honest sense to Allison and perhaps not have disturbed her as much, but talk of love deeply upset her when she was just having sex. She had assumed that since he had stopped taking her out he

17

did not really care for her. She had ignored the fact that just days before he had taken her out based on the mutual, though unstated understanding that it would not be appropriate to immediately just take her to bed. In her mind, the decision to go directly to bed was completely out of her hands and accordingly it said everything about his real interests and nothing about hers. She was a helpless romantic waif carried away by a masculine breeze. He, like many men, failed the test that she and biology had unconsciously given.

Like most women in relationships that become troubled, Allison controlled the scenario in the very beginning and then inexplicably and totally, relinquished it, thus depriving herself of the larger more protracted loving relationship on which she would have thrived. Sex is never about sex for a female. It is about everything but sex. In this case sex was about a female sales clerk who was certain that she didn't deserve to be loved and it was about a typical female who surrendered her sexual authority to a man. She quickly gave up the natural role that even she played well (despite her unusually high sex drive), at least in the beginning, and thus never found out whether her date would have been willing to love her both in and out of bed. Allison, like most women, knew to be sexually modest and selective prior to marriage or an affair in order to avoid non-marital pregnancies, but she failed to realize that after marriage or after the start of any sexual relationship the same lessons need to be applied over and over again if the relationship is to have any sense or purpose for either party.

At one point Allison was asked about her sexual fantasies. She was finally coaxed into revealing her most frequent fantasy; not surprisingly love was not a part of it. In fact she fantasized about being overwhelmed by a pack of very friendly and sexually aroused animals whose behavior needn't be described in great detail here. While most women dream of being overwhelmed and loved by a Fabio/Prince Charming type or perhaps by a genuinely equal mate, this woman had replaced those mere mortals with animals who made certain that the complicated relationship between human love and sex would never disturb her very active sexual fantasy life. In practice Allison's high sexuality actually contradicted her desire to be loved. She wanted sex as much as dinner; her mates wanted sex more than dinner, and as a result they had a lot more sex than dinner.

Her animal friends couldn't take her to dinner and so she was free to just have sex with them. It would seem that the less sex is connected with love the less civilized and useful our fantasies and behavior become. In the end Allison's mistaken perceptions about the meaning of sex prevented her from knowing how to love her husband and her subsequent lover and actually caused her to dump them both and leave herself desperately alone.

THE CASE OF THE ANGRY MALE LOVER

I happened to call Cheryl on business one day just at the time her ex-boyfriend was moving his belongings out of her apartment. The next time we talked I couldn't resist asking her to tell me about the breakup. She was very shy about just jumping in with even a general explanation. Instead she deflected the issue by asking me to tell her the theme of this book. I explained to her that the theory generally had to with the importance of a woman managing a couple's sex life as a means to insure that the overall relationship would meet her romantic and practical expectations as well as her partner's sexual needs. She then jumped back with, "well what about the case where the sex is great but the rest is awful." I then asked her to explain what she meant by great sex. This of course was difficult for a basically shy person but she managed to indicate that when he walked in the room she definitely felt something special tingle inside her. When I asked her why she had thrown the poor guy out if the sex and the general attraction to him was still so positive, she said, "he was a very angry person."

Knowing that many women perceive men as angry and that most men do have anger at or close to the surface, thanks to the testosterone that nature gave them in order that they be successful hunters, I asked, "what was the best example of his anger that you could share with me." She said, "if we went bicycling and I forgot my helmet he would absolutely blow up at me and that would ruin the whole day." When I suggested that she could have fixed that easily enough by merely refusing to make love to him again until he promised and at least partially succeeded in getting his anger under control, she began to consider the possibility. I then asked her how she could have great sex with a guy who was angry at her? She defended herself by saying, He wasn't angry at me in the beginning and by the time he began to show his anger we were already in love and sort of obligated to make love regularly anyway.

What actually happened here was that Cheryl had finally thrown the bum out because she had finally realized that there is no great sex without a great relationship. After all, if the sex truly had been great she undoubtedly could have limited their relationship to just sex and still have had something great in her life. But in her heart she knew that great sex was not important or even desirable to her without a concomitantly great relationship and so she threw him out not having a clue about what other

20

options she had.

To her, he was a big, powerful, testosterone laden man who turned her on, but also a man cast in stone who could not be corrected by a little woman. This was a stubbornly typical female attitude. She held it tightly because it did reflect her heart (a weak woman can't change a strong man) and also because it completely freed her from any responsibility in the management or demise of her own relationship. It was all his fault that she had to end their relationship. She could react destructively to a situation, but she couldn't manage it positively. In a sense she was reacting biologically. A woman, historically at least, could passively gather what nature provided for her while a man could actively hunt and build to create what he wanted. But this is not to say that she can't understand biology and use that understanding to her advantage. Her mistake was acknowledged when she said, "he wasn't angry in the beginning." A man is born with testosterone and it certainly was there in the beginning but the anger it can cause was controlled because he knew he wouldn't get to first base with a prospective mate by being angry with her.

In the beginning Cheryl was in control of his testosterone because her estrogen was in control of her. It dictated that she maximize the value of any pregnancy that might result from a prospective mate by slowly selecting for a mate whose testosterone seemed to yield the appropriate result when directed toward the outside world (primarily money in today's terms) and also the appropriate result when directed toward the inside familial world (primarily long term non-angry love). Cheryl, and her boyfriend, did what nature intended in the beginning, but afterwards she stopped insisting on loving behavior and quickly jumped into bed for what she began to think of as "great sex." In reality it was only the memory or dream of great sex. For a woman there is no great sex without a great relationship because biology requires both simultaneously as a means to insure not only that children will be conceived but that they will be cared for too. In reality she was encouraging the anger that led her to violently throw her boyfriend out. The great sex she imagined was just a sub-conscious recollection of the sex they had in the beginning, when she was doing biology's bidding, and not related to anything that happened afterward as a result of her changed behavior.

At one point I said to Cheryl, "if simple anger was the fault why didn't you just tell him that you would end the relationship unless he controlled his anger. Her answer was threefold; she said: 1) I did but he didn't readily admit that he was angry. He felt that his anger was justifiable; that I was sometimes stupid for forgetting my helmet etc., 2) I didn't really press the point because in my heart I believed he was essentially an angry person based on a long history that I was not going to change, 3) at a certain point chemicals take over; love unconsciously vanishes. I moved on to another person, or the dream of another person, or the solitude of being alone and free from the anger.

On the whole this was fairly insightful stuff but it did not even allude to a long term solution. Her pattern had long since been established and probably had been repeated dozens of times over 30 years of failed relationships. She was well educated, had a successful career, had many intelligent single friends with whom she undoubtedly discussed relationships, had read most of the relationship bestsellers, and even had a best friend and business partner who was chairperson of the psychology department at a major university, but she still had no exposure to the biology of relationships. Biology would have dictated that she stop her sex partner during the middle of the so called "great sex" and say " ya know what, just because we're going steady doesn't mean I'm your property to have sex with anytime you choose, I'm not going to finish this until I see a commitment to controlling your anger. Sex is not about getting off. It's is about getting in or getting together and I won't let that happen if you're angry. Doesn't it feel nice to love me;would you like to continue?"

This would not guarantee success of course. In certain cases, for what ever reason, anger might be more important than a relationship. Perhaps, even, he was angry because he was having sex with a woman who he didn't find inherently appealing. Maybe the anger was a way to start a conflict that would cause her to end a relationship that he actually wanted to end. Whatever the case, a biological approach to the problem would lead to a systematic and deliberate resolution. Probably a resolution that would have give her the love she craved and him a more civilized view of women and family.

Another woman I knew remarked to me that her ex-husband laughed uncontrollably when he entered the bathroom one day to find that she had lit it up with dozens of candles. He was so accustomed to getting basic sex when he wanted it, and on his terms, that her sexual/romantic interests (and certainly most of her other interests too) had slowly become totally irrelevant to him. From his point of view they were irrelevant to her too. She had given up so much of her sexual power that she barely existed to him as more than a sexual receptacle. Extend this attitude down through all the hundreds of less important interactions of a marriage, and a wife will feel completely pushed out of her husband's life. She may initially blame herself and struggle to get back into her husband's life but eventually our feminist / psychological pop culture will present divorce as the only remaining option. Instead of buying into pop culture, all this poor woman had to say to her husband was, "oh, you don't find my candles romantic today; then maybe you will tomorrow. I'll see you then." Instead, she resorted to taking a stiff drink each night before she made love to him, his way. "Sex was at least tolerable that way," she said.

Finally, she resorted to divorcing her husband, having come to believe that he didn't have a romantic bone in his body. He was completely shocked, never having been awakened from his male daze and never having been told that the sexual and emotional life they shared had long been totally unsatisfactory to her. The divorce represented her violent and thoughtless feeling that romance ought to be somehow maintained by natural chemistry and compatibility rather than with the thoughtful application of female sexual power.

Colette was a beautiful heiress debutante type, but all was not exactly right where the elite meet. Somehow Colette had turned 50. She was struck hard by the notion that she was still bereft of family and had been so most of her life. Aided by a frenetic personality she had been busily engaged all her life with the perks of privilege but in the end it dawned on her that friends and suitors had not flocked to her door as she surely thought they would.

As a child she was kept very busy with her horses and skiing. This was fine because she was really too good for most of the people she might meet. To further complicate the situation her parents didn't really like the lecherous boy debutantes in her social circle. To them it was safest to teach her that the little rich boys were arrogant punks who might get their precious daughter pregnant. They did avoid what they saw as an ultimate evil by drumming this extreme approach into her head, but the price to be paid for this approach to sex education was steep. Colette grew up to be extremely erratic toward men. She loved them (thanks to biology)and she hated them(thanks to her parents). To complicate things she was raped while doing her junior year at the Sorbonne, and again in her 40's during a first, brief one year marriage.

When she dated, the men seemed to her to be a combination of the arrogant male debutante punks who her parents had warned her about, the rapist husband who had confirmed that her parents were probably right about many things, and the Prince Charming who never quite showed up to take her to the ball. Or, they were the opposite: wimpy lovers who could be seduced and used to very quickly fill a rich heiress's empty life with marriage and children. Wimpy lovers now seemed to be her best hope of ever being lovingly connected to other people.

When Colette spoke of her ex-husband (from a 1 year long marriage) she mentioned how he frenetically spent her money and how rough he was in bed. "He pinched, he groped, he bit, he woke her up in the middle of the night and attempted to do awful things," she claimed. When I asked her how she could have married such a man she said with perfect defensiveness, "he was very sweet in the beginning." Colette was a wonderful example of intense or exaggerated femininity caused by exaggerated experiences. Her husband traveled the long journey from sweet lover to rapist in one short year and she was just along as an innocent observer. Extreme events defined her love life for her. She was powerless to understand these events let alone work toward an approach to control them.

In the course of so thoroughly teaching their daughter to resist the advances of men they had also taught her that there was nothing to do with men but to resist the strong ones, and dominate the wimpy ones. The middle ground seemed lost to her forever, but not so much because she was overtaken by a deprived childhood and some tragic adult experiences but because she lacked a simple intellectual understanding of the female's biological role. Without that understanding she was reacting out of pure emotion much the way caveman blindly reacted to the setting sun.

The extreme emotionality and ignorance which formed Colette's world view is practically institutionalized today. The recent case of the aids bandit brings this to mind. The so called aids bandit was a handsome smooth talking black guy from the big city, who happened to have aids, and who infected 13 young teenage girls from one small upstate town by selling them drugs in return for sex. When Ron Qubie, who nicely symbolizes the modern liberal elite socialist intellectual class, was asked about this his response was that we should immediately airlift a plane full of condoms and sex educators to this hopelessly provincial upstate town.

In Mr. Qubie's twisted mind biology played no part. He much preferred his own version of the way the world works. His version of biology is as follows: we don't think 13 year girls should be having sex, but if you find yourself agreeing to be raped by an adult who promises to provide you with drugs at least see if he'll wear a condom. There is always the concession to biology (we don't think 13 year old girls ought to be having sex) but then comes the resounding acquiesce to non-biological modern decadence(they're going to do it anyway).

Asking an infected rapist to wear a condom before sex is far different from asking a husband to eternally love you and your children before sexual intercourse, but Ron Qubie and much of modern culture can no longer make the distinction. Colette was never able to bring an extreme childhood into adult balance and it is certain that many of today's teenagers who are being subjected to modern versions of extreme sex will face the same problem as adults. The central problem of Colette's life, and many other lives is to acquire the biological understanding, not obtained in childhood, that will enable her to successfully manage a husband, marriage and children. Indeed this is the most important education any human being can have; yet it is something that Colette's parents denied her and something that Ron Qubie and the society he represents are systematically denying our children. Sex in the correct context leads to love as biology intended while sex in some arbitrary context leads nowhere or worse.

Susan was one of those rare and blessed women who actually was able to regularly have and thoroughly enjoy multiple orgasms. This set up an very interesting dynamic in her relationships. It made her the one who got the most direct and obvious benefit from frequent sex. More importantly, it reversed the basic sexual dynamic in the relationships. She was the sexually possessed partner who had to seek out sexual fulfillment from her men. This instantly upset the biological balance except in the case of one man who truly loved her and was happily prepared to deal with it.

But Susan had an interesting history too. Pregnant at 18, married at 19, and divorced at 20, she had never really had time to fall in love with her husband, but she was horny; then pregnant, and so she married him and hoped for the best. He definitely didn't think he was in love, but he did the honorable thing too and agreed to marry her. His disappointment at the unwanted turn of events quickly turned to anger which was mostly directed at Susan. Susan was a stunning girl. She was easy to look at and easy to love. He did care for her but it seemed hard to believe that her presence in his life had so quickly ended all his youthful dreams. A whole world of youthful possibilities had instantly vanished with Susan's pregnancy. Still, over the next 25 years he was the preferred parent although both parents dearly loved and raised their child.

When Susan finally could no longer stomach her husband's anger she placed herself among the 91% of women who initiate a divorce. Her husband responded, "you go but leave the baby." After Susan left, with the baby of course, the husband stayed in touch with his ex-mother-in-law for a full year begging that if only she would come back everything would be alright. Finally he gave up. 25 years later he hates Susan as the woman who destroyed his marriage and harmed his child. To him she was too immature to forgive and correct the mistakes of a very callow young man in a very difficult position. Susan describes her ex-husbands second wife as "a lucky bitch" because she is treated wonderfully by a husband who wants to insure that his love will never be misunderstood or taken for granted.

Susan may have wanted to forgive her ex-husband but emotionally it is extremely difficult for a physically weaker woman to forgive and trust a stronger male who has, and could again, make her live in a state of constant fear and frustration. It is impossible to overestimate the importance of male physical strength in defining the nature of female love. When women give affection it is in large part an expression of the trust they need to feel that the male's superior strength will never be used against them. This is a critical element in female love that does not exist in male love. Women may argue and fight with men but for them it is extra stressful not only because it is opposed to their maternal nature but because deep in their hearts they fear that it will lead to a physical confrontation which they desperately dread out of a legitimate fear that they will lose. This helps explain why women cannot easily forgive, even to save their marriages and children. Anyone who was ever around a bully during childhood knows how a married woman can feel. The fight that would be lost externally has to be won internally.

Susan had been a tomboy as a child who was forced to fight it out with seven brothers and two sisters. On a date, decades after her divorce, she once threw her date down face first on the bed, jumped on his back and twisted his arm up high on his back. She then said, "you can't get out can you, I'll bet you can flip me right off." It was part feminist conscienceness and part tomboy nostalgia that led Susan to find out whether her lover could be trusted in the face of extremely assertive female behavior. Unbeknownst to Susan her lover loved her, and trusted her judgement throughout the instantaneous event. He was happy that she was comfortable enough around him to be so impulsively assertive. Additionally, he was an accomplished kickboxer who wasn't the slightest bit intimidated or reactive in the face of what seemingly, to him anyway, was merely a playful or erotic attack. By not responding aggressively he passed the unusual test.

As an adult in her forties Susan was multi-orgasmic and insatiable, but still very warm and tender, perhaps because she knew how to find men around whom she could be really free and comfortable, and perhaps because she knew, and by osmosis, taught her men exactly how it had to be. For a woman with the rare physical self-assurance to drive a motorcycle this is all perhaps easier than for an average woman. But what's a man to do with a woman like Susan who has more orgasms than he has? For Susan's lover it happened naturally. He knew that with Susan his relatively infrequent orgasms would have to be secondary. This was an exact reversal of his entire previous history. But he loved Susan in part because she had many guy things (motorcycles, skiing, golf, etc.) in common with him, and because he was genuinely interested in making her happy. When he was in Susan it was not for his orgasm as much as it was for hers. He loved her and wanted to do for her above all; that was the source of his new found self-control; not mental images of Yogi Berra. For her it was ideal, and for him it worked out well too. By not coming each time they had sex he didn't go through the withdrawal that men often experience after sex. His high level of interest in Susan was then relatively constant, giving her the measure of control over him that she would occasionally need. They were both sexually very happy; this nicely set the stage for the rest of their relationship which already had the advantage of several shared activities, interests, and values.

The biological lessons here are simple. Susan's first marriage and divorce followed a perfectly predictable path because at that point in her life she had no idea how to use sex to correct and maintain a marriage that she wanted desperately. Later in life she matured as an individual thanks to feminism, an inexplicable and fortuitous meteoric rise in her sex drive, and a general maturity that had slowly developed with time. These allowed her to synchronize her body and mind with the men she dated, but deep in her heart there remained scars that prevented her from ever again making another marital commitment. She had grown up in a huge family where individual intimacy was nearly impossible; then there was the brief childhood marriage followed by 25 years of failed relationships. By her mid forties she was proudly independent and very lonely. What she lacked most was a concept of a what a sexual marriage was and the faith that such a marriage could be reliably maintained. She was good at sex, but never realized it could be the foundation of love and the other things see needed in a relationship. Her habit was that love ended as it always had, starting with her parents. She was horrible at the continuity which she prayed would somehow find her.

With each passing day she felt certain that each relationship was one day closer to its end. A decision point about what to do or how to proceed within the relationship was assumed to be the prelude to the end that was surely coming. Her reactions were increasingly defensive, bitter, and escalatory. Her inner child was defeating her biology. Without an education in this area, something that has heretofore been unavailable, marriage seemed to her like an extremely complex endeavor for which you just had to roll the dice and pray for good luck or stay lonely and on the sidelines. An endless parade of self-help books and a smug, defensive attitude about her situation further contributed to her continuing problem. Her ability to pray for good luck diminished with each new failed relationship; by her mid forties she had all but given up, feeling more confused than ever about how to proceed through a long term relationship. Her duplicitous inner child won out because that is what society encourages. You must deal with your inscrutable inner child until eventually you have a Ph.D. in inner child education and then are pure enough for the fireworks of love to go off. This is biological nonsense, but it is the nonsense we are encouraged to believe.

THE PSYCHOLOGIST WHO DOESN'T NEED A MAN TO BE HAPPY

I recently spent an evening with a sad, 42 year old, unmarried, and childless woman. She had spent years with a psychologist who charged a great deal of money to help her feel better and more secure about her situation. After the poor woman said to me for the tenth time, "my life just took a different direction," I said to her something like: "don't worry, people naturally feel bad in your position; if they didn't they wouldn't be motivated to marry and reproduce, and then they and their genes would soon become extinct." She objected strenuously because she had been led to believe that she could pay her psychologist to help her create a state of mind that would make her happy about her situation in life by successfully rejecting her basic biological imperatives. Her psychological therapy had been a lengthy, complex, and expensive undertaking indeed, and even worse, it seemed to have failed miserably in its bid to upstage biology. It would have been far easier for her to live with a normal, negative, or sad feeling about her abnormal life than with a neurotic good feeling about what she implicitly knew and felt to be an abnormal life. While being taught to feel good about what she was, she was kept from working toward what she wanted to be.

Relationship pop culture, of which she was a victim, continuously ignores biology in a thousand different ways. In doing so it ignores a basic truth about the human biological machine in order to serve a broad array of special interests including, most importantly, the ego/monetary interests of psychologists, and the political/social needs of radical feminists, but offers neither honest nor simple ways to promote, understand, and strengthen personal relationships.

THE WOMAN WHO IS TOLD THAT MARRIAGE IS DEATH

In her recent book "Revolution From Within" Gloria Steinem sounded startlingly like the above woman. Steinem points out a survey which showed that American women are tremendously insecure, but that they (American women) thought she was one of the top 10 most secure women in the country. Steinem took this to be an indication of how really bad off women are (her usual theme) since she had recently realized that she too was bad off having given her life over to "the movement" and neglected to work on her own personal issues the way a liberated girl should.

She finally resolved to take time off for herself. One night while psychotherapeutically sitting at her computer with her cat in her lap, she concluded, like the woman above, that her life too had just taken a different direction. She hadn't needed to get married she rationalized. Marriage to her was "like a little death." Feminism had made it possible for her and other women "to be the men they wanted to marry." It is hard to fathom the "inner directed" and insular nature of her thinking. For biological parents with unbounded love for their children, it is impossible to imagine them telling their children that they are the product of a "little death." Biology created sex and marriage to produce life; yet Steinem in her pathologic way equates it with death. This is the extreme to which she has to go to rationalize the tragedy of her personal life which obviously had never included a loving father or husband. Biology is the ultimate and irrefutable sexist while Steinem doggedly persists as the ultimate non-sexist. Feminism for Steinem is a way to rationalize and feel good about what she is, and a distraction from working toward what she ought to be.

Nevertheless, she is a hugely popular and romanticized figure who is always there to help a woman who needs a rationale with which to negatively understand a relationship. As a cultural hero she is there to oppose marriage for women much the way Hugh Hefner was there to oppose it for men. Neither one necessarily is directly influential, but they are there, in the background, from which place they offer needed support for divorce, infidelity, or the single lifestyle.

Many women, like Steinem, and many men too, lack the skills and/or inclinations to get married, but this does not mean that we have a social obligation to make them feel good so that their failure or abnormality can be easily ignored or even celebrated and thereby taught to others in a value free; biology free world. It is better to encourage them and everybody else to learn to live with failure, and to keep looking for love, or to keep maintaining and building the love they have. By not acknowledging failure, we forget what success is. Failure is a guide post equal in importance to success, but it is a guidepost whose pain we seek to avoid, at least on one level. Why should we experience pain if we can think up a rationale with which to avoid it, or why experience it if we can define it away? There are no old maids today, just women with the good sense to realize that marriage is death.

This is how gay people got from in the closet, to out of the closet, to gay pride, and finally to "Johnny Has Two Dads." Diversity and multi-culturalism are in, primarily because biology and discipline are out. Feminists, politicians, and psychologists among others know how to exploit this phenomena to build their own franchises. But what kind of culture can we have when cultural icons like Gloria Steinem say: "marriage is death," while the vast majority naturally but sheepishly depend on it as the basic framework of their lives. Over the long run biology will decide these issues in its favor, but in the short run a counter-biology pop-culture can and is doing tremendous damage. In the short run the divorce rate is based on the culture we elect to have; in the long run it is based on what biology demands of us. If we make excuses for divorce we can create as much of it as we choose and thus make life harder and harder for ourselves.

In the short run we can do what we want. If we make excuses for homosexuality we can have as much of it as we choose, as they did in Ancient Greece where it was common to sexually pair men with little boys. If we make multi-cultural excuses for recent immigrants who don't have the energy and discipline to learn English we can have a nation without a common language. In the final analysis America grew to be the greatest country not because everyone was free to follow any standard that they liked or the standard that seemed easiest, but because they accepted the discipline of a common unifying standard from which everybody derived strength and direction and community. The American melting pot really represented one good standard that we all escaped to from places where multiple and different standards had proved unsatisfactory. It is certainly true that biology encourages experiments like those in ancient

Greece, but now that we have seen our species successfully grow to tremendous proportions we ought to follow the model for that growth rather than bizarre models like that presented by Ms. Steinem.

On its deepest level each family is an integrated social biological system. It is for many intents and purposes removed from the pronouncements of outside special interests. Parties to a marriage must develop their own way to satisfy one another. No one can blame the other without, in effect, blaming her/himself. The family is a reflection of what all the parties have created. All to often a woman's role in the family becomes increasingly passive over time. Women, it seems, are somewhat passive by nature. They grow up knowing that they need to do comparatively little to attract male attention. Men grow up knowing that they must constantly improve their skills to maintain or improve their standing in the sexual marketplace.

Women lure men to marriage with the promise of regular sex but are often reluctant to regularly provide it, especially in the right context. Comedians often joke about how reluctant Jewish wives (perhaps the most naturally assertive of all wives) are to have sex. But they, like most women, do provide it although frequently only as an accommodation to the husband and family they love. This natural tendency for women to participate passively in marital sex complicates but does not prevent the idea of women as assertive, rational, and feminist lovers. Intelligent feminism would be a rational biological feminism as opposed to Ms. Steinem's crazy cultural feminism.

Women are most loving and the most orgasmic and the most generally pleased when they feel the most supportively connected to their husbands. If they would become actively involved in shaping their marriages they would be doing themselves and their marriage the best possible service. But women naturally resist this. They are comparatively passive due the maternal role which they effortlessly acquire as a birthright. This role can lead to economic dependence, physical weakness, more limited education and experience outside the home, and most importantly, a relationship algorithm which makes them most comfortable with the emotional, loving, and natural connections between adults that mirror their nonverbal connection to their children or to the children they were bred to bear and rear.

We can conclude from all this that biology didn't give us a very precise relationship model to follow and that the model needed to be and was correctly reinforced with cultural institutions, marriage in particular, which help define how we ought to behave sexually and even how we think about the meaning of our lives. But at a time when the divorce rate has grown from near 0% to over 50% and is peacefully and well tolerated we have to ask ourselves if we have any concept left about the meaning and value of marriage and children, and even our lives. We feel free to ignore biology and history in favor of easy diversity and multiculturalism. We have become free to dream up what ever we want without the fear of judgement or logic. The Gloria Steinem "marriage is death" approach represents just one of many silly experiments from twisted people who we no longer have the capacity to resist. We have moved from a biology that worked to a culture that doesn't.

THE WOMAN WHO RAN AWAY CRYING

The wife of Sean Connery (the original James Bond) provides us with a good example of how feminine passivity can reasonably be dealt with. She said of her first two marriages, "I let it build and build until one day I just left; which I did twice." After two failed marriages she married Connery, a very old fashioned and, apparently, occasionally violent man who once said, the night before he won an Oscar, " when a woman misbehaves as only-a woman can she needs to be slapped around a little." When asked how she was able to keep her 20-year marriage to Connery going she replied, "now, twice a year I write everything down and we get it resolved." Through painful experience and two broken homes Mrs. Connery learned that a marriage needs to be and can be easily and successfully managed, even when the marriage is to an ultra macho man like Connery. But it can only happen if the woman will actively engage in constructive management.

She learned that if she ever wanted to be a lover she had to be a manager too. Her words and behavior over three marriages acknowledge another unspoken truth: the specific problems to be managed are usually trivial. She did not even mention them. Irreconcilable differences are really silly reconcilable differences. Most 13 year olds can suggest the solutions and alternatives to typical marital problems. They don't require Einstein, and we shouldn't be tricked into believing that they do. Finally, Ms.Connery learned that a married man is not a Prince Charming from whom she should passively await a magical kiss. She learned what is elementary to a logical mind and what can be a painful but essential lesson for a more passive feminine mind.

Charleston Heston alludes to a similar popular sentiment when he advises male friends who are about to be married that there are only five essential words needed to preserve a marriage. Those words are, "Honey, of course you're right." The condescending implication here is that you had better not count on a wife to work things out with you. For a woman there is war or peace, marriage or divorce. The idea of working things out logically or verbally in some natural biological context is not readily apparent to them. Women initiate 91% of divorce because it is easier for them to passively slip away into the night rather than stay and manage a marriage which they blindly see as unmanageable. Ms. Connery was this way through her first two marriages. By the third she finally considered herself to be part of the problem and solution. Perhaps what Ms. Connery learned most was not only that women can manage men, but that men are the same and willingly manageable, within reason of course, and need to be understood by women who are generally busy dismissing them, running from them, or condemning them. One would probably not want to hear what Ms. Connery originally said about her two victimized previous husbands, who turned out to be identical to the third husband she loved so much. To be really cynical here we might say that Mr. Connery had a big advantage over the previous two husbands not only due to his position as the third husband but also because he is often considered the world's sexiest man.

Women love to be connected through language. They speak more words per day than men, they test higher than men on verbal acuity, and they think of themselves as more communicative than men. Books like "Why Men Can't Open Up" are common, but the particular verbal skills to which they refer are not related to marital management skills. Opening up, like women apparently can, to be supportive of and affectionate to their husbands or children is different from also being managerially connected to them in a way that will bring about the behavior which will keep a marriage on a steady and true course. In a highly academic study Patricia Diedrick, Ph.D. makes this point by concluding that: "it has been found that many men are even unaware of even the possibility of divorce, and that the decision is more commonly made by women Kurdek & Blisk, 1983; Pettit & Bloom, 1984; Thomas, 1982; Zeiss et al., 1989. In her book "Uncoupling" Diane Vaughan Confirms this when she writes "Partners(men) often report that they were unaware, or only remotely aware, even at the point of separation, that their relationship was deteriorating. Only after one person is gone are they able to look back and recognize the symbols. One man, married twenty years, spoke to me two months after his wife left him and was still trying to piece together what had gone wrong. He had come home from work to find a note from his wife on the kitchen table. He brought the note to the interview. It began , "I care for you, but can no longer live with you." He expressed shock and dismay; that he had no reason to suspect she was unhappy".

At another point she tells the story of a couple who called a psychologist as follows: The woman took me aside and said " I want to divorce him, but haven't told him yet." And he took me aside and said "

I used to be an alcoholic but I've reformed. I want to be a good husband. I really love this woman and I want to do everything I can to save this relationship." She doesn't go on to say the obvious, i.e. if a married man doesn't know that his wife is about to divorce him, it must be true that the wife, mysteriously, didn't tell him. This would imply rather directly that while women may like to talk it is not necessarily about difficult or important marital issues. Alice Walker describes the process of women falling in love in her novel as the process of finding a man who is little more than "a human ear" to which they connect through speech. To a woman a listener is more important than a potentially contradictory or dangerous responder. Many studies show that even modern women speak up less often on critical subjects, implying that they speak up more often on trivial subjects. They are the majority of the radio talk show audiences but men are the sex that feels conformable calling the show. This author remembers a similar point being made by a TV movie in which the theme centered around a husband who responded to his wife's' constant monologue with the refrain, "yes dear", and another in which the man, in order to avoid hearing his wife's endless monologue, learned how to cut off his hearing as he read the morning paper by simply pulling his lower ear lobe.

When it comes to real communication the "Dear John" letter made famous by the hundreds of thousands of American GI's who received them during WW II is often the best many women can offer. In a chapter titled "Secrets" Dianne Vaughan writes that; "Thus, uncoupling begins as a quiet, unilateral process. The assumption that relationships take place in each other's presence obscures the evaluative, reflective, assessing work that we do without the input of our partners." The most important aspects of a marriage are the least likely to be talked about. A woman makes the decision in solitude often never thinking that there is much that could be done with her partner before her feeling turn to the hate and contempt that must be built before the final break.

But, this doesn't mean that women don't care about the end of their marriages, it just means that they often don't care purposively. Amazingly Ms. Dietrick goes on to point out that " the pre-divorce period is more difficult for women as they try desperately to hold together a marriage, but at the same time note the hopelessness of the effort" This begs the question: how do you try to desperately hold together a marriage without telling your husband about the effort?" In truth, the agony a woman feels prior to divorce comes from not being able to do what her common sense tells her she ought to do. A woman finds herself hugely conflicted because she doesn't know how to tell her husband that her legitimate needs aren't being met; that it threatens the marriage, and certainly not that she is working over time and in silence to rewrite the history of the relationship in order to develop the hatred she needs to justify the divorce she is beginning to contemplate.

In Dr. John Gottman's landmark and ultra-scholarly epic: What Predicts Divorce, he discusses wives verbal abilities in a similar vain as follows: "This remarkable conclusion flies in the face of what generally is believed about men and self-disclosure. Komarovsky(in 1962, before sensitive men were even popular) also investigated what she called areas of emotional reserve. These are areas or concerns that are not shared with the spouse. Wives hold back most in hurts, and aspirations for herself and the family, transgressions, and reminiscences). In contrast, husbands hold back only in areas concerned with work and money (i.e., satisfactions, dissatisfactions, worries about bills, and economic concerns. Komarovsky's (1962) interviews revealed that men do not think it is manly to complain about work, to bring the job home, or to worry the family. Hence men's self disclosure in happy marriages is far more intimate than that of their wives, and in fact, appears to be more personal judging from Komarovsky's (1962) own use of the term. Furthermore, whereas wives disclose to a fairly wide support network that includes their husbands, their close female friends, and their relatives, husbands, in essence, only disclose to their wives". Disclosure, to a wide variety of essentially extraneous people, for women, serves the purpose of maternal contact but does not relate to constructive marital management something that should be taken up almost exclusively with the husband.

Dr. Gottman goes on to point out that for women it is very important to resolve things and that they will usually be the ones who will take the initiative toward this end. But how do we reconcile this fact with a woman's overall poorer marital management skills? The answer is simple. Wanting something resolved and taking the initiative to resolve it, and actually doing it are very different things. Biology provides us with a

40

direction here. A women will approach her husband as she would approach a child, i.e., with the expectation that with contact, communication and good intentions things can be resolved as she would prefer. She expects success as she expects it with her babies. She persists to the point where she finally confronts the aggressive hunter in her husband over whom she cannot so easily prevail. She feels despair and hopelessness about her long term prospects for getting what she wants out of a seemingly more aggressive husband who employs foreign communication methods, and divorce becomes the only alternative of which she is aware. To the husband it is just a small skirmish that required a little defensive maneuvering, but not a serious engagement. To the wife it is a total maternal defeat similar to not being able to sooth an infant's loneliness or pain, just as a loss in battle would be a defeat for the husband.

Mrs. Connery did not mention the role sex played in the resolution of her marital problems but we can assume it was part of the settlement. Her first two husbands displeased her and she obviously needed them to change their behavior before she could truly make love to them. But only Sean Connery, by virtue of his status as the third husband, had the opportunity to change his behavior. During her third marriage Ms Connery realized that most men are the same and that her reaction to them was the same. It finally occurred to her that a relationship is an active rather than a passive thing; that marital behavior needs to be managed rather than merely expected or talked about. In the beginning of a relationship women are biologically coy and controlling and managerial, but they often abandon this critical role shortly thereafter. They mirror Donald Trump's statement after separating from Marla Maples, "if you've got to work at a marriage who needs it."

In the end a couple bargains so they can make love; so that they can experience the feeling of love. It is the ultimate reason for the relationship; the highest and most unique expression of the value each has for the other. A lover is different from a friend. We make or create love through sex or the anticipation of it. The act of sex itself makes or manufactures the love which we find so essential. In a very real way we cannot be in love until we make love. It is during the act when the couple knows most certainly that their love exists apart from any other forces in

1.) CASE STUDIES OF COUPLES IN TROUBLE

their lives. When they dance or dine they are not making love. Only the prospect of making love in the future gives meaning to these preliminary events. What couple, no matter how compatible, would bother with them if they knew they could never be followed by love making. Men will bargain away a great deal for the opportunity to make love because love is what biology wants them to make most. The promise of making love can thus be easily used by an active woman who wants to make and maintain a relationship.

In the end though the husband will be more sexual than the wife. One way for women to cope with this is to occasionally offer sex without the expectation of any personal pleasure in return. An occasional quickie for the man is fine so long as it doesn't take precedence over the more complicated business of resolving differences and then really making love together. Another way for women to cope with a man's greater sexual appetite is to learn to enjoy sex more. Women are often surprised to find out how much they enjoy sex for its own sake once they resolve to participate. Studies show that pornography (not the kind that features violence) and vibrators often help women with sex if they can get over the poor reputation from which these things unfairly suffer. A patient husband is also very helpful, as is a wife who truly wants to learn and do what is necessary to be more sexual. Biology may require women to get started slowly and cautiously, but women seem quite able once they cross what to them is an often a difficult threshold. In some quarters modern women now talk of multiple orgasms. In a certain twisted sense this can be used, by those who hate the notion of passive women, to make women appear to be potentially more sexual than even men. In the end though, after millions of years of history, only about 30% of women orgasm regularly and less than 5% regularly have multiple organisms. This all must be taken into account as women think about how to best manage their husbands throughout the course of a long marriage.

Men literally cannot not walk down a street without tripping over their own feet as they steal furtive glances at all the women. The monogamy of marriage is a financial and sexual sacrifice for them but they do it, provided the right incentives are provided, as an accommodation to the woman or family they need and love. Each party to a marriage compromises his or her individuality to accommodate the union they have created. They become integrated social beings to create something more valuable than their individuality. For one party to blame the other when they are both equal parts of a system that was created from the contributions of each is contrary to the very nature of a relationship. Yet women are the ones who initiate 91% of divorce in the belief that they are just innocent bystanders in their own marriages who bear no responsibility for their divorces.

Another couple I know, now divorced, also violated the basic biological model. He was a very spoiled child: very bright (at least technically) very self-indulgent, and very emotional. She was almost the opposite: pretty, very educated, quiet, very shy, demure and, seemingly, dignified. Mostly, as an adult, she was retreating from tragic betrayals suffered during childhood. He suffered from too much love during childhood; she suffered from too little. In the beginning they seemed to each other like an ideal and complimentary pair. He was bold, confident, effusive and energetic in the way he loved her and the outside world. To him she appeared to have all the opposite traits that maybe, just maybe, represented a confident and dignified style that was more cool and mature than his own. She seemed to possess the quiet dignity of someone so familiar, experienced and in control that she was somehow well above the emotional chaos and petty details that always seemed to happily engulf his life.

After years of marriage they worked out a sexual compromise. He could make love to her in the dark anytime he chose; he could do anything he wanted to her so long as he didn't cause her any pain and she didn't have to do anything but lie there. Their sex life was a metaphor for their entire life. She finally divorced him, certainly the most assertive act of her life, feeling total hatred for him and the way he totally smothered her both in and out of bed. His highly charged emotional nature masked a deeply self-indulgent nature which caused him to smother his poor wife whose deep insecurity caused her to seek out a husband who would do exactly that. Her war with herself became a war with her husband. Finally, as her career, children and awareness grew, she realized that she was more than her marriage suggested that she was. She divorced him believing that he was an absolute devil who all alone had been responsible for the fourth class status she held within her embarrassing marriage. The husband, while certainly not inspired by his passive wife, did not want a divorce. He had sex, money, children, work, and a comfortable routine all of which would be gone. Without love, the wife felt as if she had nothing even though she had the same things that he had.

Her parents got away with smothering her because she, like all children, had no control over them; her husband got away with it because she slowly gave up the biological role that naturally got her away from her parents and into the arms of a husband who promised to take her even further away.

Sexuality and marriage are nature's supreme gift to us. They give us a chance to start over; to escape to the future; to control and build the family for which we always dreamt; to make the next generation a correction or improvement of the last. The above woman's big chance to rise far above a very unfortunate childhood was lost; not because her parents failed to teach her independence and self-esteem; not because she married a much more powerful man; not because she carried heavy baggage from an unfortunate childhood, but because she mistakenly assumed that love mysteriously appeared and would just go on and on without any management or understanding, through sickness and health and for richer or poorer. Millions of years of genetic evolution did its job. It drew these two complimentary mates together to correct all that had come before but it and popular culture left them clueless about the simple little steps that are necessary for a couple to live happily ever after.

To the feminists the man above was a typical patriarchal male chauvinist. To psychiatrists too he was something of a male chauvinist with the standard baggage. He was not so much the man who complimented her shy personality but just a re-creation of the parents to whom she was so accustomed. He was more the aggressor than she and aggression is considered bad even though it was what she originally sought in her champion. Besides, women are the ones who seek out and pay psychiatrists and accordingly they fully expect to be treated as the superior party. But both parties in this case were, at least according to popular wisdom, certainly in need of long therapy during which they could slowly confront the long subconscious history that had led them to such a silly sexual pattern, and then divorce.

Instead of divorce to please the feminists, or therapy to please the psychologists, she could have chosen biology. The biological model would have required her to merely zero in on her sex life and then take back the power she originally had. In this case it is doubtful that the woman ever knew of, let alone consciously used, her sexual power, but it certainly was there in the beginning where it exerted a very powerful influence over the husband who certainly did not get "it" on the first date. If she could give a professional speech in front of 300 people she could say to her husband, "sorry, no sex tonight, I'm really turned off by the way you won't listen to me anymore."

In the beginning, when they both truly loved each other, she would say to him, "have the best time you possibly can." She was actually telling him to masturbate in her body or to use her body for sex. Sex for her was, at most, a meeting of the bodies which had nothing to do with the heart or mind. Instead she merely should have said something like, "how do I feel to you?" and "what will you do for me." In that way they would have both learned that it was she as a full human being(body and mind) who was making him feel good. And, they both would have learned that he had to do something in return for her willingness to addresses him sexually. She had the opportunity to demand that he pay attention to her larger relationship needs. And, he certainly would have enjoyed sex far more experiencing it as a rare gift that is given rather than as an object taken to excess.

Certainly it would have been a more difficult process in the 18th year of marriage than the 1st or 2nd, but it is surprising how quickly men will fall into line as long as doing so leads them toward their all important sexual objectives. Unfortunately, it is an almost impossible task when the wife believes she is blameless and that her mate is truly worthy of the hatred she has very quietly and patiently developed for him. Again, the task of fixing and maintaining her marriage was not a difficult one, just one for which American culture had left her abjectly unprepared.

The couple above mirrors the current attitude of mainstream American elites. That attitude is perhaps best exemplified by Ashton Applewhite in her recent book: Cutting Loose, Why Women Who Divorce Do So Well. It is as if the recent family values movement, which perhaps can trace its origins back to Dan Quayle's criticism of Murphy Brown for having a child out of wedlock, was getting a little too popular. It was time for the liberal elites, who set much of the county's agenda, to weigh in with yet another pro-divorce, anti-family book.

In the book Ms. Applewhite points out the 75% of women initiate divorce (my own research shows 91%) and that they do it because the husbands always were, or have mysteriously become, male chauvinists of one sort or another. The husbands are dominant, overbearing, neglectful, sexually aggressive, etc. They make their wives feel as if they must walk on egg shells all the time. According to Applewhite, "cutting loose" is a wonderful deliverance. Taking their toys and leaving is Applewhite's solution to problems that she has no capacity to understand. The last thing she really wants to face is that perhaps women could learn to understand themselves and how they mistakenly relate to men. She speaks of cruel men who literally wore their wives raw from too much sex but it never occurs to her that these women simply had learned to play the wrong role and that they were capable of playing the right role rather than divorcing only to play the same mistaken role with yet another man.

Ms. Applewhite points out that second, third, and forth marriages break up significantly faster and more often than first marriages. What this really means is that biology compels women to seek out a mate, but current culture often compels them to divorce that mate, in the belief that he is a poor mate, and then marry another mate who, it turns out, is even worse than the first. We have almost a perfect contradiction between biology and culture. Biology compels women to seek out powerful men and modern culture compels them to divorce them because they don't know how to relate to the powerful men they seek out.

Ms. Applewhite covers much of the same ground that Betty Friedan covered decades ago in her ground breaking book, The Feminine Mystique. Ms. Applewhite writes, "What I didn't understand was how the illusion that he and I are equal is built into our culture. The truth is that the only time a woman's social worth equals a man's is during courtship, when the man must work to win her. Once married, no longer an object of competition among men, a woman finds that her value plummets. It's like a new car," one woman commented. The minute you take it out of the showroom, it loses 25 percent of its value. Consciously or not, many new husbands feel justified in treating their wives less well, or at least reminding them of their diminished status." Ms. Applewhite may be the quintessential hard bitten, whip toting, karate kicking, feminist intellectual but quite amazingly she has learned how women passively find that their value is diminished after marriage by men as men actively treat their wives less well after marriage. She acknowledges that equality is the ideal but then acknowledges that men are active and women are passive in their pursuit of it. Despite all her tremendous bluster it, incredibly, did not even cross her mind, at that point, that women could learn to actively maintain the social worth they so cherished during courtship and dreamt of during adolescence.

If someone's relationship skills or general intelligence are minimal, Ms. Applewhite's for example, they resort to political rhetoric or personal attacks on men rather than address a realistic solution to our divorce problem. Ms. Applewhite lost the power struggle in her marriage because she didn't really understand that she had to participate in her marriage. In her book "Turning Your Man Into Putty In Your Hands" Susan Wright writes of a very different approach: "There is a dominant-submissive quality to any sort of sexual interaction. Playing with power exchange is simply a way of openly acknowledging that fact between two lovers. Once you accept that, then you and your partner are free to try almost anything within the boundaries you have established for your power play. Whether it's through sexual play or by simply getting their lover to do what they want, many women regard the dominant role as their just returns. Often, it's seen as an expression of power that is denied by mainstream society. When you dominate a man, its a strong affirmation that you can control the events in your life to get what you need. It's an expression of freedom-a defiant and self-fulfilling gesture of independence".

This is not to merely say that women should overcome their Sleeping Beauty conditioning and be sexually-dominant. It is to say that every woman should know that she can be sexually dominant and link that behavior to the other things she wants in her relationship. To pretend, as many women do, that love means an automatic everlasting balance of power or that power and love aren't related is just silly self-deception. Love must be nourished and managed over the course of a long relationship. Long term love must be a managed balance. A woman or man who is allowed to be always dominant will not respect the other party in a loving way. Therefore love must relate to a "my turn, your turn" balance that both parties accept as the natural course of love. Women who critically say "men are this or my husband was that" are really women who just didn't know it was time to take their turn. Divorce, the political solution, just postpones the issue until the next relationship.

Even though the first divorce often leads quickly to the second divorce, Ms. Applewhite celebrates the first divorce for the first 268 pages of her book and then concludes her book with only two measly but very very telling pages which discuss, "making future relationships work better." Strangely, she admits, lastly but certainly not leastly, that "the way women are often poisons their own first and second marriages and thereby causes the marital cycle of joy and misery." All this begs the obvious question: what is it in the female mind that prevents them from learning to stop poisoning their first marriages so they, the husbands (who almost emerge as innocent and devastated victims here), and children don't have to endure the pain and long term consequences of divorce? She closes with a brief sentence as follows: "Instead of giving in to their husbands' desires as a matter of course, or expecting husbands to magically intuit their desires, wives need to articulate what they want. Many women interviewed for this book said that poor communication lay at the heart of their marital problems, and expressing themselves was the key to a better relationship. The habit of censoring oneself dies hard, but as these women have learned, it is poisonous, not only to their relationships but to their happiness." She didn't have the courage to admit that it's also poisonous to their husbands and children, nor did she have the courage to consider that if women didn't poison their husbands they would have no reason to "cut loose" from them. Her book is a huge contradiction but it is typical of the irrational clash between biology and current liberal elite pop culture that so dominates our culture.

Noted evolutionary psychologist Dr. David Buss points out that a woman's inherent need for powerful men is well exemplified by successful, powerful modern women who nevertheless seek out mates even more powerful than themselves. Dr. James Weinrich helps to corroborate this finding from another direction with his finding that in households where the woman earns more than the man the rate of divorce is double. It apparently is not in a woman's nature to say in such a situation, "now that I have money, power, and security on my own I'll seek out a mate who is, kind, sensitive, feminine, romantic, attentive and caring, etc. Instead, she seeks out an even more dominant male so that she can get back in what apparently is a comfortable and somewhat inferior position that she will ultimately hate. If this is the normal course of events then divorce is just a silly, anti-biological exchange of male chauvinists by naive women who seek power and then run from it.

1) CASE STUDIES OF COUPLES IN TROUBLE

The answer to our divorce problem lies in women learning how to teach men to be dominant toward the outside world and loving toward their inside familial world. Biology efficiently gave men testosterone for both dominance and sex. But it is largely up to women to separate the two through sexual reinforcement. It is always important to remember that men are the way they are because women bred them to be that way through the forces of evolution. To blame men is to blame themselves. But women also bred men for domestication. It is ironic that relatively weak modern women are, at least for this brief period in evolutionary history, often unable to fulfil that role despite the increasingly passive nature of modern male life brought on by the comforts of the industrial revolution and democracy.

THE WOMAN WHO WANTED
TO BE SLEEPING BEAUTY

I recently interviewed another divorced woman who just could not imagine that she contributed to her own divorce. After all, she reasoned, "I divorced him for all the terrible things he was and did." In truth, she divorced her husband after 22 years of marriage because he was a typical male. With perfect hindsight she mentioned that she began to see this even on her honeymoon. Once he had her in marriage, "his temper began to immediately flare," she said. When I asked her if she made love to him on the honeymoon after his temper flared she said, "well what else could I do on our honeymoon." When I mentioned that she was thereby encouraging testosterone laden behavior that biology had intended for the outside world and not for their marital world, she protested by saying, "but we're told not to use sex or the lack of it to control or as a weapon." Of course, this is absurd. If women were encouraged to make love when they're not in love for fear of using sex to control or as a weapon, then family and children would be nearly impossible. Women would make love with strangers for whom they had no love and the children who resulted would have no father to help insure their survival. In fact, the human female's completely unique ability to be constantly in estrus or in season evolved for no other reason than to give her constant sexual control of her husband and, derivatively, to insure the survival of her children. Concurrently, the male's ability to participate and find value in this system evolved for no other reason than to insure a constant interest in impregnating his wife and to insure the survival of his children. Love is the form of control wherein two parties control or relate to each other. If women were encouraged to make love to their husbands when they weren't in love with them they would, more accurately, be making hate or, separating sex and love. A couple grows together as the line between love and sex is blurred. Sex alone has very little value to a woman. Making love and having sex must always be distinguished.

Twenty-two years later she finally divorced her husband and was dating. She told me of a lawyer who she had slept with five times before she had had enough. Now she was divorcing boyfriends every couple of months rather than husbands every 22 years, but the pattern was the same.

1) CASE STUDIES OF COUPLES IN TROUBLE

She said that her lawyer friend's modus operandi was to declare that she looked "sexy as could be" in her tight miniskirt, take her to bed, have sex, and then quickly fall asleep. After the fifth such occurrence she was so sexually frustrated that she left the bedroom slamming the door behind her. She kicked him out and then refused to return his calls. This was much more assertive than obediently falling asleep as she had done the first four times, but it was still wholly inadequate. I suggested that she should have stopped him in his tracks and said, "wait a minute, I can't make love to you just because my mini skirt turns you on. You have to say and do and feel other things for at least a few minutes, before I can feel like making love to you. And by the way there's more to making love than just your orgasm."

It seemed as if she could not imagine herself being that assertive. Love to most women is something that passively happens to them. They often experience it as something over which they have no control. She protested by implying that I was suggesting a sort of sexual blackmail. She said, "if I tell him that I won't make love to him unless he takes me to Atlantic City for a weekend then I'd feel like a prostitute." I then suggested that that would be very similar to prostitution. Few women though would elect to use sex in this manner. Instead they might firstly use their sexual power to extract sexual reciprocity from their men so that they too could enjoy sex. Secondly, they might use their sexual power to encourage loving, supportive behavior that wasn't directly sexual thus setting the stage for a total relationship, both in and out of bed, that actually satisfied her protracted relationship desires.

This isn't to say that her lawyer friend would have instantly responded and that they would have lived together happily ever after. Perhaps he only wanted her for sex. Or perhaps loving behavior was just too foreign to him so that he could never really respond to her encouragement. In any case, by following sensible biological advice she would have got the answers soon enough without allowing herself to be used for his sexual pleasure.

THE PSYCHOLOGIST WHO TREATS HER OWN HUSBAND BEFORE DIVORCING HIM

A recent landmark survey published in Shere Hite's book, Women and Love found that 80% of women find men arrogant, condescending and mean toward them. A divorced female Doctor I know echoed this when she said of her first husband,"he cut me as if with a knife with that mouth of his." She then counseled me that only insecure men behave that way. Her explanation was typically female. She was the helpless, blameless female who mysteriously fell in love with a man who then came to be a sharp tongued and abusive bully. When I explained to her that many, if not most women experience men that way she protested that it could not be so. As I reached for the survey to prove it she resentfully said, "now he's going to prove it." She dreaded my proof just as she had dreaded standing up to her husband. In an instant we had recreated the biology of her marriage. I was the male hunter precisely using language to outmaneuver my prey or impress a woman; she was the mother passively cooing imprecisely with the language to sooth and love her child or to make and maintain a connection with her husband. While she did not mention her sex life we can be sure she provided sex on demand to her ex-husband until she finally divorced him. All she ever had to say to her husband was: "talk to me nicely or I'll see ya tomorrow."

On average women speak 5000 words a day while men speak only 2000. Men use language to communicate precise information; women use it, albeit imprecisely, to maintain a loving connection to the people around them. Female use of language is interestingly illustrated by linguist Deborah Tannen as she tells the story of a woman in a psychotherapy session as follows: "when the patient said all she wanted to say, she began to repeat herself. Her repetitions were an invitation to the therapist to begin speaking by interrupting her. One reason that speakers from some cultural groups leave little or no pause between turns is that they see silence in friendly conversation as a sign of lack of rapport."

Given this difference and many others it is doubtful that most couples could ever use language and logic to resolve complex marital problems. The task is simply too complex. Men and women don't really even speak the same language. This author recently visited the South Hampton Historical Society Museum where they are proud to exhibit 18th Century punishment devices used by their recent ancestors. One such device, called a pillory, locked the wrists and neck of a standing woman in place as punishment for talking too much. A forked stick was somehow placed on her tongue to symbolize the nature of her transgression. Economy of words was valued and women just didn't seem to understand. We obviously have made much progress in learning toleration since then but there is still a significant difference between the way men and women talk and the way in which each interprets the other's talk. Deborah Tannen, Ph.D. has written a very well reviewed and widely read book titled: You Just Don't Understand: Women and Men in Conversation, for those who may wish to concentrate on gender differences in conversation. Typical of her work is the following passage: "The element of negotiating status that characterizes many men's desires to show they are knowledgeable and skillful does not negate the connection implied in helping. These elements co-exist and feed each other, but women's and men's tendencies to place different relative weights on status versus connection result in asymmetrical roles. Attuned to the meta messages of connection, many women are comfortable both receiving help and giving it, though surely there are many women who are comfortable only in the role of giver of help and support. Many men, sensitive to the dynamic of status, the need to help women, and the need to be self-reliant, are comfortable in the role of giving information and help but not in receiving it." Ms. Tannen's work is fine so far as it goes, especially in its implicit acknowledgement that men and women are different, but it has several key limitations. Firstly, it encourages us to focus on conversational style to bring peace in the battle of the sexes. This is a big problem because 1) most of us just aren't inclined enough or sophisticated enough to go to college and study linguistics with Ms. Tannen, 2) it implies that the form and style of conversation is more important than the substance, and 3) it completely ignores that gender differences were created so that male and female of all species would come together sexually; not conversationally. In fact, most species are not even capable of conversation and they manage quite well.

Aside from the significant, and in most cases prohibitive, intellectual discipline that would be required to produce verbally induced harmony between the sexes, words create philosophical problems all by themselves. Suppose we conceded that the female Doctor above was right about her husband having been insecure and that he talked abusively and condescendingly to her as a means to make himself feel more secure. Further, let's suppose that she had a magic wand with which she gave him a Ph.D. in philosophy and psychology, a red Ferrari, a recollection of kind and loving parents, a billion dollars, a Fortune 500 company, two kids with straight A report cards, the adoration of a million beautiful women, and season tickets to the Chicago Bulls; all in order to make him more secure. Would anybody bet that this new man would love his wife more? Perhaps the fear of losing his new found possessions would make him more insecure than ever. Perhaps his new knowledge would take him to China for years at a time. Perhaps his new security would attract many new women who were more appealing to him than his wife. Perhaps he would be so secure that he wouldn't want a wife at all. Perhaps she would no longer love the new more secure man. Perhaps his new found earthly security would make him neurotically insecure about dying. Perhaps he would grow tremendously insecure as John Stewart Mill did when his tremendous intellect didn't seem to turn out brilliant work fast enough. Perhaps his higher level of security vis a vis his wife would make him even less respectful and more abusive toward her.

Insecurity is just a word. It is probably the most common diagnosis in popular psychology and yet even with fantasized magic bullets we cannot begin to describe what it means or how to fix it. It is far better to concentrate on sex. It is simple and far more essential. If he's not nice, he doesn't get it. Who can't understand that? He gets sex when she gets a nice husband, or, if he's nice he gets sex; if not she divorces him. It's the simple and fair biological deal that both parties can understand and live with happily ever after because it makes perfect biological sense. If a couple's abilities allow more breadth and nuance to the relationship then the sexual compact can be the foundation for whatever else their other abilities enable them to add to the relationship. Certainly no one would object to this, they would just caution against the complexity of it and the likelihood of failure or ongoing frustration.

It would seem that both words and sexual differences can cause communication problems. But isn't communication itself a problem? How do we even know what to communicate in order to improve a relationship? Do we communicate everything so that, 1) no boundaries exist between the loving partners, 2) one partner bears less and less responsibility for the partnership's decisions and actions, 3) the most insecure person can hide himself in the relationship, 4) the insecure person can constantly monitor the health of the relationship, 5) neither partner ever feels lonely, 6) both are receiving constant support and reinforcement. Or should we communicate very little, 1) to project an air of reassuring confidence that all is well, 2) to maintain the independent personhood that the other person originally found lovable, 3) to acquiesce to the notion that two people can never see exactly eye to eye; so it is better to avoid the possibility of a disagreement or fight, 4) in the belief that familiarity breeds contempt; that distance and mystery make the heart grow fonder, 5) to encourage the other toward independence and growth and 6) to preserve space so that periodic intimacy is special. The concept of communication itself is a vast and hugely complex thing; yet it is one thing that every person mistakenly believes is the single most essential thing in a relationship. Perhaps this is why our relationships are so poor? Let's not forget that the divorce rate is 50% (arguably 65% according to the very scholarly Dr. John Gottman) and the combined divorced rate plus the "I wish I were divorced" rate is, perhaps, 75%. Maybe our obsession with new age communication is the real problem? Dr. Paul Pearsall puts it this way: "the less dependence there is upon verbal communication in a marriage, the more likely it is to survive and grow." From his point of view much psychological folklore exists about communication. The Freudian psychological perspective inherently deals with getting to know the inner self and then communicating what the inner self is and wants. If both spouses try hard to communicate this way they are inevitably talking about the communication of difference. Pearsall takes the more rational approach that a relationship is not about the two individuals who comprise it, but rather about the new entity which is a combination of two individuals. According to this theory a couple does not equal two(one plus one); it equals 1 (1/2 plus 1/2).

Pure self delusion is also important. When Jill finally agrees to make love to Jack she may wish to believe that there is a special and unique kind of communication between them when it is really the simple lust that billions and billions of biological creatures share. Shared lust is not shared communication. When the democratically raised, psychologically oriented, me-generation concentrates too much on themselves and their uniqueness (and believes in the importance of communicating this) they lose track of the simple biological and religious based behaviors and attitudes that can provide a realistic basis on which two people can get together and stay together.

1.) CASE STUDIES OF COUPLES IN TROUBLE

In most marriages women allow or even encourage men to wield power and are naturally most comfortable that way, at least in the beginning. When O.J. Simpson attacked Nicole she fled under the nearest table in terror desperately imploring the 911 operator to save her life. She didn't calmly pull out a gun and shoot him dead, something that is very legal in all states, because she was a woman and the female psyche does not seem to permit assertiveness or the use of power, or does it ?

Another woman who I overheard on a plane was the opposite of Nicole Simpson. She said of her first fiancée, "he was a lawyer, everything had to be an argument. I should be able to have my opinion and do what I think is right even if I can't explain it perfectly each time. I heard that he made partner in his firm. My husband will never be rich, he'd rather be home with his family; he's not ruthless enough to be rich." This woman was conservative and perhaps very smart. She was willing to give up (with the help of a little twisted logic) the money, intelligence, and sensuality that women often associated with a lawyer or football player type in return for a power balance that she could comfortably maintain and manage with the ability and tools available to her. She understood that she had to have power.

Nicole Brown Simpson was not conservative. She was a gambler. She was a beautiful young waitress who aspired to be instantaneously world class through a marriage to a much loved and legitimately powerful world class athlete. Her beauty got her in the door but it didn't give her a clue about how to control a very powerful and ultimately murderous husband. His dominance of the outside world made him attractive to her but it didn't give him a clue that a wife and the outside world are two different things. He was a satiric man; she was a satiric woman, and together they were a couple who amplified the normal conflict between husband and wife for the whole world to see.

When Howard Cossell wrote about O.J. many years ago he noted how supremely self-confident to the point of absurdity he was; not only about football but about everything else too. In one instance O.J sat down to play poker for the first time with a group of seasoned players. He deeply believed and maintained absolute confidence that on the very next hand his dominance would begin to show despite a complete lack of experience and ability. For O.J. the whole world, including his marriage, was a testosterone driven football game in which he was the greatest player. If anybody could have controlled O.J. it would have been his wife and it turned out that she was very good at it indeed, but, like most women, only in the beginning of her relationship.

When O.J retired he was distraught as many professional athletes are at that time in their lives. In a half-time ceremony he introduced Nicole to the football stadium crowd of 30,000 or so and to a national TV audience of millions. This was a huge step for her given that her previous introductions had mostly been to a booth of four customers at the Denny's restaurant where she had worked. But still O.J. beamed lovingly at his new audience of one and reassured his old nationwide audience that they need not worry about him because he had the wonderful and beautiful Nicole to see him through the transition. At that point love was in bloom for them. She could sooth his troubled soul. She had control of the man who would eventually control her to the point of killing her. Neither wanted to upset what they both enjoyed as a wonderful and loving balance. But slowly she began to give up control; love faded to murder.

Perhaps in a moment of anger, frustration, or accidental rudeness, maybe after sex when his interest in her would have been at a low point, he got away with a slight insult that she let pass by unredressed believing that their perfect love would naturally reappear. Or, perhaps she made love once too often when she wasn't really feeling like participating and they both got the idea that sex was mostly to relieve him rather than to celebrate their love. Regardless of how it started, his ability to disrespect her slowly evolved and progressed according to a simple formula, albeit in an exaggerated way, until divorce and murder were the final outcomes.

Prince Charles and Diana were much the same as O.J. and Nicole. Andrew Morton writes as follows: "By any standards it was an unusual romance. It was not until Lady Diana Spencer was formally engaged to His Royal Highness The Prince Of Wales that she was given permission to call him "Charles." Until then she had demurely addressed him as "Sir." A typical date consisted of her being invited to watch him train his polo horse. She was beautiful, emotional, very young, very uneducated, and virginal while Charles was cold, old, educated, and very aristocratic. She never had the slightest clue about how to use her sexual power to make love to a husband who by any standards would have been hard to make love to. But, Camilla Bowles, an older equal, never had trouble with him.

We live at a time when male bashing is socially acceptable. Women are perceived to be victims who are justifiably balancing the scales of justice with their insults toward men. And, appallingly, the male intellectual establishment agrees quite vigorously. In his book The Ten Laws of Lasting Love, Paul Pearsall, Ph.D. gratuitously writes with absolute politically correct innocence: "Because of their testosterone poisoning men have a built-in brain bias for compartmentalizing thinking, hearing and interpreting feelings less effectively, and being consumed more with carburetors than caring. Because of their less developed corpus callosum(the part of the brain that helps our left and right hemispheres communicate with the other) boys' or alphas' brains are made to function one hemisphere at a time-what some women or betas may experience as a half-witted approach to life. They have trouble putting their right brains together with their lefts and their feelings together with their mouths. Their genitals seem to have a mind of their own, because the part of the brain controlling genital response is dissociated from caring, consideration, and caution. Their ability to know "why" they do what they do or the effect it has on those around them is not as developed as the female's sensitivities in these same areas." Wow, women and many men have participated in a evolutionary conspiracy leading to the creation of men who are regarded as near idiots? Actual Pearsall must be the idiot because evolution can not be. He blindly ignores evolution, as if women can and would want to design and built bridges, fighter planes, and automobiles. Men are encouraged to obsess over their inferior biology and freakin inner child as if it were somehow possible that they are a mistake of evolution. The divorce rate hovers at 50% not because men are evolutionary mistakes but because we don't understand why evolution created men and women; instead we understand modern psychology.

This author recalls a story from a friend who was so thrilled at having finally found a girl friend who liked sex as much as he did. Not only did she like it as often as he did but she liked to be on top too (the opposite of the dreaded woman who just lies there). A few months later he remarked that sex had changed between them such that she now wound up on the bottom most of the time. When I very curiously said, "how come," he replied that she had said to him, "when you're doing your thing on top it's different." Generally women still like to be on the bottom, they like men to pay for dates, and they don't like bridges, fighter planes, and automobiles. It seems that the more things seem to change the more they stay the same or that the more pseudo-intellectuals play with culture the more biology keeps it the same. There is a war against biology almost as if we believe it can be won by merely pretending biology doesn't exist.

Feminist insults and pretensions don't help women resolve marital problems, but popular culture nevertheless encourages women to bring them into their relationships. The famous and ultra sexy pop singer Toni Braxton recently gave an interview in which she said, "I'm sick of men using sex as a sleeping pill." Rather than think seriously about what was going wrong in her sex life, Ms. Braxton proudly resorted to feminist insults. The real issue was: what biological rationale causes men to frequently fall asleep after sex? The answer is simple:

1) sex can be very tiring for men which might be expected given the importance of it.

2) there is a sleep inducing sense of peace or emptiness that comes with the realization of one of nature's most important tasks.

3) once procreation has been attempted, it is efficient to move on to another competing biological necessity, i.e., sleep and then work.

4) Testosterone fuels the two different sides of male life: the life of sex and the life of work. The line between the two critical and competing tasks is bound to be strewn with difficulty. But the cycle of sex, sleep, and work makes sense. Estrogen, conversely, gives women two lives that are comparatively harmonious, i.e., the affectionate life of sex and the affectionate life of child rearing.

Men in love need to change gears abruptly while women do not; this was particularly true during the long period in which men evolved. Had Ms. Braxton understood this she would have looked for a way to harmonize her sexual/biological interests with those of her lovers, rather than for a way to pointlessly and defensively insult men.

The problem was not that her men used sex as a sleeping pill but that she allowed herself to be used as a sleeping pill by her men. If she feels that the cycle of sex to sleep is too short then she can, perhaps, slow it down. Years ago there was a popular song titled "Slow Hand"; (not by

1.) CASE STUDIES OF COUPLES IN TROUBLE

Toni Braxton) the main lyric was, "I like a man with a slow hand." Toni Braxton and many other women would undoubtedly like this approach to love too. But how can they make it happen? Women can sing about it and criticize men but in the end they are evolved to like dominant men and they tend to follow the sexual pace men set even though it is different from the pace they would choose if they were inclined to insist on a choice.

In Deborah Tannen's book there is a reference to a study in which a man who is encouraged to alter his love making style says something like "be quiet, I'm making love to you in my own way." Men don't look for direction in bed or when lost in traffic, generally. But, the ability of women and men to alter biology does exists. It won't happen without a thoughtful and purposive understanding of biology though. To have a satisfying love life a woman must assume and take some of the responsibility for the pace at which sex proceeds. If a man is given a choice between no sex and five minutes of extra foreplay or afterplay he'll settle for the foreplay and perhaps the afterplay, and probably enjoy the protracted experience more. Working a man up to 10 minutes of foreplay or 10 hours of affection and conversation in return for sex is not difficult. It is something that many happily married couples routinely and unconsciously manage. But it is something that troubled couples don't; often because women, like Toni Braxton, will not understand let alone purposely assert their very legitimate sexual interests.

THE WOMAN WHO GIVES HER
MAN EXACTLY WHAT HE WANTS

Another woman I knew had a husband who was like Dr. Spock of the TV series Star Trek. Dr. Spock was from the planet Vulcan where inhabitants were taught to suppress their sexual and emotional interests in favor of their intellectual or logical interests. Rather than be buffeted daily by the passion and uncertainty of sexual emotion they learned to suppress it for seven year periods after which time it was promptly and resoundingly released in an embarrassing display of raw sexuality which no man or Vulcan dared stop or witness. The husband in this case was vulcan-like. He was an engineer who preferred sex once every seven days and on Saturday mornings only. He and his wife were in the middle of a divorce.

The wife preferred sex and affection daily. During years of therapy she learned that she was more like a typical man and that her husband was more like a typical woman. The therapist was dutiful in pointing to some approaches that the couple could use to reconcile their sexual differences and perhaps their marriage. It never happened though because a therapist can't be too direct. It wouldn't be Freudian or polite or politic. The patient is supposed to learn things by herself with only the gentlest guidance from the therapist. If this happens to involve years of therapy and thousands of dollars, so much the better. If it never happens at least the therapist earned a fee and didn't offend anyone by pushing too hard.

In the end this woman, like Toni Braxton, resorted to criticism of her husband. She would complain, "he was only romantic on Saturday morning; what kind of marriage is that?" She completely failed to realize that he wanted and had sex on Saturday morning because that was when she tacitly agreed to provide it for him. He was preoccupied and nervous about work during the week, like Dr. Spock during his 7-year period of abstinence, and could not get sexually aroused or so it seemed. With sex and romance effortlessly achieved once per week at the proscribed time and place he was non-sexual and non-caring the rest of the week.

During the period when men evolved sex was a continuous adventure. Men marshaled all of their talents and energy in pursuit of many different women. They were always on the prowl so to speak. Women were actively engaged too as they asserted their evolutionary prerogative to reject those males who seemingly sought to pass on inferior genes.

1.) CASE STUDIES OF COUPLES IN TROUBLE

Humans evolved to thrive and dream and aspire and succeed in this environment and yet the couple here managed to completely remove it from their lives. It was like taking the taste out of food and the feeling of hunger out of the body. They were both miserable. The man eventually had an affair that led to the divorce she initiated. It is not difficult to imagine how natural and inspiring it must have felt for him to pursue and eventually conquer a difficult and normally evolved woman who promised to stay that way.

Oddly, the wife who was relatively masculine in her sexual/romantic needs was comparatively content in one sense. She pursued him all week to no avail, but always managed to achieve her objective on Saturday morning. This of course was the opposite of what she should have done. She should have gotten him all hot and bothered on Saturday morning and then ran out of the room shouting, "I'll see ya Wednesday morning if you're good." This would have changed his frame of reference completely. All of the sudden his wife would have transformed herself into a woman who had to be romantically pursued and pleased at a time and place of her choice. Instead of wasting time off from work worrying about work he could have been romantic instead. This, perhaps, would have made him more refreshed and relaxed for work than ever, and, most importantly, maintained a stable marriage and home for his children. But it was beyond the scope of her feminine reality.

SLEEPING WITH BILL AND HILLARY

Before Bill acquired political power he saw himself as the fat kid in the Big Boy jeans who had a difficult time getting girls. He was raised to have traditional values but he was also raised in difficult circumstances. A violent step father was addicted to alcohol, a brother was addicted to drugs; a mother was addicted to gambling, and Bill himself grew up to be addicted to power and sex. But, glory hallelujah, Bill was a smart guy who could talk about it all. At Yale he was often thought of as a glad-handing hillbilly who was somehow genuinely impressed with his State's watermelons and was certain that his classmates would appreciate them too. He was always certain of his vision. He once arrogantly talked his way into a closed museum by promising to clean up the trash while he was inside. Mostly, though he was a sensitive 90's kind of guy who was psychologically aware. He was a Democrat. He could feel your pain, and his own. As a lover he seemed far ahead of ex- Republican presidents. Nixon, Reagan, Bush, and Ford evoked no such sentiments despite, or perhaps because of, their shy quaint 1950's reverence toward emotions and their wives. To them emotions were sacred; almost marital in nature. Their emotions were in perspective unlike the modern elite view which seems to be: the more the better. I once asked a pretty psychologist friend if she thought it appropriate that her male patients often seemed to fall in love with her and express their detailed sexual desires for her during long term psychotherapy. She said, "it's fine; it's part of the process." The difference between that and prostitution escaped me. Movie stars face the same situation. They interact intensely with members of the opposite sex in exotic location away from family. Whether in a prostitute, a movie star, a psychologist, or a glad handing politician, emotions, we once knew, need to be carefully contained like a fine wine not spilled all over in every situation like water at a car wash. Certain emotions that are reserved only for marital relationships communicate that marriage is a one and only relationship.

Bill was a psychological Democrat who was not only at home with his emotions but also in every woman's bed with his seductive public emotions. He could talk about it, he could easily shed a public tear or hold it back with a strategically bitten lower lip, he could extend an affectionate arm He was in touch with his 90's feelings and everyone else's; he was the ghost of Sigmund Freud and the women of America loved him. He was a tall powerful man and undoubtedly a good lover in whose shadow they could comfortably live and yet he retained a child's ability to express the feelings a women is so programmed to respond to. He became every woman's fantasy mate. Bill, being male, firstly and primarily, promptly set out not to disappoint his loyal maternal constituency.

Hillary was the opposite of Bill. Raised with traditional but harsh Methodist mid-western values she never developed Bill's emotional range. When she brought home a report card with all A's she was not hugged. She was told "it must be an easy school." Her harsh experiences drove her inward to hide while Bill's drove him outward into sympathetic arms. While men of Hillary's generation were being shamed into being more female and emotional, women were busy trying hard to learn how to be like the insensitive men they disliked but wanted to emulate so much. It was a made to order excuse for Hillary not to develop beyond her rigid Methodist roots. According to David Brock she earned the name "sister Frigidare" in high school. But, like Bill, she too was blessed with a super high IQ and blinding ambition. Hillary was made nationally famous at the end of her senior year in college. She was selected as the first student ever to give the commencement address for her college. She shared the podium with a US Senator who she promptly shouted down for, what seemed to her, his complacency about poverty. Hillary felt that if only she were running the world centuries of poverty could finally be vanquished just the way she had vanquished student apathy about the theme for homecoming weekend. In retrospect she should have been given a spanking for her insolence and intellectual naivete and then made to repeat the grade. But hey, it was the 60's; revolution was in order, and Hillary, instead, was put on the cover of Life magazine. She was thus anointed as our future leader and she was certain divine justice had finally been done.

After College she attended Yale law school where she wore Vietcong pajamas and generally disregarded her appearance almost completely in solidarity with her more important liberal missionary spirit. That's when she met Bill. They were a perfect team, at least out of bed. Both were out of place in their way but together all the pieces were synergistically there. Hillary used conversation to steer away from uncomfortable personal emotions while Bill used it to connect and bond with people who could be made to trust his easily revealed but ultimately manipulative inner being.

SLEEPING WITH BILL AND HILLARY

Most guys didn't want to or were too afraid to approach Hillary because of her distinctly non-debutante looks and hard bitten, politically rabid attitude. Bill wasn't used to pretty girls anyway and he just knew he could charm the goatee off a angry but brilliant billygoat any day. He did and the rest is history. Today Bill is charming us into believing that he "never had sex with that woman" and that an administration which is completely and startlingly devoid of ideas is somehow legitimate. He has been amazingly fortunate politically in that he has been able to take credit for the current economic boom which clearly started in the previous administration and has been managed ever since by a the first Republican congressional majority in a generation and a ultra-Republican Federal Reserve policy. No one knows what Bill stands for because he doesn't stand for anything except his own need to rise above an unfortunate childhood. When Bill Clinton spoke of watermelons at Yale even his fellow Yalies didn't suspect that watermelons would be his only subject.

Bill gave Hillary her dream shot. He appointed her to socialize the nations health care system which was approximately 20% of the nation's economy. After health care the whole economy loomed before her the way Russia loomed before Napoleon. It seemed more complicated than being student body president but Hillary knew she was born to do it. In the end her naive and "sister Frigidare" attitude turned the nation off. She wanted to do it all behind closed doors with oh so high level meetings and then let us know our fate. She become famous all over again when small businessman asked her where they would get the money to pay the impossibly high insurance premiums she proposed. She answered, "I don't know; I can't be responsible for every undercapitalized business in America." She didn't seem to know or care that her scheme might kill off a budding Micro-Soft type company or that most of the country's new employment came from small business. The nation's economy had to fit her scheme and that was all there was to it.

Before their first presidential election Bill and Hillary went on 60 Minutes to assure the nation that their private life was the public's business. Hillary assured us that she was no "stand by your man" 1950's idiot who wasn't dealing with the problem in a modern feminist way, and Bill assured us with a tear in one eye and softly bitten lower lip that he was moved by young Chelsea's tender pronouncement that "whatever your problems were mom and dad I'm glad you worked them out." It turned out they were both lying on a presidential scale, but it was justified. Hillary needed the White House to save the world and he needed it to get babes.

But what can we speculate about their sex life and marriage? Bill, we believe, can talk about these things. He is emotionally comfortable with them and seems to have a voracious if not compulsive sexual appetite. Hillary seems the opposite. One suspects she wouldn't appreciate the true value of a genuine Cuban Cigar by any means or that poor Bill never got to stain any of her dresses. That left Bill's desires largely unfulfilled in some important ways and so his habit was to look elsewhere while still preserving the marital foundation of his political life.

Bill was in one sense a relatively hard man to domesticate owing mostly to the hugely erratic love he experienced and absorbed at the hands of his mother, father, and step-father, but he was also a very easy man to domesticate owing to his need to correct the insecurities of his youth, his extreme virility(at least as documented by Gennifer Flowers), and his overwhelming need to have a strong familial base from which to realize his most sacred ambition as our leader and President. All Hillary had to say was: "I'll provide you the appropriate amount and kind of sex you crave so much if you'll be a loyal, loving husband and father to me and Chelsea. Bill would have been especially vulnerable to this sexual contract because he needed his family for not only the usual reasons but for his career too; something not true for most men.

Hillary was not inclined to do or realize this being, 1) normally reluctant to appreciate the value of sex to a husband who was, typically, mostly consumed by it, 2) a mid-western, anti-sexual Methodist, 3) a non-giving feminist, 4) more concerned with political power than love, 5) born with the ambition to save the world rather than face the necessity of saving her own tiny marital world, 6) without the broad emotional capacity to match her husband in any way sexual, and 7) perhaps, lesbian, as Gennifer Flowers has written. So, she made a Faustian bargain accepting a marriage without biological reality and agreeing to cover it up no matter how poor an example the first family's marriage set, no matter how often she had to lie to us: her subjects, and no matter how often she had to be photographed looking adoringly into her husband's eyes. Her husband's seemingly trivial and crude sexual interests took a back seat to her complex and highly neurotic smorgasbord of concerns.

2.) THE BIOLOGY OF SEXUAL INTERCOURSE

HOW ANCIENT BIOLOGY CONTROLS OUR RELATIONSHIPS

We think of relationships as very complex indeed. Judging from the countless books, talk shows, conversations, lectures, and untotaled hours of therapy, it might seem that there are tons and tons of conflicting and complex relationship information out there to be digested and understood, but no certain or obvious path on which to proceed toward this end. Many implicitly conclude that the subject is just too vast and too complicated for the average person to tackle without a willingness to make it an exhaustive and continuous pursuit. We further suspect, and often correctly, that those who make the most thorough effort will become the worst among us at relationships having been led astray by trendy theories or the awkwardness that comes from learning something formally that others have learned naturally.

Our overall sense, though, is that the vast and diverse relationship industry is an increasingly more legitimate one grows in large part out of a supercharged economic environment. It relentlessly sells us the notion that since relationships are critically important, continuous, evolving, and complex, our spending and learning about them should follow the same pattern. The idea of a simple and thorough scientific understanding of marital relationships is quickly and implicitly dismissed as simplistic or naive in this environment.

But, can today's diverse relationship theories really be better than last year's or last decade's theories when they're both about a million year old topic that has never really changed much despite all the other changes which occurred during that period? Haven't all relationships always served the same purpose; aren't they subject to a few fundamental truths, or is each a modern, wonderful and unique creation that needs constant dissection, analysis, and direction in light of today's latest theories and opinions? Our supply side economy thinks not as it gropes forward selling us fancy psychological, political, and eclectic theories promoted by an array of trendy new age media entrepreneurs. But in the end we are more confused than ever about relationships and the divorce rate continues to hover persistently at 50%.

As a college student I asked a biology professor, who took a back seat to no one when it came to certainty about the value of her discipline in understanding human nature, "what is the most fundamental relationship motivation any living organism has." She replied, "reproduction-the more a species is equipped to succeed at reproduction the more likely it is to succeed as a species." To this day I've never found reason to doubt the integrity, veracity or comprehensiveness of her answer. She had always been purely interested in just science and was totally unconcerned and unaware of any possible political, economic or social ramifications from her thinking. Biologists stand in dramatic contrast to the psychologists, and other pop culture gurus who have somehow emerged through our complex economy to become our relationship authorities even though their diverse methodologies and unrelated perspectives preclude the possibility of a logical, scientific theory of marital relationships.

Whether or not my professor's answer was the single most accurate answer to my question, and I think it was, it does provide a very plausible rationale on which to build a purely scientific understanding of most human behavior in general and sexual/marital behavior in particular. In fact, it provides a scientific rationale far more thorough and accurate than the supposedly more modern opinions promoted by those who ignore biology to make room for their own trendy and profitable, but far less scientific ideas.

Human beings, after all, are the sexiest and certainly the most successful species of all. Of all 200 ape species man has evolved the longest and thickest penis, and a virtually constant interest in using it. The human female is the only creature on earth who is constantly in heat or in season, and continuously obsessed with sexual attractiveness. It is not really difficult to imagine that reproduction is central to many or most aspects of our behavior.

If basic reproductive biology determines our motivations and behavior in general, and perhaps in particular, then we really may not be dependant on modern relationship theories that scoff at biological truths in favor of trendy psychological, political, or business oriented theories to explain our behavior. To determine if this is so, let's proceed by developing a complete understanding of modern marital relationships in terms of basic 19th century evolution theory. This understanding hopefully will be thorough enough to explain the subtleties and nuances of relationships, marriage, and divorce, but still simple enough to be quickly understood by a large audience. It should emerge as superior to the popular, diverse and contradictory understandings proffered by supposedly more modern and sophisticated thinkers. And, hopefully it will be an understanding which children can routinely pick up from their parents at an early age, re-learn formally in school, and lastly, have reinforced through popular culture.

According to biology theory, then, humans, being a tremendously successful species, would be expected to seek out and maintain reproductive relationships with great passion and success. This seems obviously true given what each of us feels everyday and what we know about the rate of population growth over the last few centuries:

WORLD POPULATION GROWTH

YEAR	POPULATION
1650	500 million
1850	1 billion
1930	2 billion
1975	5 billion
1996	5.8 billion

It may be a little demeaning to think of our primary preoccupation as merely sexual in nature, but it can't be just coincidence that our lives tend to focus around sex and/or our sexual partners, and that we have managed to populate the earth to such a phenomenal and costly extent. In fact we might reasonably assume that sex is becoming a even more and more important part of our lives as economic development frees us more and more from what once were preoccupying survival needs. In fact we can even assume that if sex were not of crucial importance there would be no sexes. If sex is at the heart of our existence and motivation, then many of the relationship problems that we now commonly and shyly think of as broad marital, cultural, psychological, social or political problems would in reality or more accurately be described as reproductive or sexual problems. But sex is embarrassing for us and so we have generally ignored it or pretended that sexual problems were really other problems.

Of course, since we have two sexes the sexes must be and behave differently. The ways in which males and females seek out reproductive fulfillment, or, to put it another way, enact their genetic sexual roles, are very different. The extreme differences between males and females remain obvious to nursery school teachers and parents who regularly see children of both sexes. Modern feminist egalitarianism, for example, though, has grown in power to the point where biologists are intimidated from feeling that it is politically correct to acknowledge the obvious differences between the sexes, but these differences are, nevertheless, very apparent to parents and teachers who see the differences daily, and to the biologist who measure the hormones which cause and maintain the differences. The failure to recognize the importance of sex, and the failure to reconcile the difference between the sexes is what causes relationship problems and, ultimately, women to initiate 91% of divorce.

Regardless of human thought and culture the single sex approach to reproduction was tried by mother nature many times and generally never worked well. Reproductive schemes with only one sex tended to produce duplicates of the parent with minor or no variations. A parent merely recreated herself from her own genes and the species improved little with the passage of time. With two different sexes within a species, each with specialized roles and different genes, offspring were truly new creations that often contained the best genes of both parents. With new and sometimes improved offspring being created from an expanded gene pool some of the next generation were better suited to survive than others. Those who survived, reproduced another generation, some of whom were again better suited than others to survive in the then current environment, and the species thus keep evolving at a relatively rapid rate. Without the creation of two different sexes the human race would not exist. Men and women are different because nature needed the difference to make the human race possible. The difference should be understood and appreciated. It should be as natural as our appreciation of food. To insist that the sexes are the same, as much of our modern culture does, is to hopelessly trivialize an issue which is central to our marital lives as well as to our very existence.

Sexual roles are the primary roles of a lifetime for men and women. No matter what superior qualities or characteristics a human has they do not survive unless they are coupled with reproduction. This is why, for example, testosterone animates a man's sex life as well as his life as a hunter or provider. Even after a family is formed very little changes in the area of marital interaction. So much of the human machine is evolved around the sexual role that other significant behaviors, not directly or indirectly related to basic sexual behavior are not possible, without great and conscious work, at any time during the human life span. Life is sex; that part of life which does not seem to be sex is foreplay. We are sentenced to forever and constantly re-enact our primary genetic roles. Biology has given us no other role to play, and, more importantly, no mechanism with which to override the programming which dictates that role.

This would explain the whole range of post marital behavior that otherwise would have to be written off as pure coincidence. After a marriage, for example, it is still the male who initiates sexual activity (82% of the time) and the female that plays Shakespeare's coy mistress who must be seduced over and over again. When a married couple makes love within this context they achieve the highest possible form of love. Nothing could produce more joy and happiness because nothing is supposed to produce more joy and happiness. Whatever behavior exists, whether it's our ability to make love and form families or our ability to see with our eyes, it exists only as a genetic manifesto over which we have no control. It remains largely unchanged from puberty to death.

Given our elaborate cultural development it is not flattering to think of ourselves as mere biological machines, but we are, nevertheless, exactly that. The culture we have is merely that which our biology allows. To use our bodies and minds in a way that it opposed to our genetic nature is to invite pain, i.e., the feeling biology gives us to let us know that we are doing something which is not consistent with our basic biology.

Our tendency to place ourselves above biology stems from our 1) general ego-centrism, 2) position atop the evolutionary ladder, 3) ability to embellish biology with elaborate cultural trappings, and 4) ability to imagine, although not consistently achieve, behavior that is not in harmony with biology. Those who insist on value and/or belief based systems that somehow place human consciousness above biology are doomed to fight a painful and losing war against their own inescapable genetic natures. The first question must always be: is this consistent with our basic biology?

In the end, all aspects of behavior are dictated by or closely related to biology. Humans don't have free will, they have biology. We are not free to eat trees, hate our children, fly through the air, breath water, mate with fish, sleep all day, enjoy death, eat constantly, stop thinking, or understand the universe. Nature gives us a seemingly vast consciousness, but it is a consciousness based in a biology which defines the range in which we are able to perceive and make choices just as we define the range in which a captive animal is allowed to roam.

Below are some examples of behavior that is biologically driven, but for which we often forget to ascribe biological motives. Hopefully they will help get us accustomed to thinking about ordinary human affairs in biological terms.

Love: a feeling created by evolution so that humans will want to stay together long enough to raise their children. Love is not a complex thing that somehow exists independently in space and time due to magic or poetry. Love is merely a feeling which results from the chemicals that encourage us to focus exclusive attention on one mate for the purpose of procreation and child rearing.

Female Appearance: more elaborate, expensive and time consuming than men's. Much of the female psyche is dependant on physical appearance. This is understandable given that attractiveness is the primary vehicle through which women attract and retain men's attention until they have made a determination about whether a particular man is suitable as a mate.

Male Muscles: A constant though increasingly useless obsession based on ancient biology. A strong man was a better hunter/provider than a weak one and therefore a better mate. Today muscle building is a bigger industry than ever although it is less and less important for survival. Muscles remain as an increasingly obvious and reassuring visual symbol to women in an evolutionary era in which male quality is very diverse and not easily identified.

Sexual Positions: Most couples still prefer and use the male dominant position because, 1) it helps sperm to flow toward the egg, 2) male dominance of the outside world is inextricably tied to the female's interest in a dominant male in a dominate position, and 3) it favors male activity and female passivity. Effort and tension are antithetical to the mood of the female, the female orgasm, and the female's egg passively waiting to be fertilized.

Maternal Instinct: This is the dominant female instinct around which personality and the desire for family and children is based. It determines the way females play as children, the way they seek a mate, the way they relate to a mate, the way they raise children, the jobs they seek, and they way they do those jobs. Even women who get Ph.D.'s tend to migrate toward female oriented jobs. They choose fashion, family law, publishing and psychology over manufacturing and computers, for example. No matter how much women enter what was once the male world they do not overcome their feminine nature. They carry it with them, often with needless embarrassment, wherever they go.

Leisure Time: Perhaps the most common leisure time activity occurs in the fall as men watch football while their wives do minor household chores. Again, this behavior is not mere coincidence, it is basic biology. When not hunting or working, men rest and seek inspiration in preparation for the next burst of energy that work will require. Watching football is ideal because it provides both rest and the inspirational example of those exhibiting behavior that is central to the ancient male psyche. Women do constant chores, while their men watch football, in solidarity with the constant nature of child rearing.

Play: The size of the toy market for boys is four times bigger than for girls. Male toys reflect the aggressive, combative, adventurous, and skill oriented lifestyle that their hunter ancestors lived. Female children play less and therefore buy fewer toys. They grow while being far more passive. They merely need to wait and in all likelihood they will still become mothers. Their play is comparatively verbal, passive, and maternal. It has for decades, even through the recent feminist era, been centered around Barbie and other feminine toys. While boys are still developing, through play, the complex skills they will need as adults, girls are already competent at child rearing skills and at work with their

2.) THE BIOLOGY OF SEXUAL INTERCOURSE

mothers.

<u>Friends:</u> Women have far more friends than men and enjoy friendship far more than men. Having a friend for them is similar to having a baby. They are naturally equipped for it. Men are not so well equipped. They evolved to compete against each other for food and women, although they do make temporary political alliances, but generally only to achieve these ends.

<u>Architecture:</u> Men and women have different architectural preferences. Men prefer external outdoor structures such as bridges, huge buildings, and monuments which symbolize his domination of nature, something necessary for him to be a successful hunter/provider/husband. Conversely women prefer cozy internal spaces which are more suitable to love and nurture their children and husband. Female architects tend to do interior work while male architects tend to do exterior work.

<u>Blond Hair:</u> It seems that even today gentleman prefer blondes and that blondes have more fun (presumably because gentleman prefer them). Anyone who is certain they can definitively explain this one is probably over confident but it does seem that blond hair connotes youth and fertility, something very important to a man with sex on his mind. Babies start out with fair, often blond, hair that darkens with age. Very old women often look out of place with very blond hair because we associate such hair so much with youth and fertility.

<u>Sexual Speed:</u> Men are far quicker than women to get aroused and to act on their arousal. In India it is said to be common for men to smoke or read during intercourse in order to give their women the time they need to get fully aroused. Studies show that men often fall in love by the fourth date while women almost never fall in love so fast. Other studies show that women almost never buy pornography, but that when they spent some time with it they get as aroused by it as men. This female behavior is not coincidental. If women were as fast as men, as preoccupied as men, or equal to men their behavior would be mal-adaptive. They must maximize the quality of the few offspring they can bear and rear by being as

76

selective and discriminating as possible about each sexual encounter.

Once we begin to accept that all animals exhibit simple biologically proscribed behaviors we have a basis on which to understand why women divorce men 91% of the time, or why men divorce women only 9% of the time. With such an understanding both sexes will be in a position to substantially understand and prevent divorce, and redefine marriage.

One might ask why it is that biology or natural selection seems to produce such detailed premarital sexual behavior that most of us are eventually directed to the marital altar to vow, "till death do us part; for richer for poorer; for better for worse, etc.,"and yet seems to so badly direct our post-marital behavior that half or more of us end up divorced. The answer goes back to basic biology which indicates that reproduction is the key goal of all life forms, and that once the reproductive function is finally fulfilled through marriage, or simulated by a long term sexual relationship, the biological mission is largely complete. We are, realistically, machines designed to perform only one function. But what are we supposed to do when that function is completed or when we are certain that there are no significant obstacles to be overcome to complete nature's reproductive work? Hegel referred to this dilemma when he said, "the birth of children is the death of parents."

Complete in biological terms often means: death. Death performs an essential role in biology's drama. It speeds up the natural selection process. If parents never aged and died they would compete with their own offspring for scarce natural resources, and, keep passing on the same genes to the next generation. Those genes would produce similar offspring who eventually would run up against an environmental condition or disease against which they could not prevail. A species that reproduces many new generations in rapid succession is more apt to have within it diverse offspring with beneficial mutations that enable it to prevail against theretofore extinctive environmental conditions. Hence, death is a biologically adaptive imperative of similar but not equal importance to reproduction.

Befuddled post-marital behavior can then be seen for what it is: a part of the aging or dying process. Divorce does not occur because couples have irreconcilable differences as they and we simplistically like to think but rather because they are dying prematurely. They have lost touch with

77

2.) THE BIOLOGY OF SEXUAL INTERCOURSE

or have become resistant to the basic biological imperatives which so certainly and cleverly guided them through the early stages of courtship and love. As their relationships age with each passing day so too does their mating behavior. It begins to break down and die. They fall off the path on which biology once so carefully and forcefully propelled them because biology, at that point, has lost interest in them.

Oddly, the forces of evolution are mostly faulty; that is why more than 99% of all species are extinct. Even as evolution's best product, humans are still almost perfectly flawed; always poised to be wiped out by cosmic disaster, nuclear bombs, disease, environmental changes, or a general cultural failure. Evolution is flawed on many levels. It makes us die in great agony. Why don't we die with the same joy with which we reproduce? Both are evolved biological imperatives. This is simply a philosophical failure of the natural selection processes' ability to fully reconcile the need to die with the need to live and love. Joy at death would exactly contradict the evolutionary will to live and reproduce; yet death is equally important. Similarly, the physical act of child birth causes pain when it should, theoretically, cause pleasure. Sexual intercourse causes great pleasure even when it transmits deadly disease. The eye can see, but only in the day. We can fall in love but not necessarily with a fertile mate. We can think about how to bring love into our lives and into our community, but we can become Nazis. To live purposively with these contradictions we need to understand them in relation to the biology which created them.

Divorce is a cultural flaw that exists in opposition to our basic biology. It needs to be understood in that context. We can destroy a marriage but not without simultaneously destroying the foundation on which children grow. The failures, the inconsistencies and the contradictions that the natural selection process wove into our being must be understood and controlled, but in a way that never puts us at odds with our basic biology. Hemmingway said that love was ultimately a tragedy because it ends in death. Unfortunately death is one tragedy we cannot escape, and one on which life depends, but many marital deaths due to divorce can be escaped through the development of a culture which is based on harmony with a biology whose central purpose remains narrowly focused around reproduction and successful child rearing.

3.) THE BIOLOGY OF MALE SEXUALITY

EVEN MARRIED MEN HAVE NO SEXUAL LIMITS

Most males will recall that when they reached puberty their sexual dreams had little or nothing to do with love and family. The long hunt for constant sexual fulfillment begins with the young male virtually incapacitated by the expectation of a supple breast or snug vagina. It matters little to whom the breast or vagina is attached. As a boy matures he will eventually seek sexual compliance from one female, despite its restrictions, as the easiest way to satisfy his constant and long term reproductive needs, although the desire for variety often remains very much a part of his sexuality. This conversion to or acceptance of monogamy identifies the point at which the male need or interest in family is established.

None of this happens, it should be remembered, because men are either devils or angels, but rather because this behavior was adaptive during the millions of years in which the behavior evolved. In short, male behavior, and female behavior too, evolved only because it made survival and then reproduction possible. To live with modern relationship theories that do not fully incorporate this genetic inheritance is totally irrational; yet this is what we are routinely encouraged to do. We are deeply embarrassed to be mere animals. It is far easier for us to assume that lofty spiritual or psychological principles motivate us or should motivate us as we submit to all the modern special interests that tend to inspire our non-biological behavior.

For the male, the pursuit of sexual fulfillment is a long process characterized and defined by the female's far more discriminating nature. It seems that a male is genetically engineered to mate with all of the females above him in stature and many of those below him too. What does it really matter to him who bears his offspring? His investment, historically at least, was very minimal and often without consequence. Nature put him on automatic pilot with a singular mission so to speak. His most natural and basic inclination was to have opportunistic sex as often as possible and with as many different women as possible as a way to maximize the long term survivability of his genes.

Men are so genetically driven to fulfil this biological need that when women are not available they easily and often turn to other forms of simulated sex. Most commonly this involves different forms of masturbation, sex with prostitutes and masseuses, and even sex with animals. Homosexuality is popular in prisons; pedophilia was common in Ancient Greece. Masturbation is so common among male teenagers that they often discuss techniques with each other. At one point in the late 1980's the national media was warning that several deaths had occurred when teenage boys accidentally hung themselves while attempting partially asphyxiating during masturbation. Women, rather than men, are prostitutes because women don't value pure genital sex. Men do. For men, sex, all by itself, has value. A male prostitute has no value because women don't value what they sell. When a stable worker was recently arrested on Long Island for having sex with a horse the popular media was flooded with humorous tales and jokes from around the world about similar and longstanding practices with a variety of different animals. Desmond Morris, the noted popular anthropologist, points out that almost half of the boys who grow up on farms in the U.S. have their first sexual experiences with animals. When Larry Flynt of Hustler magazine was asked about his admitted sexual experience with chickens he replied, " hey, I was just a kid growing up on a farm." President Clinton's diverse sex life has made him something of a role model for the guests on the Jerry Springer show. Whether it was Methodist marital sex with Hillary, quick oral sex with Paula Jones and Monica Lewinsky, or a seemingly warm, long term relationship with Gennifer Flowers he seems to have typically diverse male sexual proclivities. There are often few limits on the breadth or intensity of male sexuality.

Men are sexual salesmen and women are their bosses. In business salesmen get paid to sell product; the more they sell the more they get paid. To sell more they'll say anything to the customer, or the boss. They contradictorily tell the customer that it's the best product in the world and then they tell the boss that he must improve the quality, add features, and lower the price of the product to make it truly salable. The boss must analyze the whole situation to see that the cost of what the salesman proposes doesn't absorb all the profit or benefit. In the end, salesmen rise above their non-salesman bosses to run most companies because they have the spirit, drive, and initiative to get out there and make something happen. Too much analysis can lead to more analysis and then to fear and passivity. Sales action is more important than managerial analysis. He who hesitates fails; he who dares wins. Men are born to dare; to act; to risk their lives in battle against a defiant universe, while women are born to cautiously and intuitively analyze prospective mates in order to select the best possible one, and then to cautiously and intuitively analyze their nonverbal offspring in order to help them survive and grow.

In the end men end up running most marriages for the same reason salesmen run most businesses. They are more aggressive. If nature made both sexes like men there would be too much sex. It would be like male homosexual sex. It would feature 100's if not 1000's of sexual contacts with no interest in slowing down for quality or family as in the case of pre-aids homosexual bathhouses. There would be no concern for the overall purpose, value, or profit of the activity. If nature made both sexes like women there would be too much analysis and too little sex. Pat Califia described lesbian sex as follows: "women's idea of a good time at lesbian music festivals consists of everyone joining hands, taking off their shirts and dancing bare-breasted around the campfire-then falling asleep, exhausted, in each others arms, before they have had a chance to do anything." Blumstein and Schwartz concluded in their study that lesbians had the fewest sexual encounters because neither partner wanted to be the initiator. In a similar vain JoAnn Loulan writes, "Many Lesbians didn't know they were Lesbians until their 20's or 30's because they didn't know the feelings they were having about their best friends-wanting to stay over every night and talk-were sexual feelings. Gay men, on the other hand, knew they wanted to have sex with their best friends."

Despite the disparate natures of men and women the human business would fail without the conflicting but complimentary input of each sex. The difference between men and women is a specifically designed biological system that optimizes the species' success. It is something that should be happily embraced; not pointlessly criticized by those who can't understand it. The difference between men and women is supposed to and often does lead to many wonderfully romantic and sexual relationships but all too often a failure to understand or naturally react to the difference between men and women leads to hugely dysfunctional relationships.

Although men are encouraged toward monogamy it is something of a compromise for them. In partial solidarity with many of their ancestral species, and to a lesser extent with most pre-modern males of their own species who survived quite well without forming permanent families, many human males remain somewhat conflicted throughout their adult lives by the notion of commitment, family, and monogamy. In a real way men are asked to give up sex for the greater joy or civility of family. Although most men do it, it is an on going compromise for them.

The long and sometimes trying search for diverse sexual/visual gratification never really ends for the male. Even if it ends physically due to marriage it still goes on symbolically. The continuous nature of it is an inextricable part of him and his culture. As the world's most successful model, Cindy Crawford is perhaps the greatest symbol of that culture. She is a visual symbol of mans' ability to identify singular beauty and his ability to generate instant sexual enthusiasm. Neither her age, skill, intelligence, reproductive capacity nor availability matter much. As a mere symbol on a magazine, box, or TV she is a rallying point around which men celebrate their disloyal, indiscriminate and ever ready sexual instinct. But what purpose does the dream of perfect beauty have? Since perfect beauty can never be found it keeps men always searching for a better and better women with whom to share his genes, and it keeps them visually attracted to women as opposed to trees or other objects or other men. The desire to reproduce, like the desire for food, was so critical to the forces of evolution that little energy was given over to mechanisms with which to regulate it let alone shut it off. Men are stuck in the "on position" so to speak. What does this mean for the knowledgeable married woman? It means that each day can be the first day of her marriage.

Male love in its natural state is, for the most part, false. Males pass through puberty dreaming of how exquisite sex would be with the girls in school, on TV, in movies, in the neighborhood, and even in the car speeding by on the freeway. One study showed that men between 14-25 think of sex 20 times an hour during the day and average 12 erections during a normal night's sleep. The sex they think of focuses on how wonderful a woman's body would feel to them; it has little to do with family or the specific woman involved.

In light of this it would be very rare indeed for a boy to honestly express his feeling to a girl. He understands that honesty would not work.

If he said to her, "pardon me but I just spent math class dreaming about sex with you; would it be ok if we skip next period and have sex," he would certainly be rejected. In conversations with his male comrades he would be more honest by saying something very similar to: "God, would I like to do her."

He implicitly understands that honesty will not work with a girl. He knows he wants it more than she does. A girl has much more generalized objectives when it comes to relationships with the opposite sex; she won't be used just for sex. So what is a boy to do? Mostly he lies, and then he grows up and continues to lie throughout his marriage. Perhaps "lie" is too strong. Maybe we should say that he hides his true feelings until such time as he is certain that they will not be rejected. But even when his sexual advances are accepted he knows that his true feeling may be a little too masculine for his mate. It is up to the female, and well within her power, to understand the nature of male sexuality. She can demand of him that he learn to connect and link his sexual feelings to feelings of love for her, his family, and community. If she is skilled she can convert the sweet nothings (lies) he whispers in her ear, into sweet somethings that demonstrate a meaningful biological love which encourages him to truly value his wife and family. All she has to say is, "I'll do that if you say and believe this."

Mae West was perhaps the most honest and sexually powerfully woman in our cultural history. She achieved that symbolic status by asking the world's most embarrassing question: "Is that a banana in your pocket or are you just glad to see me?" The man to whom that question was directed was found out. He was betrayed by his own body. Not only were his deepest and most personal desires exposed, but he was also delivered directly into the hands of a strange and powerful woman. She had the power to dash him and his fragile erection to the ground or to legitimize him and it by returning his passion. In dashing him to the ground she obtained her legendary status. She demonstrated how easily all men are controlled. She knew how easily and powerfully aroused they are; how easily she could say "no" to them and most importantly, that she could say "yes" but "yes" only so long as her conditions are accepted. Modern women have a laundry list of complaints against the men they divorce and the men with whom they end relationships but they don't

3.) THE BIOLOGY OF MALE SEXUALITY

understand that a heterosexual relationship inherently involves a contract wherein both parties must agree to acknowledge the disparate sexual nature of men and women.

Oddly, even after marriage; after a couple may have expressed their lifelong passion for one another, the male is still confronted by the Mae West biology that lives, often deep, within his wife. He must act. He must take the risk that each sexual advance will be seen, felt or heard and then rejected. But suppose a couple decided to be sexually honest with each other? In such an odd situation the male would probably initiate sex by talking much like the high school student above. He might say, "hi honey, I got really horny thinking about you today; could we please make love?" She might reply, "sorry, not in the mood," or, "ok, how about at 10 o'clock after the kids are in bed," or ok, "but would you brush my hair first?" She might also do Mae West one better and say, "please take off your clothes so I can really see how much you want me." The male would have little desire to resist, despite any embarrassment, at which point he would be totally in her hands almost as if he were again nursing at his mother's breast. If that were the road to sexual fulfillment being offered, he'd take it, and probably quite happily, but only after a little training offered by a normally shy and reluctant wife.

At some point during love making a couple must complete nature's cycle though. The Madonna/ emasculator/ dominatrix/earth mother role must be dropped and both parties must balance the equation by moving toward equality or slight male domination. In the end, neither party can be wholly dominated because nature doesn't produce losers. Such an occurrence would be a perfect contradiction. The man must be, and be seen as a successful hunter and, secondarily, a husband and father. The woman must be, and be seen as sexually desirable, and secondarily, as a wife and mother. He must reconcile his role as dominant hunter and submissive lover while she must reconcile her view of him. This need not be a complicated task. Everything goes on as before except the man is now required to pay an admission or entrance fee or, we can say, the woman is now required to ask for such a fee. In the course of openly and honestly acknowledging what they legitimately want from each other at the time of intercourse, they are maintaining the foundation of a complete marriage. Sex is no longer just a physical act, it is a celebration of the couple's entire life together.

Pornography can help us to further clarify the biological nature of male/female relationships. But first let's consider what pornography is. It is, most often, the depiction of violent sex between two adults who are not in love. More importantly, it is watched, often, by men who have been rejected by women well into adulthood. The violence represents their defense against female sexual power. They can't have sex; so it becomes something which must be taken. Men are required by their biology to reproduce. When women refuse their reproductive advances they turn to images of violent sex as a means to rationalize the only kind of sexual behavior which they feel is available to them. It puts power back in their hands. It teaches them that if they want sex they can go out and take it, even though few do. Those who wish to ban it fail to acknowledge that it provides an outlet for unrequited male genital love. When the guys at the firehouse, many of whom are happily married, watch violent or non-violent pornography they are harmlessly dreaming about a side of life that might have been had they never gotten married. Pornography rarely features people in love because those who would appreciate it generally don't need it much. They have real life lovers and they are offended by what is seemingly a contradiction, i.e., a display not only of public intimacy, but also a display of intimacy without love.

Other men who feel sexually immature or inadequate turn to non-sexual and seemingly legitimate lifestyles to sublimate their sexual energy. If they are afraid of adult female sexuality they instead love all women, and all men too. It is easier, safer, more reliable, and quite well respected. Catholic priests are the most obvious example of this. Sadly, many of them seem unable to fully sublimate their sexual energy. Some estimates indicate that upwards of 10% of the profession has prayed on powerless young boys to fulfill the sexual needs which they feared would be overwhelmed or rejected by powerful adult females. To a lesser extent most men feel the sexual power of adult women and are intent on finding and maintaining a relationship. Women ought to understand male dependence and use it to actively participate in their relationships.

The theory that male homosexuality is caused by a dominant emasculating all powerful mother fades in and out of popularity. At the moment it has regained some popularity within the psychology community although it remains extremely unpopular within the gay rights community which is obviously anxious to portray its members as very normal human beings who were naturally born gay; not created as the result of an abnormal or mistaken childhood. If they are seen as normal people they are better able to make the case that they are fully entitled to normal legal protection from any form of discrimination despite their obviously abnormal lifestyles.

The theory, though, is consistent with basic biology. The male starts out life very attached to his loving and dominant mother. Around puberty he begins to separate from his mother and identify more with his father and same sex peers who prepare him for the outside world that he must one day conquer. If he remains attached just to his mother he misses the sexual education that he would have come from his father, the most important part of which concerns the nuances of pursuit of the opposite sex. Males learn all the nuances of female pursuit and how to successfully cope with and rationalize the constant frustration and failure they encounter along the way. Male teenage sexual feelings are very strong; boys need to talk and joke about them with each other. Without sharing and normalizing such an intense experience the young male puts his sexual development at risk. It is inconceivable that a young male would go to school and talk to the girls about how horny he was. The hunter must depend on stealth to keep the real motives which would certainly be seen as lecherous if expressed generally to the opposite sex, hidden. Honesty wouldn't be a viable strategy anymore than sharing bathrooms with girls would be a viable strategy. Normal sexual development requires separation of the sexes. Each sex has very different methods and objectives, at least in the near term.

If a male is denied this separation by too little in utero testosterone or the emasculating and continuous presence of a dominant mother or by an absent father or same sex peers, his sexual development may be smothered. Honest conversations with his mother about his growing sexual preoccupation would quickly begin to seem incestuous or lecherous. The biologically driven male might focus, with disastrous consequences, on his mother if he is not deterred by his immediate social structure. Besides, a mother does not know how to commiserate with her son about his meager sex life. In fact the sex life she knows is very different from what her son needs to know. A dominant mother would unconsciously insist on a non-incestuous but important role as her son's sexual mentor with very negative effects. She would encourage him to be female and effeminate rather then male and cool, i.e., she will teach him her version of love which is primarily drawn from the way biology encourages her to love a new born child. The male version of love is quite different. It requires him to break away from his mother's loving embrace at puberty and develop male friends who understand and share his real feelings and objectives. He can eventually go safely back, but never all the way back, to fully share his post pubescent feelings with his mother. Sadly the male hunter/lover only fully becomes a man when he has established his ability to be independent of all consuming female love.

Itzak Rabin said at one point in his life that what he hated about the Arabs was that they made Israeli children into soldiers and killers. The Arabs, he felt, had added something horrible to the psyche of Israeli children. So it actually is with all men, they go back to their mothers or wives with fond memories of simple maternal love but they are conflicted because their passion for maternal love has been alloyed with their opposing passion for the male culture of hunting and war and sex. For a woman to love a man she must recognize these opposing passions and actively help him balance them.

The skill and joy of being a successful hunter requires that a man learn to cope with defeat. The hunt for food and territory is not always successful and neither is the search for a mate. Being cool in the face of this constant defeat is part of male culture. Men learn to project the James Dean image which says to a prospective mate, "I'm an experienced hunter; you see from my cool and confident style that I've hunted successfully or at least that my successes far out weigh my defeats."

For women though, defeat is not as significant a part of their culture. They are born to love their children and they generally succeed at this steadily and successfully for their entire lives. If a dominant woman alone teaches a post-pubescent male how to love she will teach him what she knows, i.e., feminine love. She may know how to identify a good hunter but she can't teach him the essence of the hunt. The joy and spirit of the hunt are lost on her. She cannot teach him how to fail with confidence because she doesn't understand it herself. Instead she will teach him to be like a woman. She will teach him maternal, nurturing love, something that will ultimately be rejected by prospective mates as homosexual or feminine in appearance. They will hold out for a hunter first and a nurturer second or third.

Male homosexuals often have feminine characteristics because they lacked the testosterone to successfully differentiate from their feminine fetal origins. They had enough testosterone to develop from a female embryo into a male body but not enough to develop a male psyche. The high income of homosexuals may indicate that they are abnormal only in that they have the best parts of both sexes, namely, the spirit and aggression of men and the nurturing and interpersonal skills of women. Unfortunately, this is an oxymoron since it completely discounts the value of reproduction. Homosexual love is not natural; it does not lead to reproduction and it does not serve nature's primary purpose, although, as mentioned above, it may serve a reproductively significant ancillary purpose. While it may imitate elements of real love it is not part of the essential biological model; hence nature has less reason to reproduce it. But, for our purposes here it serves to point out how critical the balance between male and female is. We might even conclude that female heterosexual love is little more than testosterone balancing.

Testosterone is not only the sex hormone, it is also the hunter or aggression hormone. In the animal kingdom we often see that a male who defeats another male rival will mount that male as if to have sexual intercourse. Sex and violence are inextricably linked for men by testosterone. In a similar fashion when humans want to hurl the greatest insult at one another they often say, "fuck you." A man hunts to impress a woman with whom he wants to have sex. If a man has too much testosterone, as in the case of athletes who use the hormone to improve their athletic ability or build muscles, they can become too masculine. They become aggressive to the point of being senselessly destructive and therefore unattractive to women. But if a man has too little testosterone he may become unattractive to women due to his femininity. The hormonal balance in a man creates the man. A woman who is too unlike Mae West; who instead provides sex on demand to her husband eliminates the need for his testosterone. He neither needs to hunt nor impress her because she provides sex on demand. A woman who provides too little sex frustrates a

MEN HAVE TESTOSTERONE
FOR BOTH SEX AND VIOLENCE

man's basic reproductive purpose and, ultimately, her relationship with him. She fails to recognize the duality of testosterone and in so doing she undermines the basic hormonal or biological purpose of her marriage.

Women bred men through the forces of natural selection to believe that sex and violence or dominance are alloyed; but through culture and rationale marital behavior they must teach them to separate the two behaviors even though they are associated with one chemical. We may wish that women and nature had the subtlety to create two easily controlled hormones, one for aggression and one for love, but this didn't happen. Testosterone created a male brain out of a female brain by compartmentalizing it for specific purposes. Learning disabilities are more common among males because if one compartment is adversely affected it is not easily reinforced by another whereas in the more generalized female brain this is not the case. Similarly, a stroke in the male brain produces more serious affects. It is up to us to improve upon nature's short coming.

Women bred men to be dominant because they wanted their dominant male offspring to dominate enough to survive and reproduce. Women love dominant men because they love survival. It was the single best evolutionary strategy for them to pursue. Without it they might have evolved Homo Sapiens into a trivial, endangered, or extinct species. Despite all of our problems it is still far far better to have evolved as a human than to be, say, a bug, a bird, or anything else.

Dominance is still the most common approach to love today. Here is how the famous sex researchers Masters and Johnson describe the sex life of a modern male and female: "The man initiates the mounting process when he is ready, presuming that if his partner is lubricated, she is ready. Usually he hunts for, finds the vaginal outlet, and inserts the penis; yet, the woman could have accomplished the insertion with greater facility, for she certainly would not have had to hunt and find. He selects coital positioning, usually without consultation as to his partner's preference, and she almost always defers to his decision. He predominantly sets the thrusting pattern and presumes that she will respond and will be pleased. And usually she makes every effort to cooperate with his thrusting pattern whether she is pleased or not. One wonders by what divine gift of providence the human male is endowed with such infinite knowledge of women's sexual anatomy and sexual needs. When reflecting on the degree of male dominance in coital interaction, we have a better understanding of the many pitfalls that the culture has placed in the way of an enduring heterosexual partnership for unsuspecting men and women."

Certainly it is completely absurd for them to attribute male dominance exclusively to human culture when it existed throughout evolutionary history from the crocodile to the modern monkey, but it is instructive nevertheless to note that through culture women are now asking for relief from the dominance that once was their favored evolutionary weapon. To emphasis the point Masters and Johnson further point out that homosexual couples are, on average, likely to be happier sexually than heterosexuals; presumably because they know their partners' desires as they know their own.

If we assume, as we safely can, that a man who is getting too much sex, too little, or the wrong kind of sex is not a happy camper and that a woman who is providing such sex is also not a happy camper, if only by virtue of her mate's unhappiness, then it becomes necessary to figure out how to reconcile the seemingly desperate sexual preferences of men and women. Dominance has become, partially, a vestigial evolutionary strategy that must be partially supplanted by culture. We understand that to merely dominate a woman is no longer sufficient as it was when short term survival was our primary concern. Today the planet is overrun with too many people (the result of successful reproduction and long term survival) and we have a large brain that causes us to reflect on the overall meaning of it all. Today we need to understand the way biology influences us, but we also need a way to think consistently and rationally about the way we behave in relation to our biology.

To find out what modern men think of the overall meaning of it all we can consult the Mayflower Madame, Sidney Bittle Barrows. She states, "By and large, calls involving two or more girls and one male client were about as exotic as we would get...Because being with two women at once is the most common male fantasy....more than one man told us that an evening he spent with two or more girls constituted the greatest sexual thrill of his life." Time and again we hear that this is the most common male fantasy and we see that this is so on the pages of Playboy and Penthouse. But what does this tell us about the nature of men and dominance? We might assume that if two breasts are erotic for men then four or eight breasts are even more erotic to men. Or, we might assume that the prospect of dominating or impregnating 2-3 women is more demanding and erotic than dominating one. Or we might make the more reasonable assumption that the eroticism grows out of the impossibility of dominating a pair group of actively engaged lesbians.

But, how could this be erotic? Easy. Lower animals seek, impress, and then impregnate. This fulfills their objectives' 100%, but for man this is not enough. There is no illusion that life is complete or fulfilling just because of sex. There are few internal psychology mechanisms or external cultural mechanisms which say that dominance is a complete and meaningful experience for a man. Dominance makes man king, but king of nothing. He is king of his wife for an ejaculatory moment but then above her and alone in a vast, lonely, and threatening universe in which he is an infinitely trivial part. Men may often fall asleep after sex to escape this dilemma. They fall asleep faster or runaway even faster or feel even guiltier after they have masturbated or have had sex with a chicken because this offers absolutely no escape or long term comfort from loneliness or death or the vast unexplained universe that cannot be dominated.

On the other hand, two or three actively engaged lesbians do offer an escape. They are positioned between man and the universe. He knows that he cannot dominate them, if only because he knows he can't have two orgasms in two women. Besides, as lesbians they may not even be that interested in him, let alone be interested in being dominated by him. But they could dominate and fondle him with their numbers and indifference. If he did engage with them there would be no question who would set the agenda and who would have the responsibility. This is like the old movie in which a woman ripped off her blouse and bra, stuck her torso out the window and shouted, "come to mama." In a sense lesbians are like mothers. They can provide complete maternal security, as if to a baby, to a grown man who cannot lust after his mother and who doesn't really want the responsibility and loneliness that comes from dominating a woman. A woman who is an equal becomes a sexual existentialist. She provides meaning to men by shielding them from a universe which they can perceive but cannot conquer. She provides a universe that does not need to be conquered. The lesson here for normal heterosexual women is that men can easily be made to be partners in relationships where each party equally dominates the other. Men understand that sex focuses their attention for a moment and that love focuses their attention and shields them with the quintessential illusion for a lifetime.

4.) THE BIOLOGY OF FEMALE SEXUALITY

CAVE WOMEN AND MODERN
WOMEN DATE TALLER MEN

Women are different from men. Male models make only 30% of what female models make. This is overt sexual discrimination. Although women's genetic need to reproduce is as great as man's, it is manifested far differently. No male equivalent to Cindy Crawford exists. In the 1960's, for example, when modern feminism was in its awkward infancy and at its most immature, Playgirl magazine was published with the expectation that newly masculinized women would be attracted to naked men just the way men were attracted to the naked women of Playboy. It turned out that the nation's five million homosexual men were more attracted to the naked men of Playgirl than the nation's 125 million women. Women are sexually slow and discriminating when they meet a man, when they fall in love with him, and even when they have an orgasm with him. It generally takes far more than a picture to arouse them. It takes the certainty that the man is a successful hunter, and also a supportive husband and father. Even when fatherhood is not a possibility, due to advancing age for example, female love continues to work largely the same way because love continuously exists within each of us as a reflection of evolution's overall purpose. Evolution gave a genetic definition of love to women because it was that definition of love which made survival possible. Women who practiced love according to that definition are the women who had children and genes that survived. Women are stuck, so to speak, in the "on position" in this regard. The search for a good husband and father is the genetic compulsion without which love would have no pleasure, value, purpose, meaning, or context.

Before a female is compelled to mate with a male she needs to firstly send a signal that she may want him as a mate at some point in the future. Only after she has determined that he is healthy, skillful, nurturing, and sexually loyal will she consider him as a mate. This is characteristic female behavior which biology drives her to employ in order to insure the birth and survival of her children, and the continuing support of her mate during the long developmental process. For a woman, the opportunity to conceive is sharply limited by a 9-month pregnancy and the years of preoccupying child rearing that lie ahead. Accordingly, adaptive behavior evolved to maximize the value of each precious sexual contact with the opposite sex.

This celebrated coy female behavior is an integral part of female culture. It is testimony to feminine sexual power. A woman needs that power to attract men and then make them linger until she has had time to assess their suitability as mates. The man, as the song says, chases the women until she catches him. The nature of female sexuality explains, for example, why women out spend men ten to one on hair care and clothing. The more a woman can enhance her sexual attractiveness the greater her ability to attract and maintain the interest of many prospective mates, one of whom will eventually qualify as the best possible selection. The female is just as determined as the male, but her determination is passive, indirect, and very patient as she pursues a mate because that is the behavior necessary for genetic survival.

Survival interests all of biology's creatures equally. By looking at simpler creatures we can see our true selves far easier. We may like to think that we are far different and superior to apes but in the most important way we are completely equal in that we are both able to do nothing more than act out our very similar and biologically ordained roles. To see ourselves without egocentric prejudice we merely need to look at our biological predecessors: apes. Humans are not meaningfully superior to apes anymore than apes are meaningfully superior to dogs or mice. Even when it comes to relationships, apes and humans still have virtually everything that is important in common. It is perhaps inevitable to assume that since as a species we are vastly superior at the complexities of quantum mechanics we must also be vastly superior at the complexities of love. But this is a false assumption that helps to prevent us from developing a simple and comprehensive theory of biological love.

Psychologists, feminists, and others, capitalize on or exploit this tendency by encouraging us to believe that human love is complex and superior. Complexity has economic value. Lawyers, accountants and many other professionals encourage complexity as a means to create salable and profitable expertise. Competition between these experts to demonstrate a particular or superior expertise often produces another meaningless layer of complexity. This false promotion of complexity leads to confusion rather than understanding. Who would argue that the blizzard of modern psychological truths to which we are all subjected has made us better at relationships today than we were 50 years ago? Does anybody think that psychologists have better marriages than biologists, or plumbers, or medical doctors? Why is it that Barbara De Angelis, Ph.D., arguably our nation's most prolific and successful psychologist / relationship expert was married five times before her 45th birthday? Did the overall divorce rate go up or down during the last couple of decades when psychology became so popular? Do we need Sally Jesse Raphael today more than we did 50 years ago or have we just become more psychologically oriented and less biologically oriented over those years? Psychology and popular culture in general can't change biology, improve upon it, pretend to be unrelated to it, and they certainly can't improve our understanding of biological relationships so long as they are extensively motivated by an artificial need to complicate them with artificial expertise.

An ape will share a banana or meat to convince a prospective mate that he can and will feed her. He knows that he must demonstrate his ability to provide for her, and any possible offspring, a secure world in which to live. A physicist, by bringing home a discovery about the nature of the universe, accomplishes much the same thing. He conquers the world outside of his home so that his family's place in that world is more secure. The need to eat and the need to understand the universe are ultimately the same. As food becomes abundant, the need to secure long term health grows; as health and other things are secured so too must the ever threatening universe be secured. Purposive and continuous effort forestalls the death and extinction that is eventually the fate of all species. When a woman prefers a physicist over a carpenter she is acceding to biology's hierarchy. She is creating biological happiness by securing a seemingly better place in the universe for her genes. We can't be either proud or embarrassed by this. It is simply a fact that while we are capable of more complex behavior than lower animals we are not capable of more complex motives.

The human female's mating behavior seems relatively complex, difficult, and time consuming but in the end she shares her problems with females of all species. Her endeavor never ends with a perfect result, just the best possible compromise at the time. A woman is faced with the nerve-racking choice of selecting one of the available males or waiting alone in the hope that an agreeable and higher quality male will come along before too much more of her fertility period has passed. It is very easy for buyers' remorse or cognitive dissonance to set in after the choice has been made given the impossibility of ever having the best possible husband. Complete quality is impossible to ever fully achieve. Conversely, the male's simple desire for continuous sexual intercourse is far more easily fulfilled after marriage. He may well experience disappointment for many of the same reasons as a woman, but it will not be nearly so profound. Quality for him is not nearly so important. Moreover, a man has a life outside of his marriage. After intercourse or after anything a man can and must go to sleep and then to work. His marriage is only part of his life. An average or poor marriage, then, doesn't mean that he has an average or poor life. A woman generally has no place to go that is as intrinsically important to her as her home. Her marriage is her life and her future. If her marriage is poor her life is poor. She is naturally encouraged toward divorce. Lord Byron once wrote, "Man's love is of man's life a thing apart; tis woman's whole existence." To put it another way, a woman is far more conscious than a man of the quality in a relationship. A woman's natural attention to and awareness of quality will cause her to be the one who ends a relationship in divorce (91% versus 9% for men). The lack of quality in her relationship most often occurs because she didn't know how to identify it to begin with or because she didn't know how to maintain and nurture it once she had it.

Once the female has achieved her initial goal of producing offspring, she too is less inclined to continue her original mating behavior with the same enthusiasm and self discipline because such behavior is difficult, may not seem to serve as useful a purpose, conflicts with thoughts about whether another mate might produce superior offspring, and is less effective when directed toward her then sexually secure male. It can become easier to mate more as a matter of contractual obligation, habit, or fantasize about love's early days than as a way to re-satisfy the basic sexual instincts which always remain essential to their current marital life. When, after many years of anticipation, sex finally becomes regular it necessarily becomes different. It can be a difference that tears a couple apart or a difference that maintains and builds them together.

If a man neglects or, in the worst case, abuses his wife as his relationship ages he is doing something new and different from his basic biological role. Certainly, he is not playing the same role he originally played to win his wife's affection. In fact, it is the opposite role. Somehow he has begun to act as if his fulfillment can be achieved by doing the opposite of what he once did. This is something that often happens as relationships age. Both parties get confused; they slowly relinquish the discipline of their youthful romantic roles because their basic objectives have been achieved.

A male's sexual role is the very difficult and frustrating one of controlling the uncontrollable outside world. He is supposed to leave home and bring back a banana or the Theory of Relativity. When he doesn't fully succeed he will often substitute his controllable wife for the uncontrollable obstacles outside of the home. Even though there is ultimately little to gain from controlling his wife, it still can feel good as long as he can maintain the illusion that control of his wife is similar to control of the outside world. But this is a larcenous approach. Control of the outside world ultimately gives him control over his wife. If he can get that control directly, without recourse to the frustrating and demanding outside world, he has, seemingly, found a short cut solution to his problem.

The wife often becomes an unwitting accomplice because she too forgets basic biology. She is often anxious to maintain the controlling image of her husband that caused her to marry him in the first place. If he becomes controlling toward her she will often encourage him in order to maintain her image of his control of the outside world or even to help him maintain his own image of himself. This too is a perversion of her evolutionary role from which she ultimately has little or nothing to gain.

A woman's romantic role is to provide sex to her husband, but only when he deserves it or when she is comfortable in providing it. She too has to be controlling. She must be controlling enough not to provide sex when he does not offer behavior that she deems to be in some way reciprocal. If she wants to relinquish control as the sex act progresses, as many women do, she would not be out of harmony with her basic biological objectives, but at some point, usually the beginning, she too must be in control. The age-old battle of the sexes is lost by both parties when the female gives up the discipline of control that she originally processed so thoroughly.

Teaching women the art of control, while seemingly problematic, should not be considering that it does not conflict with their basic objectives as mother or sexual partner. As mothers, women are given extreme control over their children. The more a mother loves her children the more difficult it is for her to maintain that control in the face of incessant demands. But women generally understand that they must maintain control and that doing so is consistent with love; not opposed to it. Further, the control a mother exerts is ultimately dependant on her physical superiority. What mother would like to raise a child without greater physical strength? Yet, in the case of children, control, even physical control, is not considered to be evil because love and control are not inconsistent with each other.

The physical control a woman exercises over her child is not unlike the physical/sexual control she should exercise over her husband. A woman with a husband has a great deal of control over him. A loving relationship is a controlling relationship. If she acts in an unloving way he is deeply hurt by the particular kind of control she has exercised. Love gives control and creates dependency. The balance of power in a loving relationship is established and maintained by the control each party exercises over the other. The problem we have with acknowledging the relationship between love and control stems from the general social principle that peace and civility is best preserved when no one has the ability to control and/or make war against another. This is the fundamental meaning of egalitarian democracy. It is not a means to solicit the wisdom of an intellectual electorate but rather a means to keep control as weak as possible. Control does exist however both in politics and love. In the interest of simplicity and a broad social principle: peace, we merely pretend that it doesn't. But, a teacher controls a student, a boss an employee, a General a Private, a parent a child, a police officer a motorist, a preacher a congregation, and a God a universe.

A marriage is also inherently controlling. It is a contract wherein each party vows to maintain equal levels of power or control. If the man is able to gain increasing levels of power through intimidation, abuse, neglect, or his wife's acquiesce it may, at first at least, seem desirable and secure to him. He is empowered to make decisions for them as a couple and her as an individual. In this situation she may be supportive of his power in part out her perception that love and support are closely allied and in part because she has forgotten how to control a powerful adult male who may or may not be more difficult to control than a defenseless child. In the end the support she provides begins to feel more and more meaningless to the husband, who becomes more and more controlling, because it is provided by a person who is less and less; someone not substantial enough to insist that her life too must be supported and empowered if it is to have the capacity to offer empowerment and support to a husband. A wife who can't say "no" can't really say "yes" either.

The control in a marriage does not have to be simultaneous or similar in nature. One party might supply money; the other sex, or, one party might supply emotional support; the other social status. In the end there must be a rough balance of control based on what each party values most. The details, then, are particular to each relationship. Love is nature's greatest narcotic. The control through which it works frees us from the crushing responsibility and loneliness that necessarily accompanies an independent life, but we must understand that love and control are not opposing forces if we are to understand marriage. Love is unique in that it simultaneously allows us to give and receive almost total control.

The woman who quickly and self-assuredly portrays herself as an innocent bystander to the abuse in her marriage, to pick an obvious and extreme example, is really acknowledging the decline of her own sexual ability. The man's sexual ability, being very limited in scope in the first place, in all likelihood does not decline, i.e., he continues to ask for and receive sex on a regular or semi-regular basis. The woman may continue to provide sex in such a situation, but no longer in the romantic / biological context that existed at the beginning of her marriage. She, by giving up sexual equality, gives up full participation in her own marriage. The endless sexual cycle within a marriage starts with her in control of her man, but progresses to a point at which she cedes that control to a mate whose primary role will be taking care of (controlling) her and her children.

When a woman can't get back the control with which she originally so thoroughly controlled her mate the cycle is broken; her relationship goes out of balance. Love depends on balance; on both parties giving control to the other. When a woman loses this control of her relationship her first inclination is to blame men in general or her husband's overwhelmingly controlling nature, rather than her own inability to understand the nature of love and take appropriate action.

When a loving couple has achieved a power balance they won't acknowledge that it is a balance of power. Such terminology would seem cold and unloving. But it is key to a relationship. We see this in all aspects of the relationship. For example, almost every task can be done more effectively and efficiently. This is the nature of progress. A lawyer who is trained to think logically might be inclined to find fault with everything from the effectiveness and efficiency with which his wife does the dishes to the way she talks or raises the kids. If she is not able to defend herself, both parties will find the lack of balance intolerable. If she is able to defend herself either with the natural force of her intellect and personality or by linking his overly logical mind to a diminished sex life, she will have used weapons as powerful as his to create and maintain a loving marriage. This may contradict the notion of a fairy tale love which assumes that a man will always want to be a Prince Charming to a sleeping beauty who "just lies there" or the notion that love will naturally endure just because the couple was evenly matched in the beginning, but it is the nature of real romance or of a real relationship.

A relationship with a man is similar to a relationship with a child or even another woman. If one party gradually takes control that party will become helpless, frustrated, and angry. This is characteristic of a child, a man, and yes, even another woman who ends up in control. We call a child in this position, spoiled, and nobody would argue that being spoiled like rotten milk helps either party or the relationship.

Dr. Nancy Friday eloquently forgets this point in her book: How To Love a Difficult Man. A woman I know saw this title and immediately turned to her new boyfriend and said, "are you a difficult man." She had been instantly set up by the title and pop culture to believe that it is common for men to be difficult. This instantly reinforced the notion that what ever went wrong in her 20 years of failed relationships was probably the guy's fault and thus helped to insure that she would be equally unable to improve the next 20 years of relationships.

Dr. Friday establishes her case that men are difficult in the most incredibly unscientific way. All that she says is, "if we asked a crowd of women how many of them had been in relationships with difficult men almost all of them would say: "yes." She felt no need to present any more evidence than that. If she had asked the same crowd about how many of them shared equal responsibility for the condition of their relationship or the demise of their previous relationship we can assume none of them would have answered affirmatively. But in a male bashing era her approach struck the right cord with the publishing industry and book buying public. On the positive side, the book goes on to almost two hundred pages pointing out how bad men are and what women must affirmatively do to maintain and build relationships with them. But she never stops to consider that if most women must do these things in order to love, then those who don't or haven't, aren't acting in a loving way and hence ought to be held as culpable as men. The problem is not that men are difficult, but that men and women are difficult.

Her approach though is certainly a step above suggesting that women turn to lesbianism but it is only a small step because it sets women up to always believe that their particular man may be just too manly and difficult to be controlled despite their very studied and exhaustive efforts. Moreover, it completely denigrates men while failing to make a distinction between difficult men, children, women, or even animals. Having read the book a woman is apt to say " why should I have to work so hard to control the bastard; if he loved me he'd.....". Additionally, the book fails to point out that a male/female relationship is among the easiest to maintain because sexual energy can be used whereas in other relationships biology does not provide such a powerful incentive. A book about how to love difficult people would have been far more legitimate and helpful but far less saleable and trendy at a time when feminist politics has taken precedence over love and marriage.

The way people treat each other matters. This author remembers walking up his street as a boy to see a 12 year old neighbor standing on his living room couch naked. A few moments later his mother came out with his clothes. It seems that the mother had started this routine when her son was a baby and just forget to discontinue it despite her sons advancing age. If Ms. Friday had seen this would she have been tempted to write a book about how to love difficult children? The point is the no matter how bizarre a relationship is, it's exactly what the participants have created together. To define one party pejoratively is stupid and actually counter productive.

Love is a discipline or maintained balance that offers the greatest happiness we can know. In the West we discipline ourselves to do as God says and we hope that in our faith God will love us away from our earthly problems, especially death. In the East many still struggle for Nirvana. They discipline themselves to feel a timeless love or harmony with nature that similarly frees them from normal earthly problems and concerns. The ballet dancer disciplines himself for harmony with transcendent themes represented through music and scenery. We love to see and experience this to harmonize ourselves with the same themes. When a man and woman love each other they must discipline themselves to maintain the balance which allows them harmony and escape through their partner. If love required nothing from us it would offer nothing to us.

In many conflicts, generalizations confuse specifics. To tell women that most studies generally indicate that it is common for women to find their husbands controlling and overbearing is to encourage them to think of men and their husbands in a negative way. From a political perspective this is an excellent tactic since it creates a powerful and common enemy which must be resisted through the creation of an equally powerful and opposing political movement or party. From a relationship perspective it is very harmful since it fails to recognize that each dominated woman is really a woman who failed to select a male whom she could control. If we watch children play we see that even a child bully necessarily requires a weaker child to bully. The bully instantly ceases to be a bully in the presence of a stronger child. If women volunteer for relationships in which they are bullied or even gently devalued, they need to wonder about why they did such a thing; about why they volunteered for a job for which they ultimately were not qualified. There is no law preventing a woman with an IQ of 150 from marrying a more controllable man with an IQ of 120. In the end a marriage is about the specific behavior of two people; not about the behavior of two sexes. If men are rude and overbearing toward women it may be because women so often prefer superior men. Anyone who doubts this should ask a dating service professional if a woman will accept a date with a shorter man. Similarly, it may be true that blacks are poorer and less educated than whites and that silly governmental policies may be implemented to reinforce this generalization, but this does not tell us that the individual black who walks in the door looking for a job is less qualified than a white who walks in the door. Generalizations in this area and many others serve the political interests of those who make the generalizations far more than those about whom the generalizations apply.

Women do like to make things difficult though. Most women are reluctant to love an easily controlled man. A quick look through the personal ads will indicate that they want a successful tall man. A quick look at male models will tell you that muscles are also hotter than ever although they are curiously not mentioned by the shy women who use the personals to advertise for men. Women want powerful men because throughout much of evolutionary history they were the ones who could provide them and their children with secure lives. If women want these men, something that is not inherently objectionable, they must recognize the difficult problem of controlling them.

As death defines life and a mother defines her child by the kind of involvement she has with it a woman must also define her husband and focus his very powerful and non-specific sexuality. This is what Margaret Mead was referring to when she said, "If any human society is to succeed it must have a pattern of social life that comes to terms with the differences between the sexes." The essential problem of every society is to define appropriate roles for the men." If a woman fails to do this for her husband, her marriage will falter without direction and purpose. If the man gets sex because he whimsically wants it, it has little value to him or his wife, but if he gets it as a reward for familial behavior his whole life and marriage is given purposive definition and meaning. A man wants control of the world, but only 50% control of his wife. Anything beyond 50% reduces her ability to meaningfully offer love to him.

5.) THE PHILOSOPHY OF LOVE AND MARRIAGE

MODERN WOMEN STILL
LOVE SLEEPING BEAUTY

A marital pursuit, like any other, demands purposive work and attention. The more something is practiced the more effortless it seems; the less it is practiced the harder and more painful it becomes. But, practice must be deliberate, organized and focused. A ballet dancer practices but in a very specific way, and a loving wife should practice, and also in a very specific way. If she provides sex on demand without reasonable reciprocity she is practicing in a way that does more harm than good. These are points that are obvious and above reproach when applied to everything except love. In the case of love we are greatly conditioned by generations of history to be embarrassed and shy about our sex lives. We cannot acknowledge that animalistic sex is what we enjoy most and that during sex we are nothing like what we appear to the outside world. We cannot publicly establish sexual practice rules because we are too embarrassed to do so; yet we are not intelligent enough to discover these rules on our own.

When we do talk about sex we are greatly conditioned by the dominant popular culture to blame men in political terms for their abusive, selfish, awkward, or speedy personal behavior. Women are portrayed as merely righteous victims. We often seem to attribute to them no marital failings at all. At most we are counseled that a good marriage is something that must be worked on. But who defines how you work on a marriage or why you must work at love? Love in many ways seems to be the opposite of work. Sleeping beauty didn't work on love. She merely waited for it to envelop her. Women generally prefer sex on their backs for the same reason. They too often tend to be the passive recipients or victims of male activity.

It seems that only psychologists pretend to know what it means to work on a marriage and how to do it, but they require months of expensive therapy and never have been able to provide any evidence that the "work" produces any empirical results in their own marriages let alone those of their patient's. What is missing is a concept that provides a few simple rules and practice routines regarding the proper conduct of marital sex.

Psychologists, psychiatrists, marriage counselors, and relationship experts will ask a woman to describe her relationship with her father, mother, uncle, brother, aunt, and cousin long before they will dare to ask her to describe her sex life with her husband. An already skeptical and prudish public would surely take this as evidence of their voyeurism or perversion. If the discussion of sex were a routine part of the work it would surely be seen as too much work. Politicians will scream about patriarchy, gender equality, the glass ceiling, and equal pay, but not about sexual behavior. We are very shy about it despite its huge importance to our families and, indeed, our species.

There is no voice, let alone a dominant one, anywhere in our culture which instructs us on how to use the tremendous sexual power that creates, builds, or destroys our marriages and relationships. The vague hope, if there is one, is that a woman's general self-esteem and values will carry over into assertive and forthright bedroom behavior, although we are way too shy to set up a cultural mechanism to encourage that this is so. It is far easier for us to believe that sex is a barometer for our marriage rather than to believe that sex is our marriage or at least the most important part of our marriage.

The hope that we can improve our lives and that by osmosis our sex lives will miraculously improve is a vain one. Self-esteem, to pick a hugely popular term that has grown to be equivalent to psychological nirvana, and sexual maturity, have little to do with one another. What a woman is out of bed tells very little about what she is in bed. In many ways sex is a unique and isolated experience for couples. Most do not make a connection between the quality of their sex life and the quality of their marriage and the quality of their entire life. In fact, many are embarrassed at the obvious benefits that would flow from creating an integrated life because it would involve painful growth. It would put them in a new place and that is often more frightening than leaving a horrible old place. It is in some senses far easier to maintain a routine and isolated sex life. The "when it rises I use it" approach to sex would be similar to a pill for food if such a thing were available. The problem is that if we simplify life too much as we have done with sex and to a lesser extent with food it often becomes paradoxically difficult because nature designed a certain high level of dynamic tension into our lives to help us avoid complacency. Evolution demands change because life is a race against the clock that ticks toward death or extinction. Sex is the most important and the most hidden event in our lives. It is even more hidden than our bank accounts, toilet habits, and SAT scores. Sex, in addition to being exceedingly important, is uniquely random and emotional. Being seen and heard doing or saying something unique during this most important act might expose us to the gravest potential ridicule from a society that is naturally based on commonality. If a person were to say "oh, oh," instead of, "uh,uh" it would be too easy for us to mockingly portray him as the only one in the universe doing the most important thing in the universe incorrectly or differently. Sex is something that, above all, we want to do right. Unfortunately, if we are so desperate to keep sex hidden; if we can't talk about it the way we freely talk about other subjects, it is very likely that we don't really know much about it. We say that sex is everywhere in our culture and this is quite true, but the sex that is everywhere is mostly Cindy Crawford's pretty face, Madonna's pointy bra, and The Spice Girls' sexy lyrics. Our very sexual culture is by no means a sophisticated sexual culture.

Sex is the most forbidden of all fruit. It is nature's greatest temptation. We want it desperately but we know the potential pain that can come from a failed sexual relationship and/or an unwanted child. This makes it a huge and complicated risk. Learning about it is, then, very difficult because we have so much personally at risk. History and computer science by comparison are relatively easy to learn about because we don't care about the subject nearly so much. They exist almost independently from us as we learn them. The road to knowledge they provide is straight and direct. School books in general are plentiful and we're all forced to read them, but who has ever read even one book on the role of marital sex? We are saying, in effect, that it is mere trivia while the history of Greece is somehow of solemn importance. Sex is actually too important and too little understood to be taught. We are afraid of what we know and more afraid of what we don't know.

Sex is certainly too important and controversial for public education. We pretend that it is a matter for the church or our parents to teach when in reality they know little or nothing themselves. (although we do owe them a great debt for instilling in us the belief that sex should be confined to marriage) and would be too cowardly to teach even if they did know something. To this day what we know about love and sex we mostly pick up on the streets by default and it is of highly questionable veracity. There is actually little about sex that we are certain of and even less that we agree on so it can't be taught despite its overwhelming importance. What might be agreed on is obviously very important, but it is also very embarrassing and might even turn out to be wrong too; so we forbid that it be taught. It would be a little like teaching Christianity in the First Century or evolution in the Nineteenth Century.

The sex education children have recently begun to get isn't about relationships. It's mostly about mechanics, how to avoid pregnancy and disease and the importance of accepting sexual diversity. The idea that young kids should be taught that it is acceptable for homosexuals to have hundreds of anonymous anal sexual encounters through the holes in bathhouse walls is almost perfectly opposite to the familial sex that this book recommends as essential; yet it the kind of sex education that is most common in our society which, not surprisingly, features a 50% divorce rate.

Who even knows of a book which teaches that through sex a woman can participate in the maintenance of a loving marriage. Most books prefer to keep sex safely aside as, at most, an indicator of how well the rest of a marriage is going. They would have us believe that if we can raise the kids well together or cooperatively divide household chores or agree on what's for dinner, our marriage will be healthy and happy and full of passion. True enough, there are many world famous books about meaningful sex, The Joy Of Sex and The Kama Sutra, for example, but they deal with the physical joy of sex and few women find that a meaningful basis for a marital relationship. These books don't even really address marriage. In fact you don't even have to be married to work cooperatively together or to experience the joy of sex. Marital sex presents a particularly different and delicate sexual problem.

As a result, marital sex is a ritual without any intelligent direction for many couples. If a man senses his growing dominion over his mate he will often move closer and closer toward what we now commonly call abuse, rather than further away. Rather than moving toward equilibrium the system moves toward destruction. He has no rules to follow; she has no rules to follow. He pushes her further into submission, in part because it is easier than the discipline of reciprocity and in part because he is waiting for her to assert the romantic control that led him to originally fall in love with her. His frustration at his inability to ever fully conquer the outside world can be perversely directed in the opposite direction, toward his wife. Instead of using her romantic ability to equalize this tendency and again direct his frustration purposively outward, she does the opposite. She becomes complicitious as he confuses his instinct for sex and reproduction with his instinct to provide for and secure his family. If he still can reproduce (have sex) perhaps, he reasons, his inability or disinterest in providing for and/or nurturing his mate and offspring is no longer relevant. This is marriage by default. When we don't know what to do we will most likely do the wrong thing.

When a marriage begins to go awry a thoughtful female must decide whether or not to make love and thereby reinforce the male's deteriorating attitude or show more and more resistance as her partner's behavior veers more and more off course. No matter what she does and the degree to which she does it, she must be encouraged to take full responsibility for the election to give up the complex and selective romantic role that provided the original basis for her marital relationship. In today's popular culture her choices seem myriad and complex, but with sexual knowledge her choices are actually few and simple.

Unfortunately for women, their romantic role tends to get harder as the years pass. On day one a woman has nothing whatsoever invested. She can effortlessly say, "no." On day one the male will not even ask for sex, although he certainly would if he anticipated a favorable response. He implicitly understands that biology requires women not to provide gratuitous sex. His respect and interest in pleasing her reaches a peak very early, but the second she submits to him, his inclination will be to encourage sex as a regular routine that should not be interfered with by their larger relationship. Under the constant pressure of a daily routine this approach can seem easy and comfortable for both parties, but in the end it is likely to distract them from their basic biological roles and ultimately erode if not destroy the relationship. A couple's relationship in bed is supposed to reflect their relationship out of bed. If a man senses that his wife has abandoned this view, she becomes a different woman from the one with whom he fell in love.

From a simplistic moral perspective it is not possible to hold a woman responsible for the abuse from which she suffers, but from a biological perspective, which is the more essential perspective here, it is quite possible. Biology ultimately rules. Morality is but one permutation generated from and dependant on our biology. Biology is not oriented toward morality, it is oriented toward survival and reproduction. It is the foundation which provides the basis on which morality becomes relevant.

We might ask at this point, "doesn't morality demand that men simply respect their wives and never treat them unkindly?" Yes it does, but biology makes conflicting demands. It complicates morality. From puberty forward a boy dreams on and on about the woman who will eventually submit to his sexual desires. During this period the sexual power of women grows and grows in his mind until it reaches imaginary and idyllic proportions. In this process men naturally learn to respect women and their sexual power. Women hold the key to man's reason for being, and they do not easily yield up that key.

But, if at some point during a marriage a woman regularly submits freely and without conditions, her man may well get the sense that his mate is the opposite of what his youthful dreams led him to think she would be. Indeed, at worst she can seem to be little more than a slut or whore. This at best results in boredom, disorientation, or neglect and at worst in some form of abuse. Morality can't make a man love and respect a woman who is not fulfilling her sexual obligation anymore than it can make a woman love a man who is not fulfilling his masculine obligation. In fact, the on going natural selection process makes it impossible for either party to ever wholly fulfill their sexual obligation. If they could

5.) THE PHILOSOPHY OF LOVE AND MARRIAGE

fulfill this obligation, they might well-become complacent; this would effectively bring the evolutionary process to a halt.

Evolution depends on the constant search for higher levels of quality. A wedding ring represents a peak in quality; a deep feeling that another person can dramatically improve your life and evolutionary standing. Indeed, a lover is so interesting that we hang on their every word and insist that they are the most of, or the best at whatever it is that we value most. A good marriage represents maintenance of and, hopefully, growth from that peak. A large degree of amoral sexual tension naturally exists, though, throughout such a marital relationship to encourage a couple and their offspring toward ever higher levels of quality. This is why Tony Robbins, the nation's most successful motivation coach, and a man who dares to walk on hot coals, dares us to ask out the women we really would want to marry or to be the man she might want to marry. But the more a man stretches to get the woman of his dreams the more power that woman has over him.

Where women don't exert this pressure on men: in the American ghetto, Central and South America, and the Arab world, for example, the men are less productive at best and violent or disruptive at worst. It is not coincidental that married men earn more than single men. Cooperation between the sexes that is consistent with basic biological intent produces the best environment for the husband, wife, children, and society. Morality can't fully explain this phenomenon, but biology can.

Morality, it should again be pointed out, is never sufficient to govern human behavior. Morality may discourage some of us from, say, robbing banks, but it is the police officer who ultimately makes the banking system possible. How many bank robberies would there be tomorrow if such behavior was no longer against the law? Morality, then, is but a small tool to help the policeman do his work. It encourages fewer policeman, and civilized behavior, but it alone cannot cause civilized behavior.

In the end, the failure to provide police protection is immoral too. We know our biology well enough to know how certainly the absence of police would produce crime. So it is with marriage, appeals to moral behavior are helpful but they are not sufficient to govern passionate marital behavior. A loving marriage grows out of a system in which both parties actively know how to maintain the biological balance that created the system. Focusing on morality when it is really secondary is just a way to avoid reference to our truly biological nature, a nature which we find a little embarrassing due to its basic animalistic quality and very foreign after being taught to believe in our human uniqueness and superiority. Morality may be a helpful and complimentary tool, but not if it serves to distract us from our essential biological problems.

6.) HOW POP CULTURE ENCOURAGES DIVORCE

THE THIRD PARTY WHO CONTROLS
OUR RELATIONSHIPS

Pop culture encourages us in many ways to interpret relationships in non-biological terms; this is always a fundamental mistake from many different perspectives. Out of an interest in harmony we would expect to find a growing and inherent synergy between old-fashioned biology and current popular culture; yet popular culture encourages us to ignore biology or to believe that we have progressed to a point where we can rise above it. We want each century, each decade and each day to be new so that we feel we are on an upward evolutionary trajectory; that our lives are progressing forward. The tremendous pressure for upward innovation often encourages us to produce things and ideas that are merely different, but not necessarily innovative. Successive generations of different things get us off course to the point where we forget what the original course was.

For example, each generation of kids commits itself to a slightly different culture and a slightly different clothing style to reflect that culture. Baggy pants is but one current example. The pressure to assure themselves and the last generation that they indeed have the right stuff to carry the evolutionary torch one generation further causes them to put us on notice that their youthful difference will soon be followed by mature innovation. Unfortunately, being different is far easier than being innovative. If an industry can make us feel that different is innovative, they can make millions of dollars for themselves while avoiding the excruciating and slow work of genuine innovation. Most importantly they can actually discourage our focus on and interest in real innovation and progress.

Pop culture, which is often business culture, is very powerful. It seeks us out; it is presented to us as the next best generation. It is something we need to make us feel superior to the last generation. If we don't accept it, we are made to feel that we don't belong to the present but rather to the past or even worse, to nothing. It is powerful because it is derived from our most basic biological motivation. It feels good because it provides common and reassuring standards that, when shared, bring us together like little else can. If we can identify, understand, and accept the standard we are cool; if we can't we are nerds. In the end this process is harmful if the pressure for rapid innovation overwhelms our ability to distinguish innovation from mere difference or imagery. Relationship pop culture is mostly new but not innovative. It has led us toward new relationship philosophies that encourages divorce as a means to avoid a marital problems which could be understood, confronted and solved.

Relationship pop culture, at the moment, has two dominant strains which encourage us to focus on difference rather than innovation. The first is feminist/misandrist. It holds that women have been victimized by patriarchal men who generally aren't very likeable or cooperative and that women, strategically at least, are equal to or superior to men. The second strain is psychological. It successfully pretends to be cutting edge hip in its feminist sensitivity to women (the vast majority of its' customers) and its' thoroughly modern exploration of the human mind, but is also traditionalist and sexist by often acknowledging the obvious difference between men and women. Further, it manages to do all of this in a very non-traditional moral vacuum.

The current runaway psychological best seller talks in an allegorical context about men being from Mars and women being from a totally different planet, Venus. This deceptively and cutely removes the subject from the pervasive and toxic feminist environment which cannot tolerate different but equal sexes. Both feminists and psychologists tend to encourage women to be more assertive and men to be less dominant or abusive. Neither has much use for biology except by occasional coincidence. Both are too modern, sophisticated, politically correct, commercial, and dynamic to be tied to an old fashioned but deadly and relentless biology. Biologists are left behind as nerds; they can't make a living from slowly developing innovative scientific truths while feminists and psychologists can make a living by proclaiming grandiose and phony new revolutions. Indeed, feminists and psychologists are merely inept biologists with a commercial face. They address what are primarily biological issues but never acknowledge this lest they restrict themselves to purely accurate and scientific conclusions. Their personal, economic, and political goals overshadow the truth while deceptively presenting difference as innovation.

Popular culture restricts us from many other approaches to problems and solutions. For example, it would have been quite immoral and seemingly uncivilized to criticize the Jews for the destruction they experienced during World War II. To criticize or even help a victim often makes you feel like and look like a perpetrator; so you don't do it. You would become significantly similar to the perpetrator in that you would have power over the victim. This explains the tremendous irony that made it practically impossible for the world to offer the Jews anything after World War II. It was only the Jews who were in a position to criticize themselves and then adopt a different behavior, i.e., go to Israel and build a huge army. Today Jews occasionally kill each other in fervent criticism of one another, but it is still difficult for outsiders to join in with well-intentioned help or criticism and still maintain a clear conscience. Jews however are now well organized to criticize themselves through the mechanisms of an organized democratic government and are, as a result, more secure than ever. Criticism is essential. The absence of criticism portends the absence of organization, the absence of democracy, and the absence of growth.

Criticism is one of the mechanisms through which biological culture evolves. Ideas and products appear and disappear according to the criticism and praise they receive. But, the Zeitgeist or spirit of the times determines what criticism is acceptable or politically correct. It establishes a hierarchy or pecking order to organize the evolution of our culture by selecting whom or what is most and least criticizable. Any criticism out of that order, no matter how well justified, conflicts with our society's more general objectives about the desired power relationships between groups. If a dispute between two people or two groups can be made public, usually by politicians, courts or the media, it will be resolved according to the pecking order without regard to the legitimacy of either party's particular claim.

O.J. Simpson is perhaps the most obvious murderer in the history of the world. He was freed by the most obviously stupid jury in the history of the world. Yet the jury system is so revered and therefore so high on the pecking order that the Simpson jury escaped criticism. Marcia Clark, conversely, although she did a job that should have convinced even an idiot of Simpson's guilt, has been vociferously criticized for her failings as a prosecutor. This is because prosecutors are lower on the political pecking order than juries or the jury system. The black jury felt fully justified in freeing a black murderer who killed a white woman because blacks are higher on the pecking order than whites. The electorate voted to let Hillary Clinton socialize medicine; then they vilified her for trying to do it. Then they elected Newt Gingrich to oppose her. When he tried to do it they vilified and silenced him too. The electorate constantly contradicts itself yet it completely escapes criticism because of its exalted position in the pecking order. If a black elementary school student steals drugs from a white school nurse and distributes them to her friends she escapes punishment and criticism because black children are higher on the pecking order than white adults. If a clumsy woman spills hot coffee on herself, the company that sold the coffee is criticized and successfully sued because it is lower on the pecking order than the clumsy woman. American Indians promote gambling, something that has been regarded everywhere throughout history as a vice, yet they cannot be criticized because of their esteemed position on the pecking order. From the Bible to 20th Century America, rich people have been criticized more than praised even though they have invented and delivered the goods and services that sustain rich as well as poor lives. Rich people are low on the pecking order.

Most of us absorb our attitudes and education about different groups and people from the prevailing public pecking order. If a woman is born as an Australian aborigine she automatically absorbs a vastly different education than if she is born an American Eskimo. If we apply the current public education women get in continental American to our private marital relationships we soon see how divorce can hover at the 50% level. Modern women are educated to take power in a merely non-sexual way. They are taught that they are victims out of bed who must take power out of bed. We are culturally too shy and too ignorant to have a public policy on private sexual relations and so we are encouraged to see private sexual problems as broad political or social problems at most. This moves us further rather than closer to sexual/ romantic/ marital harmony.

It is in bed that man is willing to make a deal because what he can get there is far more valuable and important to him than whatever he might be

6.) HOW POP CULTURE ENCOURAGES DIVORCE

asked to deal away either in bed or out. A recent movie summed it up with Melanie Griffith's line, " a man listens better with his pants off." Out of bed a man is far more resistant. The reward isn't as obvious, important, or immediate, and the woman will appear more like a competitor or neutral party than a lover.

A woman told to seek more control in her relationship may well find that more control feels like less love. If she controls, say, what the family eats and what the family does every night, she assumes more responsibility and quite possibly feels less freedom and love. The husband may feel better about his diminished responsibility or he may feel worse about his diminished authority. A totalitarian public education will often push a couple in a direction, but it does not begin to address whether that direction is suitable for a particular couple either in or out of bed. This is something that must be done on an individualized basis without influence by simplistic and monolithic political concepts which are too immature to address the particular sexual issues that are common to all marriages. It is easy to achieve the pop-cultural objective of feminine power by encouraging women to end relationships or initiate divorces; it is hard for pop-culture to teach women how to solve their sexual problems so that one divorce won't lead to another and another. Working out a sexual problem today can mean negotiating with the enemy rather than loving your spouse; this isn't an environment that is very helpful. It doesn't seem to matter that the same problems will be worse in the second marriage or that divorce is harmful for kids. What matters is the allegorical short term pop cultural objective, i.e., standing up to a man.

Even though sex, more than food, is clearly the more direct way to a man's heart, sexual power clearly exhibited in such women as Mae West, Marilyn Monroe, and Madonna makes them appear more as amazons or whores, in the public mind, than mature marital role models. Affirmative and public sexuality seems inconsistent with private monogamy and modern politics. To be sure, the private marital lives of these women seem to bear this out. Mae West once representatively said, "I think marriage is a great institution and I'm too young for an institution."

She was acknowledging that her kind of sex could not really find a home in marriage. It exists as titillating satire to help understand and define the kind of sex that on one level inspires and challenges men but ultimately does not lead directly to marriage, family, and civilization. In love, sex symbols are out of place. To be loved a woman must eventually stop projecting sex to enable a man to project it at her. If she lacks the skill to induce this balance of love she will experience men as impotent premature ejaculators, or as aggressive beasts who fight fire with more fire. Mae West, et.al and Gloria Steinem, et.al are equally inept as lovers; yet they are inept in opposite ways.

Teaching women about sexuality is quite difficult when our public attitude prevails over our conflicting private one. By default, independence and divorce become the easy themes to teach publicly rather than bold techniques and attitudes which might realistically encourage women to positively participate in their own sexual lives. Pop culture is not so much wisdom as it is sexual ignorance.

Our public moral system is manipulated by various groups with special interests; they make criticism of women politically incorrect and thus close off a potentially useful avenue of growth. In public dialogue women are just innocent victims; any change must be made by the perpetrators: men. The success feminists have had in portraying women as morally superior victims has discouraged dialogue between the sexes, but it has worked for them in promoting a political consciousness that has reached near critical mass. The result is that most men and many women have been conditioned to be afraid of discussing feminist issues for fear that they may be dealing with a rabid feminist who will attack them or morally rebuke them, or that they will offend a woman who is quietly sympathetic to some of feminist thinking. The abortion issue has taken on a similar dynamic. Most of us are now afraid to discuss it in the hope of coming to a reasonable compromise for fear that we may encounter an aggressive abortion fanatic. By drowning out dialogue feminists have successfully made more room for their monologue.

If both sides are willing to accept criticism; with no one claiming absolute superiority, a politically powerful majority will not develop, but private, individual solutions based on dialogue, argument, and comprise might. In the end, the absence of criticism is the absence of movement and growth. It is supportive criticism of women that will encourage them to assert their biological destiny in a way that will make them mature, assertive marital partners, rather than innocent victims of a patriarchal

6.) HOW POP CULTURE ENCOURAGES DIVORCE

society who must divorce their husbands and children, often two or three times, to become mere political symbols of that society.

Popular culture moves very fast. Things have to be done cheaply, quickly and competitively and often without regard to quality. As popular culture examines relationships and divorce it has curiously concluded that men cause divorce. This fits with our feeling that men are more apt to be adulterous owing to their greater sexual appetite and the feminist notion that men are just generally bad. Even men reinforce this assumption by attending The Million Man March and Promise Keepers rallies where they beg for forgiveness for being men. But the truth remains buried by pop culture. We cannot ask about what happens to the family as an economic unit when the gov't gives welfare to women in place of the what they used to get from men or what happens to the family economic unit when gov't waste makes it impossible for the male to still earn enough to support his family even though he was able to do it in 1950's.

The piling on goes on and on. A recent ABC NEWS special on a study which seem to have emerged as the most influential divorce study of the last ten years concluded that the main predictive factor of divorce was the man's happiness in the marriage. The study projectively measured a man's current happiness by asking about the time period during which he met his wife. If he described that period in a neutral or negative manner it was concluded that he was now viewing his whole marriage as unhappy and that a divorce was more likely to follow. I don't doubt the correlation between the man's happiness and divorce, but this does not even vaguely relate to how we might improve a marriage. The causes of why he has re-written the history of his marriage need to be understood and this so called important study does not even attempt it nor does it explain why women are the ones to pull the plug 91% of the time by becoming the plaintiffs in a lawsuit against their husbands. We are left to believe that men are moody, fickle, flaky, and adulterous, and that by initiating divorce, women are merely reacting to men who, in effect, end their marriages.

The real explanation is simple. Most men are a little unhappy, it is what biology intended. 1) They didn't marry Cindy Crawford, and 2) they have to go to work where they mostly fail in the battle against the universe. Even if they become millionaires, they still need the second million as much as the first. If they worked for parochial things like

6.) HOW POP CULTURE ENCOURAGES DIVORCE

money they would retire after the first or second million, but biology generally does not allow this. Even if they get money, they know they are losing in the battle against more money, time and extinction. When you join man's natural personal unhappiness with a natural aggressiveness, that may be partially directed toward his wife, you may well have a wife who feels neglected and abused, and inclined to initiate a divorce. To her the marriage dies because she cannot imagine herself as having the power to change or shape her family. The power she had during courtship seems to have vanished. She sees herself as an impotent Sleeping Beauty. Ironically, it is her power to balance his conflicting desires that is the very thing she is supposed to provide. But pop-culture is moving way too fast to take the time to sort these things out. Sadly, the things we know, whether it's what ABC NEWS, Sleeping Beauty, or feminism tells us about love, are the main things that percolate through pop-culture and into our marriages.

Artists are perhaps the most important purveyors of popular culture. It is from them that we seek to fulfill our ever growing need for entertainment, understanding, and inspiration. But they too function according to their own perverse relationship with popular culture. The United States emerged from World War II as the wealthiest and most technologically endowed country. Wealth created a huge artistic community on a scale the world had never seen before and technology (primarily TV) provided a means to deliver art to a broader audience that had ever seen it before. The artist's first and best task was to define what we valued most and share it through artistic expression. John Wayne who even in 1998 is still cited as our most favorite movie/TV star, is the best example of this. Other examples include Ozzie and Harriet, Donna Reed, Leave It To Beaver, Bonanza and James Bond. John Wayne and James Bond showed us courtship at its biological best. They conquered huge evils and then made love to the most desirable women around. The others showed us an idealized versions of family life. Kids wanted Donna Reed as their mother, men wanted her as their wife, and women wanted her adoring and sensitive 1950's husband. But over time these artistic creations became perfected, copied, and, finally, boring as art. James Bond was a first, but he was copied so much and so often that he lost more and more value. This left artists with nothing to do at the very time when peace, wealth, and technology had created the most demand for art and the largest number of would be artists.

The solution was simple Business 101. Segment the market to keep it growing and to make a place for yourself in it. Tide detergent was the first synthetic detergent introduced after World War II. It was a huge success because it really did clean better. In time others copied the idea and it became more and more difficult for new entrants to present anything salable to a satisfied marketplace. The solution was to introduce a detergent that emphasized new attributes such as low price, stain removing ability, cold water compatibility, environmental friendliness, or the compactness of liquid. The idea was to attract the attention of someone who had a particular interest in or neurotic vulnerability to some other characteristic than general cleanliness.

In art the same maturation process occurred, but with very important ramifications. When Ozzie and Harriet couldn't be done again, struggling artists segmented the market. Why not a TV show about a single mom? The single moms out there might enjoy an idealized version of their own lives more than an idealized version of society's version of an ideal family. And, who is to say that seeing the sad side of life made happier doesn't enhance one's perspective on the idealized side of life? A race developed among liberal artists to explore the rich tapestry of human experience in all its wonderful diversity. Gangster Rap is perhaps the ultimate expression of this. The rap artists themselves argue that this is what they know and this is what they re-create. Their Hollywood liberal allies like Warren Beatty implore, in films like: Bullworth, that "their pain must be heard." Conservatives argue that Ozzie and Harriet is more valuable in the ghetto than Tupac Shakur. Ossie and Harriet represented objectification of subjective life according to wonderful metaphysical value judgements. They represented positive art while Tupac represents negative but equally influential and inspirational art. Tupac inspires inertia, drugs, violence, despair, and death. Ozzie and Harriet inspires upward spiritual mobility; Tupac the exact opposite. Ozzie and Harriet cooperatively and respectfully worked out a mutually satisfactory time at which to end the day and head to bed while Tupac's sex education speaks of "tearing that shit up." The contrast is dramatic; yet Tupac is seem as sophisticated, urban, and contemporary while Ozzie and Harriet is dismissed as quaint, old fashioned, and sexist.

Throughout history art was in limited supply. It was controlled primarily by rich governments and rich religious institutions who used it to promote civilization. Overall the art produced was very positive and that which was presented to the general public was even more positive. Today, in our rich, free, and liberal society, the production and consumption of art is virtually limitless. An overabundance of artists live in a moral vacuum from which place they segment and re-segment the market in a continuous effort to promote their own personal and business interests at the expense of civility.

Over the centuries democracy has developed and authoritarianism in all its forms has declined. Strange gods and evil dictators once held us in there grip, but most of these strange Gods and dictators needed us to successfully reproduce if only to serve as their soldiers and farmers. They introduced us to the covenant of marriage and deeply made us believe it was sacred and could not be broken. Their definition of marriage prevailed until about 1960 at which time several trends and events converged to turn several centuries of history away from the authoritarian model.

Looking back it is hard to imagine how inclined we were to follow authoritarian rulers and ideas, even to our deaths. In the US, in the 1860's everyone felt it was his duty to fight and die for his country in the Civil War. 500,000 soldiers bravely stepped up, often brother against brother, to expend their lives in a cause, that had it been left alone, may well have taken care of itself without war as it did everywhere else. Instead, 500,000 died when the entire US population was only 31 million. One hundred years later 60,000 out of a population of 250,000,000 died in Vietnam. That's 530 times more deaths per capita (per person) in Vietnam than in The Civil War, and the country was literally torn apart because many had developed the effrontery to challenge a gov't that threatened their lives. In Europe the situation was even worse because the democratic anti-authoritarian tradition was less strong. Millions and million stepped forward to die through two world wars. It was simply their duty. It did not even occur to them to challenge external authority. By the 1960's protest in the streets of Europe against gov't authority and legitimacy were common. A dramatic new and historic view of individuality had taken hold in about 20 years. But why did individuality become so important?

A.)Birth Control-women and couples could now have sex
without anyone knowing about it (a baby for the whole
world to see would not necessarily result).

B.)Democracy- with the end of WW 1l democracy with its
reliance on the individual vote took hold around the world.

C.) Capitalism- starting in the 19th century Adam Smith taught us that a
man should be free to determine the course of his
economic life by voluntarily buying and selling goods and
services in a free market.

D.) Science- The growth of scientific explanations for things that were
one explained by religions diminished the authoritarian role of
religion.

E.) Wealth- with wealth from continued capitalism, free time was
available with which to explore and enjoy and indulge purely
individual preferences. Watergate & Vietnam- major blunders by the
relatively small gov't that still remained further challenged individual
respect for external authority. With wealth came more and more
education. Education is inherently individualistic.

F.) Counter Culture-with wealth and education comes a counter culture.
The beat generation of the 1950's may have been beat compared to the
middle class but they were not so beat that they didn't survive to
forcefully and thoughtfully challenge the little authority that still
remained.

G.) Psychology- psychology encouraged the individual to believe that his
salvation was to be found in a good relationship with his internal
psyche rather than with external forces.

H.) Assassinations- The cavalierly taken lives of John F. Kennedy, Martin
Luther King, and Robert Kennedy encouraged the belief that the
permanence and presence of even those few authoritarian leaders that
we did respect was not to be counted on.

It is against this cultural background of growing individualism that
divorce was able to become so popular. Everywhere the individual
flowered and authoritarianism died. Unfortunately for us the one thing

authoritarianism had right, marriage and children, died along with authoritarianism. Many realize this now but to change the broad historical force of culture is not easy.

Dr. Laura Schlessinger is perhaps the most visible and powerful advocate facing this challenge today. Despite having a Ph.D. she replies, when asked who she is, "I am my kid's mom." This is a way of viewing oneself, not as an Freudian individual trying to perfect a relationship with himself, but as someone who is primarily part of a relationship with a husband and child. When someone asks her about their individual problems she quickly encourages them not to worry about them but rather to do the right thing for her kids. Since she is her kids mom her joy in life comes from doing right by her kids. Other concerns become irrelevant. When we are encouraged to believe that we must pay attention to our Freudian inner child at the expense of our behavioral responsibilities we become participants in the divorce culture at the expense of our children who in the end are the best measure of our lives and the best measure of the goodness of our culture.

In contrast to Dr. Schlessinger is Dr. Mira Kirshenbaum who weighs in with her book Too Good To Leave Too Bad to Stay with her own typically modern and individualistic assurance that we that we should not stay together for the kids. Schlessinger says, in effect, people are together for the kids and it would be plain contradictory not to stay together for the kids. Kirshenbaum assures us that "kids are not glue"; that, in effect, each individual parent must first seek out his own Freudian fulfillment before he can fulfill is secondary obligation as parent to his kids. The way we choose to define ourselves determines who we are and what we do. The Germans chose to be Nazi's for a while and then they chose to be different; so it is with us. We are free to choose any spot on a long continuum. The "Kids R US" approach of Schlessinger or the "kids are not glue" approach of Kirshenbaum represent the extremes on the continuum we face today.

7.) FEMINISM AS THE FOUNDATION FOR LOVE

FEMINISTS AS LOVERS

There are two sexes because nature needed two sexes to reproduce our species. There was no other way nearly so effective. The bodies, feelings, thoughts, and behaviors of men and women are different because nature designed and built men and women to be different. Nature's division of labor didn't somehow specify that one job was superior or inferior to the other. Feminists, though, somehow concluded that it did do exactly that. Famous books at the heart of the modern feminist revolution such as The Female Eunuch and The Second Sex are shot through with 1000's of examples of the inferiority of traditional women. Biologists, having few, if any, economic, political or social aspirations, never developed an interest in or way to publicly counter this incomplete thinking about their subject. The passion, simplicity, and availability of feminist pop culture simply overwhelmed the steady quiet progress of biological science. We see this phenomenon in other areas too. Astrologers threaten to overwhelm astronomers, new age nutritionists threaten to overwhelm medical doctors, and militias threaten to overwhelm thoughtful libertarians. Truth and science generate competitors from the ranks of those who aren't well suited to the discipline of truth and science.

Feminists offered a way to be a successful victim or a way to be a successful warrior, but they never offered a way to be a successful biological lover. George Washington and Menachem Begin started careers as victims and warriors too, but over time their ideas grew more and more in respectability to the point where they could become generally popular leaders. Feminism does not appear to be on that track. Most women today will express some sympathy and support for the part of feminism which empowers them. But in the end feminism is not romantic. As a result it is something with which most women refuse a direct association. Feminism hasn't achieved general popularity because most women, and men too, sense a sexual and emotional frigidity in feminist thinking that is inconsistent with the biological love they feel for the opposite sex. Eileen McGann, wife of adulterous presidential pollster Dick Morris, expressed this sentiment well after having earned the near universal scorn of the feminist sisterhood for her stand-by-your adulterous man performance. She said, " I didn't know that feminists had decreed what the politically correct rules were for personal relationships. I did what was right for us."

Nora Ephron alluded to the same cold, loveless nature of feminism when she was asked what would happen to sex after liberation. She said, "I don't know it's a mystery to all of us."

Those who are encouraged by divisive feminist morality to feel that male culture or biology is somehow inferior or less moral than female biology and culture are simply ignoring evolution. Whatever the true nature of male sexual biology, one thing is certain. It is immutable, at least in the short term because that is exactly what women wanted. Macho men evolved and continue to prosper only because women bred them and love them; yet macho men are criticized far more than the women who love them and thereby propagate their genes. More than social, political or cultural systems, sexual systems are tied directly and inextricably to biology. It is better to discover and understand the value and purpose of male sexuality and how to deal with it than to pretend that it is possible, if only philosophically, to rise above it or dramatically pretend that we can stomp our feet and change it.

If it were true that females were morally superior based on their kinder, gentler nature then we would expect to find that lesbian marriages (which tend to feature a butch/femme dichotomy) would be less violent than normal heterosexual relationships, but curiously they are not. Men tend to beat up their wives because they are stronger than their wives; not because they don't like women. A bully beats up only a weakling for the same reason, and the stronger lesbian beats up the weaker one for the same reason. Similarly, a recent study conducted by Epic/Mra of Lansing Michigan found that in traffic, where both sexes apparently feel somewhat protected by their automobiles, women rated higher than men on aggression, anger, and punishing while men rated higher only on competition. Women take disputes seriously while men see them as natural competition. The disputes here are disputes between physically weak and strong; not problems between men and women. When feminists subvert this issue for their own political purposes they draw us away rather then toward an understanding and solution to our personal marital problems.

Sometimes we think that feminism has matured well beyond those silly days when women burned their bras in public to protest the restrictions placed on their bodies and spirits by men, but in some very important

7.) FEMINISM AS THE FOUNDATION FOR LOVE

places it has not. Bra's it turned out, after careful analysis, had naturally evolved over centuries with input from both men and women to accommodate general biological interests. Women liked them for support, warmth, camouflage, and enhancement. The braless look and feel did make some women feel free symbolically and physically, on a personal level, but that feeling was usually counteracted by the greatly enhanced sexuality it projected. Oddly, men who were portrayed as the devils who invented and promulgated the bra often supported the braless look because of the sexuality it suggested, although they only supported it on women who weren't their mothers, daughters, wives, sisters, and girlfriends.

Today we can say that feminism is generally more mature, but still there lingers within its ranks the temptation to discover that a clandestine male conspiracy is in operation against them. For example, one feminist recently wrote a book titled: Men Aren't Cost Effective. Her point was that all the stupid things men do, such as murder, rape, and rob, cost society untolled billions on top of the non-monetary consequences. The obvious implication was that women are morally superior since they generally don't do these things. No attempt was made to balance the good men do against the evil they do. The book in a way symbolized much of modern feminism. It was purely political, confrontational and contradictory. Women are taught that their lovers may really be their enemies. They are not taught to improve their marriages through understanding but rather to marshal their energy and consciousness for the benefit of the feminist sisterhood's political agenda.

Another feminist scholar recently wrote a book titled: The Politics of Meat. Her point was that ancient men used their superior ability to kill animals to gain control of the female food supply. Modern women, then, must give up meat and the blood lust which encouraged men to learn the principles of domination which they applied equally to animals and women. This is a ridiculous contortion but it shows how desperate some feminists are to use any lie to achieve parity or superiority with men outside of the bedroom. But men and women are evolved primarily for what happens in the bedroom. If women would concentrate on this, they would achieve parity both in and out of the bedroom without leading themselves further and further astray with bigger and bigger lies. Men and women were created to make love; any treatise about their relationship that doesn't take this fully into account is fatally flawed.

Feminist thinking has frequently been shallow, although it may have been politically useful to them. While it is true that aggression and deviance is almost exclusively male, it is also true that freedom and creativity are almost exclusively male. While women have been primarily focused on and tied to children, men have faced a bewildering array of choices about what to do with their lives. As death defines life, the bad choices men make define the good ones. We defend the bad choice of pornography not because we like pornography but because we appreciate the general principle that meaningful creativity and change always seems to evolve from the least anticipated places. To call all men deviant because some men make bad choices would be similar to calling women deviant because half of pregnancies end in spontaneous abortions. Nature does things for a reason. We must understand that reason before we can criticize it in a meaningful context. In fact, we might say that virtually all of evolution's creations over the last 100 million years have been deviants. All those thousands of species of silly little bugs and fishes and animals that are now extinct were really mistakes that pointed evolution toward what wasn't a mistake.

In another sense, for a woman to criticize a man she must really criticize herself. While men have been superior at murder, rape, and robbery they have also been superior at religion, medicine and business. Male evolution has been stunning in its tremendous breadth while female evolution has been narrowly centered around childbearing. In a sense nature made men more active and interesting than women. If all men were accountants, the way all women are child bearers, they would certainly be seen as less interesting wouldn't they? As humankind evolved it was really mankind that was evolving to cope with the vast array of dynamic environmental conditions he faced. The female remained tied to her body almost like an animal. Reproduction happened; it was all consuming and largely beyond her control. The food she gathered was either there or not; it too was beyond her control. But the male took the initiative. His skills, tools, creativity, and courage all mattered greatly. Each man became a distinct personality as he sorted through his particular mission in life. Thinking became masculine while feeling and subjugation to natural forces remained feminine.

127

7.)FEMINISM AS THE FOUNDATION FOR LOVE

When men mated they passed on their rapidly evolving abilities to both the males and females of the next generation, but the females were restricted from using those abilities by a lack of testosterone. They got to carry male genes for reproductive purposes but not really to enjoy and use them. But in the end a large part of their nature is derived directly from the male just as a large part of male nature is female. Accordingly, much of feminist criticism tends to be merely political rhetoric rather than sensible argument based on biology.

Despite their maleness, females were to passively stay at home to bear and rear children. They got to be spectators one inch removed from a man's world. This is why, for example, not one single German or Japanese woman was willing to step forward and die to prevent the slaughter of 60 million people in World War 11. Women gently support the thoughts and behavior of their men. They look inward toward their children while allowing men to become their intermediaries with the universe. It is difficult to understand how thoroughly a woman feels the need to thoroughly assume the role biology has given her. Biology has made women morally neutral throughout history. Modern feminism cannot instantly appear on the scene and declare men to be the enemy without considering their own evolvement or lack of it in all that has happened. At the very least, women are culpable as the mothers of all those bad men. Feminists should mark their recent appearance in history with a sensible proposal of accommodation with men that recognizes them as partners; as mere evolutionary reflections of one another; not enemies. Men and women evolved as one system. A recognition of this would leave an opening through which a sexual accommodation could be proposed.

One hundred years ago women were fully occupied with home and children. As male inventions gave women more and more leisure time and better and better ways to spend that time, the feminist revolution became possible. Ironically this process came to fruition in the sixties just as govt. spending on massive social programs stopped the growth in family income. Women still had leisure, and they also felt the lure of creating and using all the new male inventions, but, thanks to gov't waste, they had no money with which to take advantage of the new environment. This, more than feminism, propelled them into the work force, and at the same time explains why a large majority of mothers who have high incomes, or access to high incomes and exposure to feminist rhetoric, still prefer not to work.

Whatever changes may take place for women outside of the bedroom due to the current political environment it is clear that those changes won't necessarily affect what happens in the bedroom; the place where marriages are consummated and maintained. While genes cannot be expected to change in less than 1000 year periods it is certain that culture and people can change overnight. At this point, barring total war or some other cataclysm that could dramatically set back our standard of living, we would expect that future development will continue to benefit the relative power of women. We all have an interest in that development, especially if it comes at a very rapid pace. But how can we expect real development if we don't consider changes in the way the sexes have sex.

Perhaps the best example of how cultural changes can dramatically and quickly change sexual behavior is provided by the ancient Greeks. Elite Greek intellectuals like Plato believed that women were to be used primarily to produce babies. They weren't worthy of love because they, it seemed, hadn't demonstrated that they could do more than just have babies. Post-pubescent boys however were, it seemed, worthy of love and tutoring because they could grow into the great thinkers, artists, and warriors who would propel society forward. To this day many scholars reluctantly acknowledge that a tiny number of very elite Greek bisexual/homosexuals, in a tiny amount of time, somehow produced ideas and institutions that formed the bedrock of Western Civilization. Of course, this can be dismissed as just another example of aggressive and creative male behavior, or it can seen as an indication of how much flexibility or aimlessness there is in male sexuality. The opportunity for women to control male sexuality is vast. Women created it through natural selection for their own benefit, but then they lost the knowledge and discipline to control the very thing they created and needed most.

There are precious few, if any, examples anywhere in history of women being as sexually aggressive and experimental as Greek men. Perhaps the best example of female experimentation occurred in the U.S. in the 1980's at some of the elite Eastern women's colleges. These colleges always had an anti-male streak believing that women would be better educated in an artificial environment where men didn't overpower them with their aggressive sexual and academic tactics. With the advent of modern feminism some of the colleges decided to go coed or merge into nearby male colleges. But some decided, partially due to geography, to stay female only. These schools at one point produced historic rates of lesbianism approaching 80%. In the long run though this lesbianism did not stick. Apparently it was short term feminist political behavior rather than long term sexual behavior. Still, it is frightening to think that at one point many of America's elite women were on the road to homosexuality. Perhaps, in the case of women, cultural behavior like that described above will one day overcome genetics. Or, perhaps women are too passive for any really revolutionary changes that might affect the course of future evolution?

In the course of ignoring the lessons of women's biological history feminists conveniently miss much that they really don't want to see. They may ignore moral issues or just not talk about them, but it is quite another thing for women to address moral issues and to die for them as men have dutifully done throughout history. The drama of life and death, and of morals and ideas has been almost exclusively male while women have been confined to the very safe, but morally neutral world of children.

This is why Camille Paglia, a lone but highly intelligent feminist, persuasively argues that modern feminists should study and get comfortable with the likes of Napoleon and Caesar rather than Greer and Friedan. Modern feminists must decide whether they want to overcome their testosterone deficit by loving manly qualities or hating them. At present it seems that they hate men but love masculine qualities. If in the long run they maintain their love of manly qualities and the well-constrained male qualities within themselves, as Ms. Paglia would prefer, perhaps, in the upheaval, they will for the first time also elect to address the power balance in the act of sex itself.

Feminists have generally ignored sexual intercourse because they are afraid of it. They are afraid of the passive woman sex object in the inferior position on her back. They are also afraid of the aggressive woman sex object in the superior position because her identity is still seen in relation to men and she probably wouldn't be truly happy, as in the case of Marilyn Monroe, anyway. But, feminists have not proposed anything constructive. They have not managed to develop satisfactory sex lives, or a sexual philosophy, based on the "different but equal concept" or on the "equal/equal" concept and so they remain at odds with basic biology. On a purely practical level a rapprochement with men, while the source of their political power has always been distaste for men, would be suicidal and they know it; so they do nothing but cling to their political power. "Power" feminism and "victim" feminism have made "love" feminism highly problematic. Feminist leaders elected to fight men for equality in the work place rather then the bedroom because they weren't lovers; they sensed that their future is in work rather than love.

Feminism hates biology because biology seems to restrict its "true believer" political objectives by defining the female mind and body around sexuality, reproduction and motherhood. They have not come to terms with the notion that there are two sexes so they can have sex. Feminists rally against the hated notion that "biology is destiny." In so doing they are concluding that female sexual power is less worthy than male economic and political power. In effect they are saying that raising a child is less worthy than raising a widget at the factory. From a biological perspective, sexual, political, and economic power are all essential links in the chain. All are of equal value. The feminist lust for political and economic power seemingly is more a reflection of the perverse life circumstances of NOW leaders than a reflection of objective thinking. Patricia Ireland, for example, the current president of NOW, is married to a man, but mostly sleeps with and lives with a woman. NOW's philosophy of liberation, which often translates to liberation from family and children, and subjugation to work, more reflects an imbalance in their own lives rather than objective scientific reality.

When Madeleine Albright was appointed Secretary of State, Patricia Ireland said that the women in her NOW office were hooting and hollering and whistling in great celebration. This is fine, but why isn't Ms. Ireland also hooting for the woman who raises three kids all of whom go to Ivy League schools, and why isn't she hooting for the women with successful marriages. Aren't these legitimate roles for a woman to play too? How can we argue that the women who make it in NOW's world compensate for all those who must now sadly say, "I'm just a housewife" wasting my time at the meaningless job of raising the next generation.

7.)FEMINISM AS THE FOUNDATION FOR LOVE

Wealthy educated women who, it is supposed, have the most exposure to feminist thinking, overwhelmingly elect harmony with their basic biology by staying home to raise their children, when they have children. Poor women and wealthy pre & post child rearing women do often need or want to work. They, through perverse coincidence, can thank the unusual women of NOW for many of the opportunities that have become available to them. Oddly, it seems that when women need feminism it is there for them, and when they don't it's there to embarrass them.

The inability of feminism to understanding biology or to recognize the necessity to reach some kind of accord with it is reflected in Germaine Greer's famous book The Female Eunuch. She writes:

> When she had sucked the marrow from my bones
> And languorously I turned to her with a kiss,
> Beside me suddenly I saw nothing more
> Than a gluey-sided leather bag of pus!

According to Ms. Greer this is an example of how men genuinely hate women and why men must be opposed as enemies. To be sure the phenomenon of which Ms. Greer speaks is very real and something to which most men can attest. This author has heard a Billy Crystal comedy skit in which he humorously asks a widely sympathetic audience to explain how it is possible that merely having sex with a woman can transform her from an enchanting seductive goddess into a creature from whom he must desperately and immediately escape. For feminists the answer is simple. Men inherently hate women and have no use for them after fucking them; therefore men must be opposed politically and every other way as the enemy. For biologists, most of whom approach their work detached from any possible political consequences, the relationship between men and women is seen from a very different perspective.

Firstly, what biological purpose could possibly be served if men evolved to hate women? It seems clear that love rather than hatred between the sexes would be the obvious adaptation necessary for marriage, sex, and child rearing. Hatred of men is more likely an adaptation particular to Ms. Greer's unfortunate personal life (and to many of the lives of the more strident feminists) and so she wishes to generalize about men as a kind of self-psychotherapy. It is very stunning that women with such unusual personal lives have been relatively successful in shaping the consciousness of women with comparatively normal lives. If a male presidential candidate lived with a man but was married to a woman it is doubtful that he would get even one single vote. Feminist leaders get away with their subversion of biology while somehow maintaining tremendous power in a very anonymous way.

Biology would seek a scientific rather than a political or male bashing explanation for men's seemingly odd post-intercourse behavior. Men and women, like most other biological creatures, are not necessarily monogamous. Throughout much of their evolutionary history they pursued the very successful strategy of reproducing their genes by mating with as many partners as possible. In testimony to this, male ejaculate was and, to this day, is comprised mostly of killer sperm whose job it is to kill or block sperm from other males. Only a small number of male sperm are specialized for the purpose of fertilizing the female egg. Those men who had the most powerful sperm and mated the most, passed on the gene for that particular behavior and hence the behavior survived and spread. Today monogamy is enforced culturally, but the feelings toward promiscuity are still present, particularly in men.

For feminists, this biological behavior boils down to an emphasis on male dominance or hostility; this gives feminists what the pursuit of political power demands: a simple treatise and an enemy: men. It's true that men like to control women. But this is not a random and evil need that just happened to find its way into the male psyche. It is the need to insure that the children they invest in carry their genes. Women love these controlling men most because they know they will have the greatest interest in protecting the offspring that grow from those genes. A mate who is unsure of or who doesn't know about the genes of the offspring from his partner will be inclined to leave or, at best, be a less enthusiastic parent. Despite the development of killer sperm and a loving or controlling nature the attractiveness of non-romantic sex remains in men perhaps as a manifestation of his inability to ever fully control any one woman.

Unfortunately the duality of male sexuality grows more complex as we factor in the biological necessity of it. In the event that a spouse dies,

7.)FEMINISM AS THE FOUNDATION FOR LOVE

leaves for any reason, or is infertile, men still need to fulfil their destiny through reproduction. While women generally prefer to control/love the one man who will best insure the survival of her genes she too must have the ability to adapt to different males depending on her potentially changing circumstances. It would seem that evolution creates love but it also creates many caveats. If we understand these caveats the course of true love need not be strewn with obstacles.

Each mate has the lingering, adaptive feeling that he/she might produce a superior offspring with another partner. In the fifties Marilyn Monroe made a move called The Seven Year Itch. Studies later confirmed what this movie suggested. After seven years the rate of divorce peaked because by that time children had survived what throughout evolutionary history had been the period of greatest vulnerability. It occurred to some women at that time that their genes in combination with those of a new male might produce offspring superior to those from the first lot.

To teach that all of this obvious biological behavior is motivated by random male hostility just to score political points is to lead us further from resolving the battle of the sexes. As someone once said, "the battle of the sexes is largely just a battle over sex." It is not a battle over politics. Feminists have taken good old fashioned sex and transformed it into something to be used for their own political ends.

Gloria Steinem provides an interesting example of how far some feminists will go to avoid the truth when they think that it may contradict their political agenda. She states that, " we must question the very purpose of sociobiology." Sociobiology is a recently developed subject area that concerns the way biology influences groups of people to behave. Specifically, she is concerned that among the groups to be studied will be men and women and the conclusion will be that the current patriarchal state of affairs is more biological than cultural and therefore inevitable. Even though sociobiology is almost exclusively an academic phenomenon, and even though most academics are overwhelmingly leftist, liberal, Marxist, and feminist she is scared at even the remote possibility that if women are studied as a group, by persons not explicitly and solely feminist, they are liable to be labeled as biologically different from men. Accordingly, she wants the whole subject and any valuable truths it may produce, abandoned. She wants us to pretend that the subject does not

134

exist. Feminist studies apparently is ok with her because its exclusive purpose is to promote the feminist agenda, which apparently is indifferent to the truth. It seems to her that there is no chance that feminism as a subject could get out of hand so long as truth is secondary to the essential political agenda. In the end it may turn out that she is relying on something less stable and predictable than she cares to believe.

Ms. Steinem and others in the sisterhood (especially the 300 lb. arch feminist Andrea Dwarkin) always go to great lengths to inform women that "fat" is a feminist issue too. Women who want to be thin to attract men are falling into the male chauvinist trap, they claim. Naomi Wolf weighs in here too with her mistaken conclusion that tens of thousands die each year while starving themselves to be thin for men. To feminists it is ok for women to die prematurely of fat related cancer and heart disease as long they resist the biological common sense of men (and, recently, scientists) to find thin healthy women attractive.

If we look at the current Women's Studies curriculum at Wellesley College we see that they are currently considering the notion that the logical goal oriented thinking and thought processes of our Judeo/Christian, European/Greco/Roman heritage is exclusively male and as such, very bad. At one point feminism seemed to say that if a man can do it a woman can do it too, and perhaps better. But, over the long run that position has been a problem because it acknowledges that women should want to play the male game and that perhaps they have not played it in the past because they have not been as well suited to it as men. The truly feminine approach is to invent their own female game. And so the curriculum at Wellesley stresses emotional, intuitive, and dynamic thought processes over those originated by dead, white, European males. This approach seems problematic for women because it: 1) retroactively embraces the feminine qualities that originally tied women to husband and child, 2) it does not prepare women to function in the male economic world where they will increasingly find themselves and, 3) it escalates still further the men are bad; divorce is good mentality that is already too prevalent. Wellesley, women may survive their college years to marry, but only to discover at the first hint of trouble that their old college professor was right all along about men. Feminism serves a few women politically while it does a great deal of damage to a geometrically larger number of families and children who have no political interests.

Given that the rise of modern feminism exactly parallels the rise in the divorce rate and the rise in the number of children (half of whom are girls) growing up in broken homes why can't some feminists consider that the truths of sociobiology may offer more value to all humans than feminism? The matter seems especially compelling in the face of Judith Wallerstein's recent landmark 25 year study on the damaging effects of divorce on children. For feminists, opposing men has been more important than supporting children. They have managed to persuade us that it is ok for children to grow up in an environment where the parents they love, hate each other. They counsel us that a divorce is better for the kids than the sight of parents fighting, but they don't counsel us that if we love our kids we will find a way to stop fighting. Children, they argue, are resilient little creatures who can handle it while adults are emotionally weak creatures who need divorce to cope. We might call this trickle down parenting.

Feminism has taught us that female assertiveness, no matter how blindly exercised, is more important than child welfare. Their little social experiment has been a significant factor in raising the divorce rate from 1% in 1960 to over 50% today. It has taught millions of children the exact opposite of what a society should teach about love. It has taught that family and love are merely temporary . It teaches that love is a trivial thing that comes and goes like the wind. It teaches us not to rely on love but to find other more important things.

It is not surprising that when we turn on MTV we see what we wouldn't have seen in 1960. We see hugely popular groups like the Spice Girls(unanticipated but perhaps natural manifestations of feminism) who emphasize raw assertive Mae West sexuality rather than long term tenderness and love. In a sense they offer victory to men in the battle of the sexes. They offer them the short term, uncommitted, non-familial sex that was typical of pre-civilized human and animal societies. In contrast, when President Kennedy had an affair(in the 1960's) the press didn't report it because it was too horrible for our kids and impressionable adults to hear about. Today our standards are low; we don't care what our kids hear about and then they grow up to manifest our lack of concern..

Women who adopt the attitudes and behavior of uncivilized men are not responding purposively to the behavior of men. The feeling of distaste or simple boredom that a male often experiences after intercourse may be the biological feeling that compels him to go home (if, say, he is with a prostitute) or to go to sleep in preparation for the next day (if, say, he is with a wife) or to go to another woman (if, say, he is purely responsive to that part of his genetic programming which thrives on variety). Feminists need not be offended by normal biological drives. They merely need to understand them and then to fashion a non-judgmental way of dealing with them. Ms. Greer's thoughts suggest that feminists are more political and neurotic than loving and philosophically insightful.

For women, separation after intercourse is distressing; not so much because they have often have not reached orgasm but because it breaks the connection which is the basis of feminine love. A woman needs to lie there without pressure or tension in a non-muscular position to be slowly enveloped by her lover. As a fetus slowly overtakes her body so does the male sex organ. To ask a woman, "was it good" is to ask a male question. For the woman it is not good for just a point in time, it is good forever. The woman exists continuously with her family while the man must leave for the hunt.

A popular TV marriage therapist uses the ripples from a stone thrown in a pond to teach men the effect of an insult on a woman. An insult ripples through a woman forever conflicting with the constant feelings of affection that possess her. A man misses this point because his love and life lacks continuity. He is hunter as much as lover. For him the season of love and the season of war exist concomitantly and in opposite relation to each other. Biology seems to explain the complete cycle, from the man on his knees begging for marriage or sex, to the disappointed woman who must separate prematurely from her lover. Cultural refinement is necessary to complete the picture. Feminism does not seem to be helpful.

Betty Friedan, probably the single most important living feminist voice, recently made great progress in acknowledging the contradictions of feminism by saying:

> even if women are sorely handicapped by lack
> of testosterone, it is inescapably necessary for
> women at this stage in human evolution
> to move to equality in society.

7.)FEMINISM AS THE FOUNDATION FOR LOVE

This is, at least, a grudging admission that men have more testosterone than women and presumably more aggression and creativity. From there she would presumably agree that testosterone or the lack thereof gives women the minds, hearts, and bodies to bear and raise children while it gives men the minds, hearts and bodies to build bridges and watch football. But, to suggest that women are handicapped by a lack of testosterone is silly; it is similar to saying that men are handicapped by an inability to bear children. A difference is not a handicap but neither is it something that can be ignored. It is something that should be understood. What appears to be a handicap to Ms. Friedan was not made to be a handicap by biology. It would seem that Mesdames Greer's and Friedan's handicap is not a lack of testosterone but rather an inability to fashion an accommodation with men that is more rational then emotional.

Men don't make the argument that they are advantaged by testosterone. Why would they? Testosterone makes them absolutely dependant on women for offspring and family. A man's job and place in the family can be displaced while a woman's place is relatively secure and permanent. Women, conversely, especially in today's service oriented and highly efficient economy, can have offspring and family with only minor input from men. Men don't make the argument because they are happily resigned to and accepting of their dependence on women. They even get down on their knees and propose marriage to them. It is difficult to imagine a feminist on her knees proposing marriage to a man; yet women are everywhere successfully promoting their victimhood and testosterone disadvantage versus men. They should, instead, face up to the poor social/ sexual/ intellectual skills which are really preventing them from successfully relating to the male half of the human race and substantially contributing to the divorce epidemic.

Freidan loves to claim that that the spontaneous eruption of Feminism in the late sixties was due to the fact that so many women were just plain miserable as house wives back in the fifties. Her book struck a cord with that group and there was no turning it back. But the children are mysteriously left out of the picture as Friedan the mother described the headaches and backaches that reflected her boring, wasted, frustrated life as a housewife and mother. It is hard to fathom how uncomplimentary this must have been to her children. Perhaps they said something like, "my mom hated being there for me and that's helped me in so many ways. Or, what's good for mom is good for me."

Suppose Ms.Greer and all those who she has consciously and unconsciously inspired had elected to understand male sexual behavior rather than to presumptively and arrogantly start off on an anti-social tirade against it. As it turned out, a large part of liberation for women meant liberation from children. If we look at what happened to children from 1970 (the start of the modern women's movement) to 1995 we see that SAT scores went down while drug usage, teen pregnancy and criminality went up. No one would argue that the period was a good period for kids. Things went wrong for kids not because women stopped caring for their kids but because they cared a little more for being like a man and a little less for being like a traditional woman who was exclusively devoted to her children. Prior to the modern woman's movement women saw their lives as centered around their children; consequently they supervised them closely enough that there was little opportunity for misbehavior and much opportunity for positive growth and development. A family, it turned out, is a complex and delicate system. Any change in that system toward more working moms is simultaneously a change against children and the marriage of which the children (half of whom are female) are such an integral part.

It is interesting to note that the relationship about which Ms. Greer was generalizing was obviously not a successful marital relationship. It seems that she chose to draw her conclusions from a relationship which was more representative of her particular experience than the normal marital experience of the larger general population who she so eagerly influenced.

Certainly, there are basic strategies to deal with male post intercourse behavior without defining it or men as evil. A woman, who wished to maintain and build a relationship with a man who had a tendency to fade away or fall asleep, would simply not be well advised to anticipate much pleasure after her husband's orgasm. The best time for hugging and talking or whatever, would presumably be before intercourse at which time she could have anything she wanted for as long as she wanted. And, any sexual variety she provided would, seemingly, also function as an informed strategy with which to exercise control over her man's biological inclination for such variety. Lastly, talking and thinking about the issue from a biological viewpoint, as only humans can, might be enough to discourage a man from believing that his sleepy feelings mean that he dislikes or is disinterested in his lover, and a woman from believing that his sleepy feelings mean that he dislikes or is disinterested in her.

Perhaps the most talked about experiments to document the natural inclination toward male promiscuity were the Coolidge experiments. They were done at a chicken farm where the roosters were given the choice of either mating a second time with the same chicken or mating the first time with a new chicken. It turned out that there was no interest in mating with the same chicken twice, but as long as new chickens were provided the rooster, like a bull, could go on and on. When President Coolidge heard of this he advised the scientists to make the information available to his wife. Without looking up the marital history of the Coolidge's we don't need to assume that he wanted to commit adultery but that he wanted his wife to understand that, owing to his male ancestry, he should at least be permitted an occasional roving eye and a varied but monogamous sex life. Cattle ranches are similarly instructive. Before the days of artificial insemination they had to hire groomers whose job it was to carefully comb each hair on a cow's behind at just the proper moment in order to insure that no hair would harm the delicate and overworked bull's penis during its sisyphean and very polygamous labors of love.

Extreme reactions to male sexuality like the one detailed above from Ms. Greer's book probably reflect the realization that not only did the male need to move on to the next woman but that the current woman was the wrong woman with whom to make love. Does Ms. Greer believe that each woman is the right woman with whom to make love or that what a women does has nothing to do with whether a man wishes to hang around? Modern man is somewhat conflicted by the need for a family and the need for sexual variety. In a moment of passion a man's judgement can be clouded to the point where he is moved to mate with a woman who could not provide a suitable family. This is why most women, but not most feminists, are biologically very well aware that for a man sex and love can be two different things. The revulsion, albeit temporary, that men often feel might partially reflect natures legitimate way of telling him to raise his standards in sexual partners, or to simply go home and love the family he already has, or not to stick around to help raise the children when he could be out finding other women to impregnate.

But, in the long run we must face the possibility that NOW represents a significant aspect of human evolution. According to the dominant theory of anthropology, human females encouraged marriage only when the point in their evolution came which rendered them unable to simultaneously bear and attend to their offspring, and economically provide for them too. With govt. redistribution, the high rate of unhappy marriages, anti-male feminist rhetoric, the prominence of value free psychology, and a highly efficient service economy that is less and less dependant on male muscle, it is certainly conceivable that the mother-child family which is dominant throughout much of nature, and was once dominant in human nature, will continue to become more and more important.

Oddly, while we generally agree, despite the Dan Quayle, Murphy Brown imbroglio, that this trend is generally bad for children we do not seem able to develop an approach to reverse it and we won't until women realize that men are actually very simple and easily domesticated sexual creatures who can be made to be responsible marital partners. A woman who divorces will often reason that it is better for the kids to be from a broken home than an intact home in which the parents are fighting. The man will respond, in disbelief, that they can learn to stop fighting. The difference between marriage and divorce is the difference between the masculine will to do, and the feminine will to be; to be part of and accepting of an immutable universe.

While Gloria Steinem and some of the other pillars of the 1960's feminist movement go about their business of creating a leftist, matriarchal, lesbian society others are taking a more mature and cooperative approach. Naomi Wolf is perhaps the leading young feminist. Her recent book Fire With Fire is filled with what can only be called feminist hallucinations, but in the end it does offer hope for an intelligent feminist future with which reasonable people can generally agree. At her worst she points out how young girls used to flock to the stores to buy little toy horses called, My Little Pony. Wolf somehow concluded that this behavior represented their hidden desire to be brave, aggressive, and powerful women with the natural boldness to control large animals (and other things-perhaps men) between their legs. No basis whatsoever was provided for the connection between the little toy horses and female aggression. It was simply Ms. Wolfe's feminists projection of what she would like the real explanation of the phenomenon to be.

This is a typical mistake that most of us make. We look for and find support for our ideas almost everywhere while we reject and ignore everything that contradicts our ideas. Without scientific exploration it is reasonable to assume that soft, feminine colors and hair, or the loving and kind way they were portrayed on TV, or the phallic shaped horn on the pony/unicorn head was what really attracted little girls.

But, Ms. Wolf goes on in a more positive manner. She points out, to the consternation of her older and radical feminist mentors, that the place in life where she feels most at home is next to the male body of her husband. This is a big step forward for feminism. It at least acknowledges the overwhelming mutual attraction between men and women and suggests that women, even feminist women, can get along with and love men. Ms. Wolf points out that she too hates sexism, but that she doesn't hate sex or men as her feminist colleagues often do..

While Ms. Wolf does not talk about her sex life she seems to imply that she feels comfortable, at least part of the time as the passive woman lying on her back. Perhaps her marriage works because her husband knows that his modern feminist wife will assertively divorce him unless he satisfies her traditional sexual desires and her liberated sexual desires too. Or, perhaps it works because Ms. Wolf fought to maintain or develop her ability to feel at home being aggressive in bed and thereby communicate to her husband that she too has sexual and broader relationship needs that must be met in order for her to meaningfully and equally participate in a loving relationship. Either of the above two feminist approaches to relationships and marriage is superior to the traditional approach which holds that: 1) a woman must actually divorce a man or end her relationship with him in order to control him because she doesn't know how to do it any other way, and, 2) the next man will be so loving that I won't need to control his behavior at all.

Perhaps feminism has been so easy to pick on that it has garnered more criticism than it actually deserves. If we look back through the divorce records of this century we see that feminism may not be so important. If modern feminism had its bra burning birth in the late sixties then how do we account for the 59% increase in the divorce rate(according to the US Statistical Abstracts) from 264,000 in 1940 to 483,000 in 1947. Apparently one million GI's who didn't get killed in WW II came home only to get killed there. WW II seemingly gave women the opportunity to 1) forget about their husbands 2) find other lovers to replace their husbands, 3) discover that they didn't need their husbands, and/or 4) escape marriages in which they were unhappy. WW II wasn't feminist but it may have provided the same set of incentives to women that feminism did two decades later.

A next huge jump in divorce came in the late 1960's, just before feminism was well established and influential, when the number of divorces rose 69% from 419,000 to 708,000. Our civil rights failure and foreign policy failure (Vietnam) encouraged us to question all the underlying assumptions that could have led to such failures, and women to questioned their assumptions about their husbands. But this, again, was not feminist since it largely preceded feminism.

Interestingly from 1970 to 1975 the divorce rate shot up another 46% from 708,000 to 1,036,000. This increase might be attributed in part to feminism; in part to residual and lingering affects of the 1960's, and, again, in part to war time separation. But it cannot be said from this data that feminism was the major contributor to divorce in this century. Rather, it would seem that feminism gave expression to an underlying process that motivated women throughout the century.

After 1975 the number of divorces settled in at around 1,150,000 and will probably stay in that range through the end of the century on the assumption that no significant new changes will affect the way women view marriages. We might assume that the divorce rate is now stable in part because many current marriages might be deemed feminist and therefore not belatedly subject to feminist revisionism, but at historic highs because many women conveniently discover their feminism after marriage or as a convenient substitute for the effort of marriage.

8.) HOW PSYCHOLOGY CAUSES DIVORCE

HOW WE LOST THE WAR
BETWEEN BIOLOGY AND PSYCHOLOGY

Psychology, like feminism and most of pop culture, also hates biology on many levels and for the wrong reasons. Biology precedes and dominates psychology; it makes psychology almost adventitious. At one point psychology was supposed to be a kind of bridge from biology to the social sciences. It was supposed to explain the biological basis behind those human behaviors which transcended basic functioning. This didn't satisfy psychologists. It was very limiting, non-intellectual, and non-profitable. They yearned for a larger role that freed them from the encompassing constraints imposed by a biology which seemed to explain too much. Rather than settle for being biologist / psychologists they strove to be psychologist/philosophers.

They wanted human behavior to be a matter of free will and they wanted to appoint themselves as guardians of our free will. In reality, biology, at least as it relates to human behavior, is simple and fairly complete; as such it just won't support a huge industry the way the disingenuously fabricated complexities of psychology/philosophy will. In biology there is no great mystery to a feeling or a behavior, it is simply a thing created by nature, like a hand or foot, for a specific purpose. If psychology was able to offer new and meaningful explanations and insights into human behavior we would expect the human condition to have dramatically improved over the last few decades as the psychology industry has grown from nothing to tremendous proportions, but it is very difficult to come up any with hard evidence whatsoever that it has made any contribution or achieved any measurable results at all. Indeed, psychologists have not even been able to proscribe successfully for their own personal lives, let along everyone else's.

The psychotherapeutic model which, in various incarnations, is still in widespread use today was largely developed in the 19th century by Freud. He believed that his scientific research had proved that most behavior was motivated by unconscious sexuality. In fact, he believed that men have an Oedipal complex which gives them an unconscious desire to kill their father, who supposedly is a rival for their mother's love, and then make love to their mother. Biologists believe that such a desire is absurdly counter evolutionary given that the death of a father would drastically cut the son's probability of survival and reproduction.

Freud developed the theories at a time when it was culturally difficult if not blasphemous to talk about sex. He was forced to ask customers (usually wealthy, bored, frustrated Victorian women) about everything but sex in an effort to find out about nothing but sex. Even in today's comparatively promiscuous, liberal environment it would strain the psychology industry's fragile reputation badly if the first question out of a therapist's mouth was, "please describe your sex life in great detail?" Biology avoids all this complex, unproven pseudo-science and the social taboos by merely focusing on current behavior or more specifically on current sexual behavior and its consistency or lack thereof with basic biology. A woman doesn't need to go to a therapist. She can read biology from a book and then ask herself whether her sexual behavior is consistent with basic biology.

Unfortunately, a woman who wishes to consider this subject today is almost always sent toward a psychologist who most probably will attempt to take her on an endless ride through her subconscious. Unfortunately most psychological theories, in addition to being based on largely disproved Freudian or Freudian related theories only explain past behavior while ignoring a biological, religious, or philosophic basis for future behavior.

What you really get in the end from a psychologist is the only thing possible, i.e., the psychologist's personal value judgement which emphasizes the individual over the family, and the paying patient over that patient's family. The value system which created civilization in a dramatically short period of human history asks of us that we vow, " till death do you part; for richer or poorer; in sickness and in health, etc." Psychologists do not subscribe to that social/philosophical/religious value and they do not subscribe to the value of science either. More than anything they subscribe to the their own values and to the value of money.

8.) HOW PSYCHOLOGY CAUSES DIVORCE

The best that can be said is that they are substitute friends who we pay for their good listening ability. It seems odd but we would rather speak ill of ourselves than not speak of ourselves at all. If we don't have a lover we can pay a prostitute; if we don't have friend we can pay a psychologist but in the end more is needed.

Anyone who has seen a divorce trial knows that either party can have as many psychological experts testify on his behalf as he can afford. Money makes psychological truths very flexible. It gives psychologists flexible values as well as a disregard for science. In their value free, science free world they are "free to be you and me" to use a pop culture title which attempts to relate America's most cherished concept, freedom, to the idea that any individual should be free to do anything he wants without regard to values. Psychologists are part of the I'm ok; you're ok" world of cultural relativism where everybody and every idea is ok regardless of truth, logic, or values. Biology, conversely, leaves very little room for freedom.

This explains, for example, how Woody Allen, our most lovable neurotic, was able to attend therapy his whole adult life and still not know that he it wasn't ok to seduce his own daughter. The incest taboo is and was respected by virtually every primitive tribe and modern society on earth; yet Mr. Allen was shielded from it through 30 years of therapy. With the release of "Thriller" Michael Jackson became the pop culture icon of the decade and by some measures the pop culture icon of the century as his androgynous sexuality educated us that it was then ok and even preferred for the sexes to be the same. When it turned out that he was, allegedly, a pathetic child molester we got another warning that basic biological parameters exist for a reason.

Psychologists attempt to defend themselves from this by saying that they treat the patient for what she is or from where she is at that moment. They say it is not their job to judge or to direct behavior Instead, with a series of Socratic/Freudian questions they slowly make the patient aware of more and more truth, and finally what is best. If that happens to include divorce then it includes divorce. This is the exact opposite of civilized. Civilization formed and grew around values that were codified through centuries of cultural evolution until they had the power to be imposed on us by our Gods and laws. The idea that each of us can walk

146

into a psychologist's office and develop a new personal culture on the spot contradicts the very process of civilization. By talking about divorce it is legitimized as value free. The culture which says, "till death do you part" and "thou shalt not covet thy neighbor's wife" is laughed at as something from an primitive and immature past. If marriage had been presented as merely a legitimate lifestyle option, the way divorce is presented today, rather than as a required institution through which you live and love and reproduce, civilization would not have been possible.

Culture unfortunately is a severe and often painful discipline. When a woman walks into a psychologist's office to discuss divorce she has found a new, instant, and competing culture to enable her to do what the old one wouldn't. It may be true that we need divorce to prevent slavery and abuse, but we don't need it to describe civilization as fraudulent and children as meaningless pawns.

Perhaps one of the greatest differences between biology and psychology is that biology can be truthful because it is so impersonal. If a biologist gets to a point where he might offend personal or cultural sensibilities he can make his case by generalizing about all humans or he can just as easily talk about animals instead. A psychologist is stuck in a one on one relationship which is lengthy, detailed, and gives rise to very personal questions which lead to more lengthy, detailed and personal questions. This is eventually supposed to make the customer/patient aware of the real but theretofore unconscious motives behind his behavior.

Once the customer is made aware of the unconscious motives behind his behavior he then is free to think, feel and behave in a way that he consciously dictates. The conscious decision to be, say, a killer or lover would then have to be made on some new basis or foundation; that basis or foundation would have to be biological or biological/cultural because there is no other choice. Psychology then is, at best, a distraction on a road that leads straight back to biology or the culture that grows most directly out of it. One recalls the dilemma faced by Nazi psychologists who trained the Hitler youth to kill the pets they had raised from birth in order to demonstrate their total militaristic devotion to the State. Without values anything was possible. Psychology itself then and now has no moral dimension and supports no specific behaviors. It can be used adjunctively to support any behavior. Civilized behavior, on the other hand is specific and comes from biology.

8.) HOW PSYCHOLOGY CAUSES DIVORCE

Even if there had been some truth in what Freud said, what is the point in whining about your history or your mommy and daddy to a psychologist when you know what you want to do in the end anyway. You want to be a doctor, lawyer, artist, mother, president, athlete or spouse. The energy wasted dealing with your "issues" on a psychiatrist's couch is energy that could be better spent studying law, playing with the kids, practicing your hook shot, or sharing something nice with your wife.

A combat veteran may recoil the rest of his life at loud noises which he unconsciously equates with life threatening combat noises; an abused child may unconsciously recoil at authority all his life; a normal child may grow up with unresolved Oedipal ambivalence toward all men and women; we all supposedly grow up with "love maps"(unconscious imprinting during childhood that determines the kind of adult we will fall in love with), but why should we go to a psychiatrist to delve into these processes?   Firstly, the processes are to complex to be understood. No one can discover the processes that cause them to, say, prefer beautiful blondes over sultry redheads. An abusive parent might cause someone to recoil at authority all his life, but an odd combination of thousands of unknowable and normal experiences might cause someone to develop the same response to authority. The anti-authoritarian passion of Bill Gates and George Washington is not in question is it? If George Washington had gone to a psychiatrist and miraculously discovered that his hugely abnormal passion against King George III was really displaced passion against an uncle who had been nasty to him at summer camp, would he then have fought for us, and would he have had any passion left at all. In a very real way to understand passion is to destroy it. Biology wouldn't have given us passion if reason alone were sufficient to motivate us. Passion is necessary; if we think about it too much we risk destroying it. The better course of action is to recognize and enjoy our passions, whatever their origins may be, and work to direct our behavior in a socially constructively way. When our behavior was more directed by the 10 commandments and the Boy Scout manual we were essentially doing this rather than looking for an inner child that really can never be found and would be largely irrelevant if found.

Our culture, which thankfully is still somewhat based in simple biology, prevents a psychologist from embarrassing us too much by asking

8.) HOW PSYCHOLOGY CAUSES DIVORCE

directly about, for example, the anal retentive part of our psychosexual development. Instead they ask us to projectively talk about whatever is particularly important to us and then they use the psychologist's popular refrain: "how did that make you feel?" The patient says: "angry." The psychologist then asks more questions: "why does that make you feel angry," in order to slowly help the patient to realize that the anger might be, say, generalized anger that stems from an unresolved childhood Oedipal anger toward his father or anger perhaps because his father beat him too much. The patient, upon realizing this, then resolves his self-defeating anger (to be psychological) or stops being unconsciously reactive (to be Scientologist), or learns to "know thyself" (to be Socratic) toward someone who is not really his father, and then becomes a happier, wiser, and more productive person.

The problems with this are myriad. After 100 years Freud's theory that our feelings reflect an unconscious sexual reaction to our parents has grown weaker rather than stronger. If you assume that it is important to know yourself, but that this may only marginally involve your sexual relationship with your parents, then you are left with ancient Socratic concepts which rightly presupposed that an inability to think or to know thyself was primarily caused by insufficient training in logic or the dialectical method. Freud may have contributed nothing at all. He didn't invent thinking, he only invented silly thinking about our sexual relationship to our parents.

Freud tried to lock us into one little theory that would support his grandiose impression of himself. Suppose he occasionally could make someone happier. Would that lead to greater contentment which in turn might lead to less productivity and then less happiness? When psychologists free us from our primary demons what motivation are we left with? Somehow we survived many demons even without psychologists. We survived freezing and starving to death in winter when we had no heat or food. We survived being suffocated and eaten alive by wild animals when we had no defense. We survived the deaths of our parents when life expectancy was only 25 years, and still we evolved and prospered. Why is it that now we need psychologists to properly motivate us by overcoming the petty demons we still face? Wasn't it those very demons who motivated us to make the progress we made in the first

149

place? Freud wanted us to believe in his very particular little demons in part because they were the only new demons he could find and in part because he didn't realize or want to admit that there are always new demons of equal evolutionary importance to slay. Without such demons there is only complacency and death. Civilization is much more concerned with slaying demons of all kinds than with idly contemplating them.

Freud taught us that feelings are windows to the soul. Today television talk shows endlessly glorify the feelings of ordinary people; yesterday they glorified the behavior and accomplishments of famous or ideal people. Our capacity to self-indulgently explore our feelings has become a meaningless way of life for many and a significant part of our culture. We pretend that by focusing on our feelings we are working on significant psychological problems (issues) when really we are only wallowing in them. Sally Jesse Raphael and Ricki Lake and their clones can be everywhere if we choose to expend our valuable time and energy on them. We can identify our feeling, explore our feeling, and resolve our feeling but they or new feelings will always come right back. Our choice is to wallow in them continuously or to go out and do something positive and productive.

To Freud, feelings were the essence of human experience the way a twinkling white star is the essence of gravity and time. A feeling was the light coming from the compacted star. With the psychologist's guidance, the patient merely needs to follow that light back in time to discover his true self. Feelings have become the psychologist's stock in trade. They have empowered themselves as the sultans of feeling. When their telescopes pick up a few rays of our feelings they instantly pretend to know our souls. They use psychology on us the way an advertiser uses it if he wants to sell us toothpaste. They pretend to know us better than we know ourselves. They can trick us into buying toothpaste or discovering our souls. Whether they interpret the feelings of a patient or create the feelings an advertisement projects, their intent is always deceptive. The don't tell us the truth. They make it magically appear before us as if it were our own creation. It is the perfect confidence game.

When a patient is done with his psychologist; when he has understood that feelings have layers and layers of subconscious meaning how can he know whether the feelings and emotions he next shows in public are real or just manufactured advertisements. In an important sense to know feelings is to destroy them, but how can psychologists do this when we depend on feelings as our most simple and extensive form of communication? Biology adjunctively gave us the ability to examine our feelings as part of an over all mental capacity, but too much use of that capacity where it is not needed can cause us to lose sight of the simple and important meaning for which feelings were given to us in the first place. The Buddha, for example, may ignore the simple and disgusting feeling of urine rather than interrupt his search for Nirvana, but general civilization would not be possible if everyone learned to attach there own non-biological meaning to feelings.

Fortunately, most customer/patients have neither the time nor money to delve deeply into the layers of subconscious meaning in their feelings. Instead a generation of women is being encouraged to rely on half of the psychological process. Rather than endure the time, expense, and difficulty of interpreting and understanding their feelings in a biological context they are taught to rely and act on whatever feeling they have as legitimate reflections of the true nature of their souls. Support groups are all the rage; not because they help women understand and control their feelings, but because they validate feelings according to emotional new age value judgements. In theory a woman who felt like killing her husband would get support for this feeling at a support group. In a support group you feel pressure to be supportive; not thoughtful or value conscience. Everywhere psychology teaches us to "trust our feelings." A woman contemplating a divorce is taught to look at it as a means of personal expression and evolution. It is a wonder that a woman who is contemplating suicide is not taught to rely on her feelings that her life is useless. In that case they are still able to make a judgement about what it right or wrong behavior. William J. Doherty, Ph.D. summarizes this nicely when he says that "therapist-assisted marital suicide has become part of the standard paradigm of contemporary psychotherapy."

Interestingly, marital therapists often become the enemy of men who are being divorced. The men often smell a rat early on. They avoid marital therapy sensing that their wives are using it, instead of talking to them, as a means to wiggle out of the marriage with official third party approval and often with the direct assistance of a therapist. As the man

8.) HOW PSYCHOLOGY CAUSES DIVORCE

pulls away, like the lamb being led to the slaughter, the therapist cruelly steps in to hint that if he too is willing to work on his "issues" perhaps the marriage, and an additional fee for the himself, can be saved. The therapist offers to be the wetnurse and the butcher, but sees no conflict of interest. But in the end the wife, with her paid co-conspirator often follows through with the divorce. The therapist is often willing to do the dirty work of breaking the marital vows that the wife cannot brake on her own.

The therapist can actually be seen as the party who enables or makes the divorce possible. A woman who balks too long is often encouraged by her therapist to work on her personal issues further until she gets to the point where her dread of breaking her marital vows is finally seen as an act of personal development rather than as an uncivilized betrayal. She is told not to feel guilty about her sacred marital vows or the agony of her husband as long as she is doing "what's right for her" and the therapist's fee. In the end the woman generates the highest fee and the therapist stays with her to the end and beyond. A therapist who doesn't gently lead the divorce minded wife ever closer to divorce runs the risk of losing his customer to a competitor. In the 1960's and 70's divorce was seen as an unequivocal treatment failure and few women elected to pursue it through therapy. Today divorce is seen as a neutral, and as a personal development process and the therapy industry is booming. In the end men are criticized and made to feel guilty for not being nearly as willing to work on their issues even as the therapist becomes the enemy co-conspirator who actively participates in the demise of the marriage and children. None of this is to say that therapists act in isolation. Society in general has adopted the idea of no-fault or neutral divorce.

Therapists are in part chicken and in part egg we might assume. As soon as State Legislatures define marriage as something that can end with no-fault they are saying its ok for a marital relationship to end. Nobody will be at fault; so why not divorce? Historically, gov't viewed marriage as exactly the opposite. They wanted to tie people together; not out of stupidity, but to benefit children. The State's position was that divorce was negative. The party at fault in a divorce was penalized. Being tied together in marriage meant that a couple had to work together to be happy together. This is the essence of civilization. No fault divorce has meant that working with people is not necessary or valuable. It holds out the false hope of relationships that just feel good without work, organization, or discipline. Given the higher rate of divorce in second marriages we know this is mistaken not only for adults but, more importantly, for children too. The govt.'s no-fault laws indirectly tell kids not to take the thing they thrive on most: love, seriously, because it may well be temporary, and then their wonderful parents show them first hand that this is so. Gov't no-fault laws and psychological insights don't create marriages. They harm them, in the case of Gov't, and are irrelevant to them in the case of psychology. A marriage is created only by the definition we give it. If one society defined and imposed marriage on its citizens (as we once did) as a till death do you part institution and another defined it as a 5 year commitment after which time it would be very acceptable to re-evaluate and move on if desired, we would find vastly different rates of divorce and vastly different values placed on all human relationships. In the end, people who divorce don't find it leads to greater personal happiness, because in the final analysis it is more civilized and more meaningful to have policies that support children over those that favor mistaken notions regarding parental happiness.

The new world of work and marriage, in which modern women need to assertively participate, is not a therapist's support group either. A business meeting is not a support group. Ideas need to be presented and critically analyzed. Feelings have little place until after the success or failure of an idea has been determined. A couple may marry in support of where each other is at that moment, but in time they need to analyze ideas together so that they can grow together and in the same direction. If they just support each other they will grow slowly, and probably apart. Love is a mutual idea. Marital feelings celebrate the shared evolution of good ideas, but by themselves they have no meaning. Working to stay together rather than supporting random feelings is the essence of civilization and marriage.

Not coincidentally, at a time when we have emphasized our individual feelings over ideas, responsibilities, duties, and behavior, our behavior as manifested by general criminality and general rude behavior has dramatically deteriorated. Everywhere we are taught that self-esteem is the feeling which is essential for children. Black leaders were made to believe that self-esteem was the feeling that white oppression took from black children. Black children were then taught to have high self-esteem, and then nearly seventy five percent committed crimes and fifty percent were sentenced to jail. The cause and effect relationship is so clear that many now refer to it as a form of genocide derived from a mistaken psychological conclusion.

Ghetto children are taught to "dis" (disrespect) whites and even each other, perhaps because respect for whites had kept them as slaves too long. We say to them, in effect, "you're feelings are ok; if you think he's ugly go right ahead and tell him so; get in touch with your feelings; trust your feelings." Respect for "the man" gives "the man" control. Frighteningly, professional wrestling, which once featured matches between good guys and bad guys, now only features bouts between evil and more evil guys.Fans love the display of evil feelings so much that wrestling now dominates Cable TV. Even when the jet set gathers to watch tennis it is now common for them to boo a player who has made a mistake rather than politely support their favorite player. The fans are taught to go with their feelings no matter how disrespectful and uncivilized they may be. The fans don't owe the inferior player respect as an integral part of the civilized meaning of community; instead they owe themselves free expression of their most base feelings. Still, though, as a culture we persist in believing that good undisciplined expression of basic feelings leads to good behavior rather than that good proper behavior leads to good feelings.

Ironically, as feelings have become so important to us we have invented the hugely popular Prozac to make us always feel good. In the future perhaps the only reply to the psychologist who says, "how does that make you feel," might be, "you know my Prozac always makes me feel good." Without a patient who no longer feels badly about wanting to kill his father and sleep with his mother, what's a psychologist to do? She'll have to focus on thinking and doing, something about which it will be difficult to claim saleable expertise. All the Prozac in the world and all the good feelings in the world won't make someone more civilized or a better marital partner. Only thoughtful biological behavior will. Perhaps it was not that Freud was wrong, but that he stated his conclusions in a way that separated the sexes rather than in a way that united them or in a way that encouraged a healthy respect for one another's differences. It's just not loving to imply that deep down women hate their mothers and love their fathers, but can eventually get over it. Among Freud's other conclusions was that notion that women felt like inferior or castrated men. What woman would want to go through life fighting the feeling that she was an amputee? What parent would want to treat their daughter as if this were so? And what man would enjoy sex with a wife who felt so afflicted. And why was there so much focus on the individual's feelings over his societal behavior?

If it was all a sinister psychological plot to drum up business for future generations of psychologists it worked. But from a biological viewpoint Freud was absurd. Disliking genitalia would be counter-evolutionary, just like disliking arms or legs. Similarly, Freud's Oedipal and Electra Complexes were absurd. Disliking a parent or genitalia would be counter-evolutionary. It would make survival more rather than less difficult. Nevertheless, Freud should be given credit for what at the time seemed to be brilliant discoveries but for what later turned out only to be half-truths. Perhaps, though, he points us in the right direction with his brilliant but largely mistaken idea that women saw themselves as castrated men. This idea offers us a plausible explanation as to why women don't participate creatively, aggressively, and equally in the bedroom. The modesty and secrecy surrounding sexual organs was designed, he suggested, to protect little girls from discovering the horrible truth that nature had left them without sexual organs. At puberty this truth could no longer be hidden. A repressed, prudish, femininity was the result, according to Freud, but it was not a volitional result caused by men. It was a fact of biology over which no man had control and it presumably left women with little sexual authority or expressiveness.

While Freud's scientific reputation was never established and while he has been roundly vilified by feminists, who deplore his notion that women are essentially inferior men, his empirical observations have been hard to ignore. Freud felt that women were sexually repressed. Betty Friedan (100 years later) felt similarly that they were repressed and depressed in marriage. Friedan's theme quickly grew to assume political proportions with "male chauvinism" being the catch phrase to describe men who took advantage of the female's plight. Politics offered instant and guiltless political power to depressed women. This was a wonderful escape and certainly more fun than a women helping women theme or a pro-family theme or a how to successfully love men theme.

A careful reading of de Beauvoir and Friedan (two of the most important feminists) shows that they, like Freud, believed that women themselves were at least partially responsible for their relationships and their marital depression. Susan Faludi in her book: BACKLASH details the depression still found in post-Freudian/Friedanian marriages. Noted depression expert Ellen McGrath M.D. calls female marital depression "psychology's dirty little secret." Dalma Heyn, in her book "Marriage Shock", says that women viscerally refuse to choose between their authentic sexual selves and their perceived relationship responsibilities. Women, she correctly claims, appoint themselves as guarantors of a happy, successful relationship and in so doing lose their true selves in service to their husbands. Nathaniel Hawthorne made a similar point in his novel, The Birthmark. It describes a husband who became obsessed with the unsightliness of a birthmark on his wife's face. The husband's obsession was then matched by that of his dutiful wife who eventually dies from inept surgical attempts to remove the birth mark her husband so hated. A women's impulse to please a man grows out of the maternal instinct that enables her to please her children and help them survive. Women bring too much of the estrogen that is intended primarily for their babies to their husbands, so to speak, just as men bring too much of the testosterone, that is intended primarily for hunting, to their wives. Heyn says that women now have a modern political solution: divorce. But she neglects to point out that it is a solution which completely avoids rather than addresses the problem. What about the children and the higher failure rate of second marriages? Freud, Friedan, and even their most recent successors are remarkably silent on how to address this most important of all problems because it is merely a personal problem while they are concerned with much more important political problems no matter how great the destruction in personal lives.

Women were given estrogen to be mothers who raise children while men were given testosterone mostly to impregnate women and to hunt. Not surprisingly men often have intimacy problems and thereby fail to live up female expectations, but women get severely depressed even without men. The Center For Disease Control reports that in 1996 there were 22,000 reported cases of attempted teen female suicide (despite or because of the most feminist and most psychologically oriented mothers in history) and only 600 reported cases of teen male attempted suicide. Interestingly successful teen male suicides exceed teen female suicides by 20 to 1 adding support to the notion of female frivolity. Boys and men adjust more easily to their environment thanks to the broader motivational influence of testosterone. They can pursue girls (even though it is just practice), play sports, and learn computers while girls are somewhat out of place and depressed with too much estrogen and too few children and too few childlike boyfriends. Females it seems need to learn how to handle their estrogen even more than males need to learn how to handle their politically incorrect testosterone. If women are independently and comparatively depressed it is not surprising that they initiate 91% of divorce. They search for children but often find men.

If Freud had said that women often envy men for their testosterone and all the exciting things it encourages them to do, he would have been far closer to a sustainable theory. Modern women have always seemed to feel that being a baby factory wasn't a complete end it itself. They never rebelled much because they mostly got what they wanted, i.e., sex, babies, and support. For the most part they were shockingly loyal to men who were often little more than their masters. But in the end comparisons with the men, with whom they shared virtually identical genes, were inevitable. They envied men for their masculinity; for their ability to take power and for the vast creativity and energy they used to explore and conquer the seemingly more diverse and exciting outside world.

Women especially admired men when they were at a time in their lives when they were not directly or fully involved with children. The masculine world often seemed a little better than the feminine one mostly because it was a broader one containing more possibilities. A woman knew her child had to be, but more importantly, she knew that it had to do, especially if it was a boy, and so she needed to know about, if not participate in a man's world.

Doing, was the acknowledged masculine ideal that gave the final and greatest meaning to the whole process. Even the act of sex itself, around which so much of culture was centered, seemed to be under the control of men and enjoyed primarily by men. It was initiated by courageous male courting and ended by the male orgasm, or, when the active male sperm found the passive female egg. In this context it is possible to understand what may have led Freud to overstate his conclusion that women felt like castrated men.

In reality Freud's specific hypothesis was wrong. No scientist ever proved that he was right, and presumably all gave up trying long ago. It is no wonder though that truculent feminists vilify Freud for having set their movement back by 100 years. In truth, it is hard to know whether psychology or feminism set back marriage and sexual relations more. Both dealt extensively with sex and relationships but neither had an essential concern with the preservation or support of biological marriage.

Dr. Joyce Brothers tells us that half of all women fake orgasm half the time to please their husbands. Apparently they feel a greater need to please their husbands than to please themselves. If we couple these women with: the other woman who "just lie there", the passive Japanese and German women of World War 11, and the fact that infertility doctors tell us that where female egg gender typing is possible males are most often selected by female mothers (there is no female equivalent to, "it's a boy!"), there is a strong Freudian case to be made that penis/testosterone envy is a significant part of the new divorce/feminist female psyche. Feminists don't want a revolution to do something new and feminine, they want a revolution to do or be something old. They want to be masculine. They want to enter the testosterone filled male world. Fighting with a man for the right to be his colleague though makes it harder to peacefully lie under him or beside him as a lover, but love has been largely irrelevant to the larger themes of psychology and feminism. It is remarkable how destructive the great heroes of psychology and feminism are to marriage and children. It is more remarkable how little they cared about a subject that towers above theirs in importance.

Today Freud has become something of a liability to psychology. It is a risk to call yourself a psychologist because it, may identify you as someone who believes in a rigid Freudian, or some other, wacky theory, or that you were led to the field by your own severe psychological problems, or that your behavior can't be normal because you've studied behavior so much. Adler carved out his own market niche after Freud with a much safer and more generalized theory which held that life was more than libido. He believed that a more generalized "will to power" existed which caused man to seek dominion over more than just sex. Life was a relationship to the outside world in addition to the internal psyche. According to Adler, failure led to inferiority feelings and then to antisocial neuroses. This was all well and fine except that it was ground that philosophers had covered directly and indirectly for centuries. Without Freud's bold ideas much of psychology's intellectual energy came to a dead end.

In recognition of psychology's complete failure to justify its founding father's revolutionary theories many modern psychologists more realistically describe themselves as marriage counselors or relationship experts. This is much more folksy; it doesn't imply that they have a magic Freudian bullet that will cure and explain everything. It merely implies that they may have thought about psychological issues and relationships more than average, not that they have any demonstrable scientific expertise that leads to specific treatment.

Alongside the trend to legitimize feelings, women are further led astray by conflicting economic pressures. As the energy consumed by children becomes less and less due to advances in medicine, greater economic wealth, greater life expectancy (fewer generations) and fewer children per household (due to overpopulation concerns), women are inevitably doing more than bearing and rearing children. They know that a maternal mentality has a diminished value when there are no children around whom to be maternal. Moreover, much of the future work to be done will suit women more and more as it becomes less and less physical. To be sure, lower testosterone levels will hurt them in the short term but who is to say that recognition of this problem won't solve it all by itself? Who is to say that women can't get their creativity and aggression through mental discipline to the extent that it is not available hormonally?

Perhaps women will even come out on top of men despite their maternal attitudes and all the time spent with children. Faceless male hormones produce so much deviance and wasted manic energy (sports, for example) that female mental discipline may prove to be a more efficient source of creativity over the long run? Or, perhaps women will come out on top as they force themselves to reconcile their desire for both creative work and children. Despite a lack of testosterone women are creating their own businesses in greater numbers than men; often so they can reconcile their conflicting interest in both work and children. The self-imposed pressure they feel to create these businesses may actually be greater and better focused than the indiscriminate hormonally induced pressure that men feel. We can't really say what the future holds, although the trend seems clear, at least outside of the bedroom. Sadly, though, we must acknowledge, that much of the pressure to work is merely a reflection of a woman's inability to get a man to work for her and her children. Statistics always seem to show that when a married women has sufficient money she generally chooses not to work, especially if she has kids.

The industrial revolution has brought and undoubtedly will continue to bring great increases in the amount of wealth we have, what role each sex contributes to that wealth, and the overall level of knowledge (psychological, feminist, and otherwise) we can afford to accumulate. It is very difficult to speculate about what all of this will suggest to those in marriages but it is certain that the way couples works out their sexual life will continue to be central to the health of their marriages in this very dynamic environment.

From a biological perspective relationships are simple, but they are so complicated from a broad cultural perspective that a continuous amount of information can be and is generated about them. Most of us have been persuaded by this avalanche of information to give up the notion of a simple, practical, biological relationship concept and to embrace the relationship industry in its current generalized form; often on a daily basis. Those who generate this endless information thus get paid more on the perpetual installment basis. One very famous psychologist, not satisfied with an already huge market, claimed that 96% of us come from dysfunctional families and, accordingly, 96% of us need his books, tapes and TV shows. Psychologists further encourage us by telling us the opposing lie that it is healthy people (those healthy enough to see that there is a problem) who seek a psychologist, in order to help prospective customers over the stigma that is normally and correctly attached to people who patronize psychologists. The profession wants to expand the market completely, not only by insisting that we are all healthy and simultaneously dysfunctional, but also by insisting that we all need treatment on a daily basis.

Perhaps the ultimate manifestation of the above mentality is found in the DSM-IV(otherwise known as the fourth edition of the Diagnostic and Statistical Manual of Mental Disorders). At 886 pages it is the bible of all known mental disorders authored by hundreds of the industry's leading professionals. Each disorder is accompanied by a billing code so that interested insurance companies, govt. agencies, hospitals, and other bureaucracies can make easy reference and assign treatment fees accurately. According to Harper's Magazine among the illnesses are frotteurism (the irresistible desire to sexually touch and rub against one's fellow passengers on mass transit), fugue(travel in foreign lands; often under an assumed name), bad writing(self-explanatory), coffee drinking including coffee nerves, bad coffee nerves, inability to sleep after drinking too much coffee, shyness, jet lag, snobbery, tobacco smoking, nightmares, clumsiness, playing video games, snoring and failure to clean up one's room.

DSM II said homosexuality was an illness; DMS III said that believing one's homosexuality to be an illness was an illness. Neither said whether those who once taught that homosexuality was an illness were ill. Similarly, penis envy disappeared, as did the belief that schizophrenia was caused by bad parents. Nowhere do we learn what normal healthy behavior is. We are simply left to find an illness that fits and go in for treatment. Or worse, to fear that someday the govt. will use DMS IV to find us mentally ill in order to justify some action against us. The constitution protects us from criminal self-incrimination but it offers no protection against psychological incrimination. We are all now mentally ill according to greedy psychologists.

In 1950 the number of mental illnesses was a paltry 26. In 1986 when DSM II was published the number of illnesses had grown slightly, but more importantly the word "reaction" had vanished and the science of Psychology had vanished. Previously an illness had to have a discernable cause like a biological condition or a specific occurrence. Science needed to see a consistent cause and effect that were measurable and repeatable

8.) HOW PSYCHOLOGY CAUSES DIVORCE

before a truth could be believed. As of 1968 they formally gave up trying to prove that women felt like castrated men, and that we all want to kill one of our parents. Not only did they find that science was very difficult but more importantly that it dramatically interfered with a rapidly growing and profitable market. If mental illness could be sold more and more easily why not do it? Why not make everyone a potential customer? If someone does something a little odd, like travel in a foreign country under an assumed name, why not encourage him to come in for treatment? The harm in all this is that it is done more for money and the self aggrandizement of the profession than to help people. They are willing to be non-scientific experts on everything for a fee. What the public then gets, especially in the divorce/relationship area, is values from people who aren't trained in values and who don't recognize the importance of values.

Their ability to exploit us has been made easier by our natural feeling that something as important as a our marital relationships might well deserve daily consideration. After all, if something is important it must be important all the time; not once a year. In truth, scarcity is what gives value to many things. A couple can't make love every day, celebrate Christmas every day, have a heart to heart conversation every day, or buy a new car every day. If they could, the essential value and definition of these things would be lost.

Politics provides a similar example, 18th century American politics was torn apart by the Jeffersonians who hated govt. and the Hamiltonians who loved govt. The exact same dichotomy still is the focus of 20th century politics. But, despite an ever growing political information industry, Americans are further than ever from knowing whether they like Democrats and big govt. or Republicans and small govt. Today you can watch C-Span 1 & 2 and almost literally watch everything including the mice run loose during the often empty closing hours of a "Special Orders" session at the House of Representatives. This tremendous overexposure hopelessly trivializes and buries the hugely important and essential issues which are few in number, easy to deal with, and very inexpensive to promote. Many of us learn countless facts and percepts about politics (and relationships) from all this disorganized overexposure, but few ever focus on or decide the essential and age old big govt./small govt. debate.

Barbara De Angelis, Ph.D., is probably our country's leading

162

relationship expert. At book stores she often has more shelf space than any other author. To capitalize on her success she has an infomercial in which she sells a sort of do-it-your self-psychotherapy kit. She begins by talking very directly about how her knowledge has empowered her to find real love in her personal life. She does not mention that she found it five times through five marriages. She goes on by pulling out a baggage cart that is overflowing with baggage. This is her way of symbolizing the psychological baggage that people acquire, mostly during childhood. They then carry the baggage unconsciously, but influentially, into their marriages and this prevents them from achieving true and lasting love, etc.,etc. In her case, despite a Ph.D. and a life time of personal and professional experience she, according to her own definitions, must not have discovered and understood her own voluminous baggage.

This is because the process is too difficult (as discussed earlier), and filled with philosophical contradictions. Ms.De Angelis is living breathing testimony to this and she is not atypical of her industry. The people who speak the most know the least. Curiously, one of her marriages was to John Gray, Ph.D., also a relationship author whose book "Men Are From Mars Women Are From Venus" is currently the best-selling relationship book of all time. If it continues to sell at the current rate it will easily out sell all of his prolific ex-wife's books. It almost appears as a battle of the divorcees to see who can pretend the most that they know the most about marriage.

But more importantly, these books sell well because, 1) we can't help but believe that a Ph.D. in psychology must have learned something in all those years of study and, 2) we believe that we know something, when we do not, and that it will be reinforced and expanded by the particular book we buy. The Mars/Venus book is better than the traditional "baggage" books because it is something of a biology book. It is a very simple and fun book, intended for a large audience, that is essentially a list of baggage that came to men and women from their respective biology's rather than from the way they were treated as children. While it does recognize that biological baggage is far more important and far easier to understand than psychological baggage, it does not prioritize baggage into categories of importance, i.e., sex and all other. And, it does not provide a biological/cultural/philosophical basis for long term love, perhaps because the author does not think in those terms.

Gray's most talked about example has to do with a husband going into his cave (or the TV room) after a hard day at work to be alone while a wife will want to be together with her husband after her similarly hard day. Dr. Gray counsels the wife that it is natural for the husband to seek the shelter of a cave after a hard day out in an insecure world and she should let him go rather than seek conversation or housework from him. He claims the husband will eventually and naturally come out at which time he will be a more willing spouse. Gray claims that this is natural evolutionary baggage for a man to carry. While this does recognize the biological truth that men and women are different it might well exacerbate the problem between them by encouraging men to stay in their caves more and more. But, he also advises men to take the time to listen to and stay connected to their very talkative wives. Teaching us a series of gender based mechanical interactions is, possibly, a tiny step in the right direction but it does not address the actual problem.

Before Dr. Gray's therapy a wife might say, "he watches TV too much and listens too little;" after Dr. Gray's therapy the a wife might say, "he watches TV more than ever and consequently listens less than ever." Watching more TV and listening to his wife more is a contradiction. The couple might well be back to where they started. Dr. Gray leaves them on their own, where they always were, to find the balance of activities that suits them best. The real incentive for the opposite sexes to be together is sexual. Biology gave us sex to draw the sexes together; without this incentive the sexes would be happier apart as in the case of pre-pubescent children. Men and women exist only so they can have sex. Therefore, the promise of sex can make a husband an attentive listener; the promise of attentive listening can make a wife an attentive sexual partner.

Without the biological model, relationships just can't be made sense of by psychologists. Sandra S. Vogel, Ph.D. demonstrates this in her book Women And Divorce, Men And Divorce. This was a book that I was originally very optimistic about given that it was scholarly and one of the very few that even considers gender and divorce, but it turned out to be hopelessly limited by its total psychological orientation. The summary of the first chapter reads as follows:

Remarried men and women were more oriented to a balance between self-interests and the other's interests in the remarriage decision than in the first marriage decision.

> In depth interviews showed these men and women used a similar balance when making the remarriage decision but that they arrived there by different avenues. The balance came from the women beginning to include self-interests more and the men beginning to include the other's interest's more. These remarried men and women also perceived themselves to be more non-traditional in sex role orientation at the remarriage decision. Gilligan's Ethic of Care, a cognitive theory was used to explain the change in self-other and sex-role orientation. Recommendations were made for using this theoretical framework in marital therapy.

A few sentences later the author asks the following question: if the conditional commitment to remarriage is based on the expectation of equity in all aspects of the marriage, then would this balance of self/other orientation really be a higher level of moral reasoning? The author's conclusion is really quite simple. After all the high faluten academic language she is really saying that by the time of remarriage men have grown morally above their male chauvinism and women have grown above their submissiveness. The authors would apparently conclude that second marriages are wonderful and equitable evolutions in human relationships. And on the surface this makes perfect sense, especially to a Ph.D. looking for an easy politically correct theme to latch on to, and to couples marrying for the second time who need a reason to believe they can succeed the second time around. Who would quickly argue with the notion that people may well learn from their first marital mishaps?

It all seems to make perfect sense, except that second marriages are shorter than first marriages. In their enthusiasm to find support for feminist ideals of sexual androgyny they manage to overlook that essential fact. The logical conclusion from their data might actually be that marital

8.) HOW PSYCHOLOGY CAUSES DIVORCE

decisions based on equity lead to divorce faster than marital decisions based on the traditional male chauvinist/submissive model. In a theoretical sense second marriages aren't natural because they're not optimal for the kids who are after all at the heart of biology's larger plan. This is why second marriages with kids from previous marriages are the shortest of all marriages. Perhaps second marriages fail faster because biology can't very well reward those who fail their children. If nature could have found a way to make equitable androgyny work, it would have because it's a far simpler concept. These authors might then have been tempted to argue that while second marriages may not be longer, they're better, at least for the shorter time they last. As long as you forget biology's basic purpose the argument can almost seem to make sense.

The question these academic psychologists could not ask is: how do you have sex or make love in an equitable way or how does a man pursue a woman in an equitable way or how does a woman choose a taller man that she wants to be on top of her during intercourse in an equitable way? These just are not questions of equity; they are question of lust and passion which really provide the substance of a relationship. In academia a relationship is apparently good and equitable and wonderful so long as the house work is divided equitably or each provides equal input about the next vacation site. This may be important but it is not sufficient to make a marriage.

It is easy to know and observe and measure how equitably a couple makes dinner or mows the lawn, but these are not the things that alone make a loving marriage. A wife does not say to herself or to anybody else, "I'm so in love with my husband; you should see how well we divide up the household chores." While such a man can certainly be appreciated in moderation, in time most women would begin to think of him as a nerd if he seemed to believe that that was the way to win and keep his woman's heart. Women primarily select a mate for his inequitable supply of money, masculine competence, and tenderness toward them while men primarily select a mate for her inequitable beauty and sexual promise. The commitment to eternal adoration of the other spouse's inequitable characteristics is what makes a marriage.

Ph.D's in psychology come in all shapes and sizes. Perhaps the most elite of the elite are the research Ph.D's. For them nothing can be considered the truth unless it has been tested with a scientific experiment that can be described and then duplicated by others. To them any conclusions reached by any other methods are not scientific and therefore not reliable.

In the case of relationships this usually means survey research and statistical analysis. A certain group, who are carefully selected to be representative of a larger population, is surveyed for characteristics that, if found frequently enough, are assumed to be found at a certain level in the overall population. A psychologist who sits in an office all day and listens to patients without careful and systematic record keeping, and draws generalized conclusions from that small sample population is deemed to be unscientific or to have mere opinions which are unsubstantiated by fact. The patient group as a survey population might be atypical of the over all population because of size, ethnicity, religion, wealth/poverty, geography, education, or achievement.

The problem with real science and relationships though is that passion is not an easy thing to quantify scientifically. Perhaps the best example of the logic and folly of scientific psychology comes from Dr. John Mordechai Gottman's supposedly epic book: What Predicts Divorce. It is 500 scientific pages devoted to the science of what really predicts divorce. The thinking presumably was that if you could predict a divorce in advance you could also intervene and prevent the divorce. But right away the arrogance and failure of scientific psychology becomes evident.

On page 6 Dr. Gottman proclaims, with a queer mixture of bluster and humility," I can now predict, from just six variables coded from this interview, with 94% accuracy, which marriages are headed for divorce." But on page 7 he says that, "Put simply, accuracy of prediction (94%) does not mean that I understand the process involved in the maintenance or deterioration of a marriage." With that Dr. Gottman is free to bury the reader with 500 pages of blinding statistics all of which, despite our fervent curiosity, don't tell us a single blessed thing about how to avoid the divorce he can supposedly predict. So who should care about this prodigious scientific effort from the academy? Perhaps we are expected to hold our breath waiting on Dr. Gottman until he leads the scholarly community and the rest of us to the discovery of the magic correlation between prediction and prevention?

8.) HOW PSYCHOLOGY CAUSES DIVORCE

After further reflection it seems that any fool can come up with six variables that predict divorce. Alcoholism, physical abuse, emotional / verbal abuse, chronic unemployment, adultery, and hatred / indifference, it would seem, ought to be high on anyone's list, but they are not on Dr. Gottman's. Other possible predictors of divorce are listed as, parental divorce, premarital cohabitation, age at marriage, premarital pregnancy, marital fertility, the husband has a lower income, the husband was a stepfather, the wife had low income and low educational level, the couple had a history of divorce, the couple did not pool finances, the couple knew each other only a few months, the husband and wife held dysfunctional beliefs about relationships. Examples: 1) disagreement is destructive to relationships, 2) sexual perfection is expected, 3) the wife is low in self-reported conscientiousness, 4) the wife was low on satisfaction with perceived social support, 5) the husband had many external motives for being married, 6)) the couple had large discrepancies on autonomy and external motives for being married, 7) parental disagreement about child rearing practices, 8) relatively high internal orientation of the man, 9) interest in art, 10) dissimilar physically attractiveness, 11) extroverted, 12) less clothes conscious, 13) unconventional, 14) neurotic, and 15) poor impulse control. The list of predictive factors and the scientific ways they are analyzed goes on and on and on until the reader cannot possible have any faith that anybody could ever organize and understand them.

At one point Dr. Gottman even gets down to measuring the blood pressure of a couple while they are teasing one another. He concludes that teasing can be bad. At other points he discusses the several other scientific methods of measuring and recording data on married people. There is the MICS, the Marital Interaction Coding System. He says, "this observational coding system is designed specifically for use with conflict-resolution discussions. It includes codes such as problem description, positive solution, negative solution, agrees, and disagrees. It also includes codes that describe the listener's behavior (attention and engagement or disengagement). Then there is The Rapid Couples Interaction Scoring System (RCISS). The author says, "it provides a means for classifying couples into regulated and non-regulated types. It employs a checklist of 13 behaviors that are scored for the speaker and 9 behaviors that are scored for the listeners on each turn to speech. A turn at speech is defined as all utterances by one speaker until that speaker yields the floor to vocalizations by the other spouse (vocalizations that are merely backchannels yields the floor such as "Mm-hum" are not considered as demarcating a turn). RCISS behavior codes can be scored in terms of an underlying positive-negative dimensions. In the present study, only speaker codes were used to classify the couples. These speaker codes consisted of five positive codes (neutral or positive problem description, task orientation relationship information, assent, humor-laugh, other positive) and eight negative codes (complain, criticize, negative relationship issue problem talk, yes but, defensive, put down, escalate negative affect, other negative."

After RCISS there is the SPAFF(Specific affect Coding System) and on and on. Once data is coded this way, out come the computers and statistical analysis. But in the end the results are paltry at best. Perhaps the hope is that this is a new science (which it is) and that in a few decades or centuries it will yield clear and actionable results (such as preventing or minimizing divorce) much the way other sciences did. But more likely it will never yield meaningful results because it is a conceptually disorganized science.

Thanks to the legal system most people who get divorced know why they get divorced. They get divorced due to irreconcilable differences. Maybe in the future followers of Dr. Gottman will testify at divorce hearings that couple X is seeking a divorce because their ratio of RCISS positive codes to negative codes was 69%. But this does not even attempt to help with what we need to know most, namely, how does a couple stay in love and have reconcilable differences? The answer to this question is not psychological/scientific; it is biological.

Dr. Gottman seems proudest of what he calls his Four Horseman of the Apocalypse. He says, based on very scientific analyses, "The process cascade I propose, which predicts marital dissolution, is the following: Complaining and criticizing leads to contempt, which leads to defensiveness, which leads to listener withdrawal from interaction (stonewalling)." At no point in the book do we learn how to reconcile Gottman's Four Horseman with, say, the two horseman: alcoholism and physical abuse. If a person who is an alcoholic stonewalls do we address the stonewalling or the alcoholism. These are basic question but still they are beyond the scope of even Dr. Gottman's epic work.

At another point he talks positively about behavioral research which treats marriage as a contract in which each party must learn how to negotiate for what they want. This was fascinating to me since this book is a proposal that couples learn to negotiate the sex that men want and the affection that women want, but Dr. Gottman never went beyond acknowledging the work to tell us how important the work was and how it could be reconciled with the absolutely disparate work he was doing. In this case there was one horse of the Apocalypse: not knowing how to negotiate, but the reader is given no clue about how to integrate all these horseman into a coherent actionable picture. Dr. Gottman was very long on percepts and very short on concepts. His work is perhaps most of all a reflection of the academic environment in which he operates. It is mathematically superior and methodologically rigorous in order to be rated as scholarly; it is comprehensive enough, in terms of listings and describing competitive research, to be a significant reference resource for his colleagues, but very short on the meaningful conclusions that would but him in an arena where he would inevitably be exposed to questions regarding the essentially non-scientific nature of his subject.

Dr. Gottman is not alone. Throughout academia there is an attempt to turn soft science and non-science into hard science. The emphasis on science gives academia a market position above those who tackle the same work, often with better results, without the supposed benefit of hard scientific analysis and it gives academia an easy way to rank work, people, and institutions which merely requires that they check for scientific rigor rather than that they understand the final conceptual value, if any, of the work.

Almost anyone who looks at any depth into marriage and divorce stumbles across the issue of sexual relations whether it suites their purpose or not. Almost unanimously they ignore its importance to marriage and divorce despite its constant intrusion. Dr. Gottman is certainly no exception. He happens on to what is the perfectly quintessential couple and then ignores the lesson to be learned. He writes: "They finally settled on discussing the sexual issue. He said he is extreme in not showing affection. She said she is less responsive in bed because it is the only time he does show affection. He thought that was a problem too. He said he is wrapped up in his work, not relaxed. She said she has responded over the years by becoming detached, and that sometimes she feels terrible about her detachment. They continued:

Husband: If sex didn't seem like something so out of, I don't mean, I shouldn't say, out of the ordinary, but it's sort of separated in a way from regular life and it's the place for intimacy and the other isn't .

Wife: I guess.
Husband: Well, you know neither of us come from families that do very much, have very much physical contact among themselves and I always felt........
Wife: We kids always did with my mother.
Husband: You kids did?
Wife: Well we never did.
Wife: And I have a lot of physical contact with Nick (their son)
Husband: So do I at this point.
Wife: I don't know. It doesn't bother me as much as it did... used to. I mean, people make a big deal about having sex, sexual compatibility and so on, but I think in the long run it's probably more important that we have our other compatibility's.
Husband: Yeah.
Wife: If our sex life was wonderful and we disagreed about everything else, we'd probably be considering divorce.

To Dr. Gottman this classic couple was merely classified as "conflict avoider". He speculates that it is probably a bad sign in a marriage but is blissfully and scientifically unable to conclude that the sex/affection bargain a couple strikes is the central most important aspect of their marriage. While most non-academic psychologists are eager to use their psychological background to justify their own personal and non-psychological marital values Dr. Gottman is fastidiously uninteresting in his own values and seems to have perfect faith in the ultimate value of the science he applies to relationship theory no matter how faltering and irrelevant it seems.

8.) HOW PSYCHOLOGY CAUSES DIVORCE

At the other end of the spectrum are those who skip the discipline of scientific research and the truth of biology in order to get straight to their own personal conclusions. This approach is perhaps best exemplified by the prolific popular author Dr. Herb Goldberg who states: "The common contention that the differences between men and women are deeply rooted in genetics and biology derails us from an awareness of how we prevent little boys and little girls from expressing their humanness to the fullest. If indeed we are programmed genetically to be masculine and feminine, then the programming is enormously damaging psychologically to men and women, and we need to question and work toward altering the destructive course we are on. Indeed, a healthy relationship of genuine intimacy and growth becomes impossible in direct proportion to the degree a couple fits the ideal model of masculinity and femininity."

It is difficult to refute something that is so philosophically mistaken. Mr. Goldberg was trying to capitalize on the current wave in pop culture which holds that androgyny is superior to biology, but in no sense can it be said that he was thinking rationally. The idea that biology prevents humanness is similar to the idea that the sun prevents light. In truth, the sun produces light just the way biology produces humanness. Without the sun, light has no origin; similarly, without biology humanness has no origin, existence or meaning.

Humans don't create their humanness. It is given to them by their biology. We didn't determine, according to some arbitrary man made standard that murder is bad and love is good. These are concepts that are consistent with our biology just as using our eyes to see is consistent with our biology. Without reference to our biology we would have no perception about life or death or anything in between. The war on biology draws us further and further away from an understanding of who we are and what marriage is supposed to be and why women initiate 91% of divorce.

It is certainly true that by creating two different sexes evolution has added the task of sexual relationships to our life. But how can this be bad when sexual relationships make life possible? Biology gave us legs but we do not say that this is bad because we have to struggle to learn how to use them. It would be like saying that swimming is bad while ignoring that the alternative: drowning, which would be a thousand times worse. The water exists; we have no alternative but to swim in it. Evolution created sex to make life possible and it succeeded more with human sexuality than with any one of the millions of other species that came before. Why should we resist nature's most successful creation? In the end Mr. Goldberg must know that he isn't likely to one up the forces of evolution and create a third superior sex or make the two current sexes androgynous.

To keep the patients coming in, all psychologists must keep biology in its place. This started on day one with Sigmund Freud. At one point he was informed that one of his conclusions seemed to contradict a biological fact; he replied, "don't worry we have our own science."

One of our problems with biology is that it embarrasses us. It teaches us that we are mere animals with little or no free will. The notion that men want sex and women want affection when they marry just does not suit our noble ambitions and dreams. We delight in art and science, and sex and affection. But in our minds we use art and science to define ourselves. We can justify killing and eating animals because we know that their flesh can provide energy for our oh so very important art and science. We imagine that our sophistication versus mere animals means that we don't mate just like they do, but this serves only to divert us from our need to mate just like they do and for the same reasons they do.

Our embarrassment at biology was objectified well by a TV program hosted by Dr, John Gray who wrote: Men Are From Mars; Women Are From Venus. A woman in a troubled marriage was asked to consider what she wanted out of the marriage. She replied at the end of the program after long thought and some months of therapy, " I keep asking myself: is this all I want out of life and the answer keeps coming back, "yes." She was referring to the little tokens of affections and appreciation that she wanted from her husband. If it is embarrassing for a woman to admit that she thrives on affection, it is excruciating for a man to admit that he wants to be out there screwing like some barn yard pig. Hence we have a potent incentive to embellish our needs and desires with a vast array of hypocritical complications.

The ability to reason and make choices; to contemplate our own biology and existence doesn't mean that we are more than mere biological machines as psychologists, pop culturalists, and feminists would like us to think. A fish doesn't know what caused the ocean; a human doesn't know what caused the big bang or if there is one universe or a billion universes. We know more than a fish because our biology is more, but we don't know much more. Moreover, since we don't know all we don't even know if we know significantly more than the fish. Sure, we can experiment with problems and solutions but in the end we know little more today than ever about where we came from and where we are going. As religious explanations have faded in the face of science we have not even invented another compass to guide us. Over the centuries we have experimented with all manner of ideas. Any political, economic, sexual, cultural, or familial idea you can think of we have tried, but in the end all of our self-righteous passions were just so many failed experiments. Perhaps we could say that we have emerged as biological existentialists. Now, just like a million years ago, our existence all over this planet is freed from all the failed great new ideas, like those advanced by feminists and psychiatrists, and is focusing more and more on simple biological imperatives because they are constant and inescapable and most consistent with our actual nature.

9.) A CONVERSATION BETWEEN FRIENDS

WOMEN ARE NATURAL RELATIONSHIP EXPERTS

Teaching people about that which they know little or nothing is very easy. For example, if you say to someone that Bell's experiment demonstrated that if you alter the spin of a photon here on earth then you would simultaneously be altering the spin of another photon billions of light years away thus proving that the universe is connected in a way heretofore undetectable to human beings, it is doubtful that that person would have the knowledge base from which to argue. But, if you try to teach them about something with which they have daily experience, it can be very difficult indeed. Everyone, sadly for this author, already considers themselves to be a relationship expert, although everyone knows very different things about relationships. Even the so called experts who have their books lined up on bookstore shelves all know very different things about relationship and agree with one another on nothing; not even key facts or methodologies with which to approach the problem in a common way so that knowledge can accumulate and evolve. The subject has yet to develop the mathematics of science or the logic of philosophy.

Women, in particular, fancy themselves the greatest experts of all. No woman will declare herself ignorant on this most maternal and essential of all subjects. A relationship book like this one, then, faces an uphill task. The easy temptation for all of us is to rely on the information we already have rather than to learn new information which to a certain extent may contradict or enhance the information which we have grown accustomed to think of as accurate and complete.

This was brought home to me very directly in the course of corresponding with an editor about the subject matter of this book. Normally he is the most delightful and Platonically intelligent person in the world with whom to correspond about a book idea. In his spare time he is a very accomplished avant guard poet. I have always liked his very unusual orientation because it always gives his criticism a fresh and detached perspective that didn't owe any allegiance whatsoever to the status quo except, of course, when it was justified. I was shocked when no matter how hard or how long I tried, I could not get through to him regarding the important points of this book. I would have figured that if anyone would have been able to understand them it would have been him.

9.) A CONVERSATION BETWEEN FRIENDS

But on this subject he had no capacity to get beyond the status quo.

Below is a summary, in question/answer format, of the debate we had. From my point of view it stayed on a very elementary level, but perhaps it was a threshold level that, once penetrated, will open his mind, to the general theory of this book. On the assumption that most readers will have similar and other blocks in their minds derived from an ingrained or imagined relationship expertise, I have reprinted the text of our interactive debate in the hope that this format and methodology will somehow make the point in a way that will supplement the previous format of this book. I have often found that in the course of learning about something we often come to believe that if we can just ask one very central question of the supposed expert we can defeat his arguments, like Perry Mason, and go comfortably back to our own theory. So then, this is an opportunity for the reader to imagine herself in the debate, or at least to see if my editor asked the same question that she would ask.

To: Bob(editor)
From: (author)

Dear Bob,

It's as if you are writing to me about the book in your head rather than the one I wrote, i.e., the one you're supposed to be editing. I know this is much easier for you but please try to remember that you are commenting about my book; not all the little disorganized thoughts that have randomly accumulated in your head over the years. And why do you insist on going over the same ground and in the same depth over and over again. I am almost forced to conclude that you cannot confront the arguments in the book because you know doing so will force you to rethink everything you thought you knew about relationships. I know this must be very hard on a poet - on the Dr. Of Love, but please try for the good of the project. In the past your input was always the best there was. I'm really onto something here, but I fear getting beyond everyone's prejudice will be an impossible task. Besides, knowing the truth about love will make you a better poet, won't it? Or, perhaps your fear is that poetry and biology are fundamentally incompatible, and that biology is superior?

On this subject you've become a one transaction guy even though in all of our previous correspondence you have assumed that the truth begins to emerge only after the third or forth transaction or written exchange of questions and answers. Below please let me force you toward the more organized Platonic format that we have always used in the past. At this point I'm beginning to assume that your inability to confront these simple ideas points to how inherently comfortable we all are with our personal and often mistaken, approaches to dealing with relationships.

Issue #1

Bob: If sex is everything in a relationship then a prostitute could be a substitute for a wife?

Author: No silly. Sex with a prostitute cannot be everything because it is not conducted as biology intended. Sex was to be conducted in the long term context of a family where kids are conceived and raised. My book argues exclusively for complete biological sex; not just for sexual intercourse. Some men might be comfortable with just sexual intercourse, but very few women would find this
compatible with their long term plan for a loving family. You must not have understood the book.

BOB: I guess you're right.

Issue #2

BOB: What if a man is a gambler; how will sex cure him and make him a good husband?

Author: This is really insulting, it seems as if you didn't really read the book? If the woman withholds sex and threatens to end the relationship until the man stops gambling she will have exerted the greatest possible influence on him. Biology intended sex to be more important than gambling, hence most men will stop gambling for sex. The problem is that many women do not trade sex for good behavior. They should start on day one so the thought of gambling will not even enter a man's head.

BOB: I really think you're on to something.

Issue # 3

BOB: Should she use sex to get what she wants and thereby make him miserable out of bed.

Author: What they both want most is what biology wants, namely, love, kids, and family. As a general principal these are the things that biology plans to make them both happiest. If your girlfriend wants you to give up poetry because you don't earn enough from it to support a family why not consider her point of view. Poetry may seem valuable to you but kids are valuable to her, and you will be surprised to find how valuable they'll be to you too. The issue is that she too will be miserable if you don't give up the poetry. It sounds like she grew to love you with the normal expectation that you would be willing to do what was necessary to sanctify that love, i.e., marry her, and then have and support children. If you had no plans to lead a normal biological life then you should have told her in the beginning. Of course, she should have known enough to ask you about his too. In the end she is fully justified from a biological point of view in not making love to a man with no money, or a man with no plans to earn money. The poet Shelly saw the world in a grain of sand and we should see all of biology in the simple act of sex.

BOB: I'm beginning to understand, how dense of me.

Issue # 4

BOB: I see. So in the strange world you inhabit all there is is sex and biology! Why does biology care about reproduction and why should I care about it?

THERE IS NOTHING BEYOND BIOLOGY

Author: In a practical sense all we need to care about is biology. Beyond biology there is only physics. It demonstrates to us that one element needs another; that one electron needs a nucleus or that one nucleus needs a electron, etc. Humans evolved as clusters of elements and therefore have the same needs for affiliation as elements. Beyond that, the new physics teaches us that all people and all particles in the universe are not separate entities, rather that we and they are intricately connected even to the extent that what we see of the universe is actually created by our perception of the universe. In the new physics perception creates reality. Physicists can now demonstrate that a light photon can pass through what humans think of as a solid faster than it can pass through air, and that one photon can instantaneously turn into two despite our inability to explain how this might be possible, and that by altering the spin of one photon we are simultaneously altering the spin of another photon billions of miles away . Thus, what we see can literally be built or constructed by our vision. Your wife, if you had one, may literally be a creation of your perception. Physicists conclude that existence is something probably far stranger than human beings can imagine. Some psychologists are using this new information to argue that true marital harmony is ultimately a function of true physics and I can't quarrel with that. So then, sex, love, biology, and physics are all connected. So you should care about biology and physics. If you did what you had to do to finally get a wife you would be happier due to greater harmony with the universe. A priest may love God and a poet may love poetry, but they both would probably love a woman more.

BOB: I see what you mean about all that science stuff, but my God, do you think I'm gonna get a wife by talking about biology and physics. You're very cold. Love is about feelings.

Author: Please, my book isn't about courting (although you certainly seem to need such a book). My advice, frankly, is to follow your penis. It will point toward a woman(won't it?) and suggest to you that a relationship with her will be far more wonderful than a relationship with a rock, or tree, or another man, or poetry. If men and women weren't created for sex then there would be no men and women. Just remember that what she will want most is simple nurturing which she will return to you and any children you may have. It is as natural for her to desire nurturing as it is for you to desire sex. I agree. Love is about feelings and nothing evokes more profound feelings than sex or the promise of sex.

BOB: That's just so eloquent and poetic. I can't decide if there's more Keats or Shelly in it.

Author: Gee thanks.

BOB: What if a wife uses sex to discourage me from being a Republican Senator or starving poet or anything that I really want to do?

Author: In the first place, a woman who consented to marry you would presumably be content with what you did for a living. A wife who doesn't want a Republican senator should be divorced or never loved in the first place anyway because a Republican senator, generally speaking, bodes well for her kids. Ultimately work and affection are what a woman selects for. If you are young, when most mates are selected, but still not successful you can probably land a wife even as a poet, but as an unprofitable adult poet it would be very difficult unless you found someone who was self-sufficient (although these women generally want someone who is more self-sufficient than they are) or someone who regarded an unprofitable poet as superior to, say, a successful waiter or another unprofitable poet. You face a difficult choice when you've gotten some of your sexual fulfillment from poetry and then the real thing comes along. Biology does not force you to fall in love with a woman who doesn't support your work no matter how unprofitable it may be, but it sure does let you know that you may have wasted your whole life if you go on and on despite never hitting the poetry jackpot Besides isn't it silly of you to fall in love with a woman who doesn't support your poetry. It would seem that the relationship was about sex, and that you and she never looked to extend your sexual harmony beyond the bedroom. It really does sound like you're in it just for the sex anyway and she's telling you: "enough, I have larger biological priorities."

BOB: You've got me again?

Issue #5

BOB: Most men are disgusted with women who use sexual manipulation?

Author: I'm in the business and I've never heard this, let alone seen evidence of it. In high school we used to say that certain girls were cockteasers but this was mostly an expression of our horny frustration. Besides, what on earth does that mean anyway. Men universally acknowledge that women have the right not to be raped. If a woman asserts this right is she being manipulative to you? The selectivity of women creates love; without it there would be no love and no families. Men would always just be moving on to the next woman.

If a woman says, "let's get the lawn mowed before we make love tonight," what's wrong with that? If she says go rob a bank and then we'll make love she's not acting within the bounds of the marital/ biological contract and the man should obviously resist. In sum, manipulation is good so long as it supports the family; in fact it is what makes the family possible.

BOB: Darn if you're not right.

Issue # 6

BOB: Men resent manipulation.

Author: Manipulation is a pejorative term that I never use because it has no application here. Try to think deeply about this Bob. If people work together on a team and encourage each other in the course thereof they are not manipulating each other; it is much closer to loving each other. As long as the woman is encouraging her husband to do the things biology intended she is loving; not manipulating. Such behavior elicits love from a man; not resentment. If he's not helping the team, then he should be punished or denied. If he feels resentment, it's his problem for

not being part of the team. The problem is that women are often too
lenient, sometimes to the point of being beaten, before they
assert themselves. If you want sex with no conditions you can
masturbate, but why do you suppose few men find this to be satisfactory?

Issue # 7

BOB: What about women who use sex for the wrong reason?

Author: Again, I'm in the business, and have never seen any evidence of
this. You are probably repeating yourself anyway. Isn't manipulation the
same as "for the wrong reasons". If you mean prostitutes and artist types
like the Spice Girls, I agree with you. Assertive female sexuality in a
non-familial context is certainly bad to the extent that it teaches non-
familial sex. This is the opposite of what biology intended, but to the
extent that prostitutes and the Spice Girls teach women to be sexually
assertive they are doing something good.

BOB: Sorry, I wasn't thinking!

Issue # 8

BOB: You have to say more about choosing spouses?

Author: Not really, the book is about why women initiate divorce and
what they can do to prevent it, although why and how they choose mates
is extensively covered anyway because choosing a sexually compliant
mate is one good way to reduce the possibility of divorce and its
attendant consequences on the children. Besides, choosing a mate for a
woman is simply a matter of finding someone who is sexually compliant
and someone whose looks and money will improve her social position. It
is inherently problematic since two equal people generally cannot improve
each other's social status. Generally a bargain is made if the man is
willing to give up a little social
status for sex and the woman is willing to be forthcoming sexually in
return for improved social status.

CHOOSING A MATE BIOLOGICALLY

BOB: OK.

Issue # 9

BOB: Women choose their mates poorly.

Author: This is true; I suppose a first marriage divorce rate of 50% and a second marriage divorce rate of over 60% proves it. But why are you telling me this when it is covered in the book. Women choose a guy to whom they have a chemical reaction, and a guy relative to them who appears to be: handsome, rich, tall, powerful, smart, and nurturing. When they don't also select for sexual compliance they make a big mistake because the man will then treat his wife as if she is less handsome, rich, powerful, and smart. The wife will resent this, fail to correct it, and then initiate a divorce. Women choose poorly because they have no model in mind that allows them to proceed rationally in a relationship in light of biological imperatives. But the problem is not so much in the choice since men are generally compliant anyway, the problem is that women don't know how to keep men compliant.

BOB: I'm really sorry.

Issue # 10

BOB: Should a wife use sex to make a man give up Monday Night Football or rock and roll.

Author: Haven't we been over this ground before. If you've seen women with their babies you know they generally do what biology expects. They love them and encourage them to grow up
and be independent, etc. They are generally very fair with their husbands; if they decide rock and roll and football is too much, for whatever reason, they generally are right. It is usually the man who welches on his part of the marital bargain, but only because the woman fails to even know what the bargain is, let alone enforce it. In the beginning the man is compliant

and responsive to get sex, after the marriage he seeks sex without compliance. A self-destructive wife acquiesces to this only to find that she has exacerbated a very tiny problem to the point where a divorce becomes the only alternative.

If they're incompatible in the first place (he, for example, lives in Minnesota and she in Mississippi or he spends hours a day on football while she hates the game) then of course they should not get married. The plan to be lovingly together is what makes the marriage; and sex is the glue that a woman must use to keep it on track. But it is not a glue that is sufficient in all cases.

BOB: I think this is over my head given my limited experience but maybe you should think of me as a typical reader.

Issue # 11

BOB: What if they find they have nothing in common but good sex?

Author: Earth to Bob, come in please. Very few women settle for just good sex. For women there is really no such thing as good sex without the context of a good relationship in which children can be raised. While you were having good sex your goofy girlfriend was imagining that you had a good relationship. When she found out that your poetry was far more important to you than the relationship she dumped you. People get married because they have things in common. They live in the same State, remember. After the marriage, the list of things in common should grow as the wife says things like: lets clean up our house tonight; together, before we have sex. If the list does not grow it is because the woman has given up control. Biology does not allow us to have just good sex; if it did there would be no families.

BOB: I'm beginning to understand, but what about people who have extensive personal lives before they are married. How do they merge and what does this have to do with sex.

Author: I suppose that's the question about whether a couple is two halves of a whole or two separate wholes. In the later case each is using the other to enhance his or her personal life. "I hate playing golf alone; now that we're married you can play with me". In the former case a couple finds new activities together that are actually new to each of them and therefore more an extension of their love. If a couple is too preoccupied with what each did previously it makes the marriage more an adjunct to their lives rather than a new life. The act of choosing various preoccupations together is a marital act while using a partner to share your activities is not so much so. Almost anyone else can share a pre-existing activity and so such activities can diminish a loving relationship, but no one can share an activity that is specifically created or engaged in for the specific purpose of providing a unique shared activity. A marriage ideally should be about the couple; not about the separate activities of one or both partners. Sex is ideal in this sense but when it is a celebration of a couples unique marriage.

But these are trivial matters that psychologists especially like. They represent fine tuning and nothing more. A husband can participate in any activity he wants (his , hers , theirs), even solitary activities. The important thing is that the wife not let the activities, behaviors, or language get excessive to the point where she can't or won't regulate them sexually. Women initiate 91% of divorce, remember, because they lose control of their husbands. The ultimate common interest is the act of sex and the nurturing male behavior that should precede it.

Issue # 12

BOB: What about if parents disagree about religion and college?

Author: Most people know to resolve these things before marriage. Remember they have to live in the same State and have common interests and values before they would want to get married. I don't claim that sex can start a relationship(although it certainly can encourage it a great deal). If they don't agree on basic things they must argue, consult, make love, and compromise. But, if a neighbor pulls out a gun and shoots the husband, the wife can't use sex to revive him. Even sex has its obvious limitations! Besides, a loving wife or one who would be a loving wife

9.) A CONVERSATION BETWEEN FRIENDS

knows that asking a husband to compromise his religious faith for sex, even the broadest meaning of sex, would not be acceptable. And, hopefully a man would have enough presence of mind not to comply with a woman on things that each should be willing to change. If she wants him to mow the lawn instead of watching football that's fine assuming she is directly or indirectly making a similar contribution to the family. If she wants him to change his religion then she should be willing to do the same or something of similar magnitude.

BOB: Sorry, that was a cheap shot

Issue #13

BOB: Once married, however good the sex, incompatible couples will not become compatible?

Author: A ridiculous premise, A woman should check for compatibility before the marriage, i.e., does he live in the same State, etc. You only get married because you are compatible and because you believe you will stay compatible. Sex keeps you compatible by being a reward for such. A woman will decide she no longer loves her husband because she allows herself, after the marriage, to be ignored or abused over and over again. Why do you keep on insisting that it is possible to have good sex and be incompatible? I've explained over and over and over again that sex and overall compatibility are directly related such that you should not allow yourself to have one without the other. If it were possible then a good prostitute would be sufficient to satisfy a man. You are absolutely stuck on the idea that sex is a thing apart when it is the last thing that should be a thing apart.

BOB: Ok Ok, this stuff is just over my head.

Issue # 15
BOB: Aren't compatibility and communication important?

186

Author: No, sex is important, but congratulations you selected the two most mistaken impressions we have about relationships and marriages. If people didn't share compatibility and communication they would never get to the first date. Just for a first date a couple needs to agree on where to make the date, when to make it, what to do on the date, when to talk before the date to arrange it, how to arrange transportation, back up plans, where to meet, where to sit, etc., etc. Before a relationship commitment or marriage there are literally millions of demonstrations of compatibility and communication. These are things that, for the most part, even an idiot or two idiots can manage. A couple doesn't mysteriously lose their ability to compromise. The problem comes when the man finds that the woman will now provide sex without all the infernal and constant compromising on which she thrives. Biology needed families and it gave us sex to provide the incentive for men to communicate and be familial. Good sex occurs when love is present, i.e., when the woman provides it in return for things the man is made happy to provide.

Issue # 14

BOB: You have to define what people want out of existence and how marriage fits in for your book to be more than pop pap.

Author: Wow, a poet and a philosopher! Why are you resisting so much. In point of fact what people want is food and love/sex and kids and simple religious beliefs. When someone has kids his life is more simple, pure, directed, comfortable, complete and meaningful than ever because he knows more certainly than ever exactly what he must do. He must happily do biology's bidding. I'm sorry that I can't encourage you to spend more time reflecting large on philosophical issues, but I'm afraid that for most of us these are very simple questions.
BOB: Come on, I've been a poet /philosopher all my life, and you do want me to edit your book don't you?.

Issue # 15

BOB: For women love and sex is about giving; not taking

9.) A CONVERSATION BETWEEN FRIENDS

Author: That's the greatest delusion of all. It started in the Bible based on the accurate but simplistic notion that a world of givers is far better than a world of takers. But in the world of sex if women were just givers civil society would cease tomorrow. Men would attack. The pre-conditions for sex actually define happiness and the organization of civilization. Even in the context of marriage, if sex becomes a free gift it will destroy the civility of that marriage. Women must give sex primarily to get love and children. When women don't insist on something they get nothing. They initiate divorce because they get too little.

BOB: Right

Issue # 16

BOB: Freud did not invent psychology and he was a crank.

Author: He invented psychology in the sense that he codified it first, although people always thought about it. Ok so he was wrong about psychoanalysis, Copernicus, and Shakespeare, but, most importantly, he was right about how central sex was to everything.

BOB: Ok, right.

Issue # 17:

BOB: We should turn to a wise person for psychological help, even a bartender could be better than a psychologist ?

Author: A wise person would be better than a dumb one. I agree with you there. How did you figure that one out.? I remember one day I turned to a night watchman with a romantic problem. He put his hand on my thigh and said, " Ted, get yourself a man." All things considered, Bob, I'd still pick a Ph.D. over a bartender or night watchman, but in the end I'd pick a biology Ph.D.

MAKING THE ISSUE TOO COMPLICATED

Issue # 18

BOB: You say sex is intrinsically valuable. What's intrinsically valuable about anything. Sex and chess are essentially the same.

Author: It seems to me you're trying to hide behind philosophy. The value of things is sexual. We want to know the earth and the universe so we can survive in order to have sex. Sex is different from chess because it is our most important function; that's why everyone does it and virtually no one plays chess. I suppose that the people who devote themselves to the game imagine that it is a substitute for sex. If you take sex out of its proper biological context, as you insist on doing, you have a life that is adrift with too many questions.

Issue #19

BOB: What's the point of marriage?

Author: This philosophy stuff is too much for me. Some of your questions reflected the answer; so why ask the question over and over again. Women will not engage in sex alone because they know marriage and child support is necessary for the kids that the sex will produce; so that is the point of marriage.

BOB: Now I see.

Issue # 20:

BOB: Depression and psychological depression are often caused by genes; so why should we be slaves to our genes..

Author: They can be, but this does not mean that genetically induced behavior is generally counterproductive. Without the right genes or genetic condition you can have depression or even two heads. This is obvious. You said that psychological satisfaction was important; much like sex. What you didn't understand in your haste to make a quick debating point was that good sex will alleviate depression while bad sex

189

will cause it, assuming you were born with normal genes. In sum, if sex is the most important human function then it will also be an excellent weapon with which to avoid depression and other common psychological maladies. Similarly, if eating is also an important genetic human function then eating will be a great way to alleviate the deadly effects from not eating. Depression generally doesn't exist independently. It exists in relationship to something, and in our modern era where many of our historical problems have been solved it will exist more and more in relationship to sex, although there are many different kinds of depression some of which are purely physical in nature.

BOB: Ah, yes.

Issue # 20

BOB: Good sex is of course possible with a prostitute if you use sex to mean copulation.

Author: Sex or copulation with chickens, prostitutes, dead people or yourself cannot be considered good. It is considered a simulation. Why couldn't you describe what was good about it? When Larry Flint of Hustler fame had sex with chickens as a poor southern farm boy what did he say and think during the act?
"Thank you, thank you, your feathers really turn me on." No, that would have made sex impossible. It was simulated human heterosexual love. He was thinking of a human female. In someway he was pretending that it felt the way he imagined human heterosexual love would feel. You can't have sex without thinking about what biology wanted you to think about. If humans could get turned on by chickens there would be no humans. But this would be like eating rocks instead of food.

BOB: I see.

Issue #24
BOB: Women like bingo, harmony, safety; not quarrels or competition.

Author: Women talk as easily as men breath, but they talk to make a maternal connection; not for truth . You have to love them for what they are and not hope for something that is generally not part of the package. But, if you want a women who can help you grow intellectually you can find such a woman. Quarrels and competition are more natural for men because they are similar to hunting prey or fighting off a sexual rival. If a woman's nature was somehow deficient, as you seem to imply, how do you explain that they do what once were men's jobs so well? This will become increasingly true over time. And besides, most men don't really hunt and fight any more, intellectually or other wise, they get ahead mostly by pleasing their bosses and this is distinctly feminine.

A recent bestseller says that corporate women are very easy to seduce because they are particularly in need of the maternal warmth and security that the male world does not so readily provide. Perhaps this indicates that they are not really fulfilled by male work, but most men don't seem to be fulfilled by it either. Modern life is more androgynous than ever before, but each sex retains profound links with its evolutionary past.

Issue # 25

Bob; But I got flat out dumped by a woman who in the end couldn't maintain her love for a starving poet who couldn't take her out for dinner and do other normal courting rituals. Out of the blue she just said good-bye. If women initiate 91% of divorce as you say how can you insist that they are passive participants in their own lives?

Author: Haven't I covered this before? Ok, here's a letter that a woman wrote to dump a guy after their second date. It's exactly like a divorce. Keep in mind that she has all the usual complaints about his overbearing behavior even though she was an equal contributor to the behavior. Also keep in mind that she is an feminist era ivy league graduate and an attorney who seemingly should have been able to participate in the direction of her relationship; yet she seems unable to imagine this. For her, like many women, her roll is to "be" while the male role is to "do." When the male inevitably does too much of the wrong thing, even if it is well intentioned, the female can't imagine herself influencing or working with the male to correct his behavior, even if he loves her desperately, and so her only course of action is to leave and pray for better luck next time. Here's the letter:

Dear John,
I enjoyed meeting, and initially liked you very much, but, unfortunately, my feelings changed because of that missed train. I met you through a chance encounter and not through a mutual friend, and in such a situation, I think that a certain amount of reserve is necessary until you get to know more about the other person. In our case, we'd had one brief meeting near Grand Central Station, and then a second date. Staying overnight at someone's apartment is something that(I think) should be discussed and agreed to ahead of time particularly where two people hardly know each other and have no acquaintances in common. I know some women would feel otherwise, but this is the way I feel. I do of course want to wish you the best in all your endeavors.

Sincerely,
Susan.

I can't say for sure what was really bothering Susan about John but the explanation she used to get rid of him was quintessentially female. She was passive about everything but dumping him. Below is another correspondence between a very articulate woman and myself in which the woman explains her divorce in a purely typical, although very elequent, feminine way. Interestingly this woman is in her forties, a graduate of a famous Seven Sisters college (where she was steeped in the whole macha, feminist, left-wing, lesbian tradition), author of four books, and mother of 4 daughters. She writes, and I answered, about relationships as follows:

Anonymous woman:
I don't think doctors these days are as gung-ho about fitness as they once were unless it is accompanied by emotional well-being. If thinness were the answer to health there wouldn't be diseases such as anorexia. With

the welfare of four daughters to think about, I've tried to emphasize inner worth, independence, intellectual pursuits and moral and spiritual values. Health, if you look the word up, has its roots in wholeness.

Author:
Well all right already, but still, there is just no denying that "thin" turns men on when a woman walks into the room. We can't help it. God or evolution made us love health, and for good reason. Moreover, there is no connection between being thin and healthy, and, anorexic and sick. The things you emphasized to your daughters are wonderful of course, but beauty is not a competing either/or thing. There would be no point in emphasizing beauty as a parent since it is for the most part something that "is" and certainly is beyond parental control. It cannot be controlled or emphasized to any great degree. Homely women may be troubled by beauty when dating, but poor men are troubled by money too. Neither sex has it harder or easier than the other. We may be uncomfortable with the competitive nature of social intercourse, but, like it or not, all living creatures are living beneficiaries of the competitive nature of evolution.

Anonymous woman:
My ex-husband was from a very small and conservative town in Wyoming, and, despite 2 degrees from Harvard, retained some antiquated ideas about what women were all about. He had a need to control everything, including me. He was also manipulative (which is somewhat different). In any event, when the children were young and demanding I had little energy to devote to this growing problem in the relationship, but as they began to leave home I became more conscious of it and less accommodating. Eventually a crisis occurred that put his behavior patterns into focus so sharply that I could no longer pretend this was just going to go away. When you live with a tyrant it seems you have only two choices: give in to keep the peace or go crazy, and I had been doing a bit of both. After my youngest left home (for college) I began to challenge his authority in all things big and small. This was a domestic revolution. His initial response was to become more aggressive and unreasonable but the 'jig was up' once I began to see through him. Bullies are cowards under all the bluster. He left because he couldn't get

me to change back into the doormat he wanted me to be, though the sad
thing was that if he had been able to budge an inch in his "my way or the
highway" approach to living, the marriage could have survived. My
therapist, after months of observing the two of us, determined that Joe
hadn't wanted the divorce at all but was simply trying to frighten me back
into familiar patterns. Walking out, she guessed, was a grandstand effort
that backfired.

Author:
I feel very bad for all you went through but it is just not possible to use a
simple feminist explanation rather than acknowledge your role or the lack
there of. He did, after all, remarry a high powered corporate attorney
who,you said, certainly was not a doormat? Your relationship was a joint
creation; a joint evolution, and there was joint inability to make it work.
Would it have all unfolded the same if you had been in college more in
the feminist era 1969+? But I thought Vasser was always feminist. For a
time the world was alarmed that they were so much so that 70% of the
girls were experimenting as lesbians, or am I mistaken?

Anonymous woman:
It is hard to negotiate when you are talking mostly to yourself.

Author:
It sounds like you let your husband win the negotiations from the
beginning with his silence. Isn't that a common negotiating technique?

Anonymous woman:
Vasser did get weird in the 70's and on into the 90's, which is why my
kids didn't choose to go there. However, at the time of my marriage I
was as evolved in the feminist direction as anyone -- not radical, just
expectant of equality.

Author:
Isn't equality something you continuously demand rather than something
you are passively expectant of?
Anonymous woman:

9.) A CONVERSATION BETWEEN FRIENDS

It's hard for people to comprehend an abusive relationship. Why on earth, they wonder, would someone stay in it! What they don't see is how the person who is abusing you works at making you believe in them, and how effectively he/she eliminates all avenues of escape. I don't think the conventional wisdom of sharing responsibility for the success/failure of the mutual creation applies. One person is doing all the creating; the other is just trying to survive.

Author:

All salesman work to make you believe them. It is up to you to decide whether to become destitute or keep some money in your pocket . Neither party is more qualified to eliminate avenues of escape unless one party concedes that ability to the other. If one party is doing all the creating then the other must be allowing it. All of your comments are shot through with underlying inferiority, powerlessness, and victimhood. It seems to me that if you understood the biological process by which you got in the inferior position you would know how to avoid it in the future and then have a chance at real love. But I just can't understand how someone with your background got in an inferior position? It seems that if it can happen to you it can happen to any woman. I've heard your story from so many women that its tempting to it believe it is genetic.

Anonymous woman:

Is your divorce book about legal issues or is it more of a social approach? And does that 91% refer to who left, or who filed?

Author:

The book explains why women file for divorce and what they can
do to save their marriages. 91% refers to the % of female plaintiffs in divorce actions. It's not so ambitious if you understand the biological foundation of heterosexual relationships. Men want sex and women want affection (generalized sex). If each negotiates for what he/she wants the relationship is supposed to work out according to evolution's plan. Today we forget about evolution in favor of ignorance or our inner child, and women, while they start out in a relationship as supreme negotiators, just stop negotiating and surrender to their men only to regret it.

Anonymous woman:

I seem to have lost the copy of your note that detailed the theories you are interested in, but if memory serves, you wanted to know why women tend

195

to get caught up in the down side of abusive relationships. It's hard to add to a subject which has been so over-discussed, but here are a few random thoughts.

Author,
Thanks for the effort. It is much appreciated and as always I pray it wasn't painful for you. If you had got me on the last book I assure you we wouldn't be discussing this, at least not at my provocation.
So then, you say the topic has been over discussed but it seems to me that it has not been meaningfully discussed and that is why it is still the most common cause of divorce.

Anonymous woman,
Perhaps women fall into the negative role because of such circumstances as these: conditioning as children to be conciliatory and non-confrontational; society's low expectations; poor self-esteem; abusive patterns present historically (parental domination); and an inability or unwillingness to take responsibility for one's own happiness.
Often, I believe, negative relationship cycles begin innocently, as: a newlywed couple discuss options for going out to a movie; he wants Bruce Willis, she wants Sleepless In Seattle; no one wants to compromise; then she, being more concerned with what she perceives (or has been trained to value above self-interest) as the good of the whole, gives in and they go off to see Bruce. Where it goes wrong, however, is in the man's perception of what she has done. The wife believes that she is acting as an equal in a partnership; the husband sees compromise as weakness and thinks he has won an encounter in a relationship which, since it involves winning and losing, is not a partnership but a struggle for control.

Author:
I agree, both have made a mistake for the relationship.

Anonymous woman:
Once established, this pattern of a power struggle in a relationship created for mutuality is hard to dislodge and a formula for disaster.

EVOLUTION VERSUS OUR INNER CHILD

Author:
Here I strongly disagree, (if I may) if the wife understands her husband's testosterone driven need for control and sexual fulfillment then she is in a position to correct the problem unless she is passive and impotent by genetics.

Anonymous woman:
The wife eventually realizes that her love for her husband and her desire for equality are being used in an emotional karate game against her. Her partner is misusing intimacy to undermine her self-confidence and insure an increased dependency on himself, while at the same time chastising her (she's imagining things, pre-menstrual, just like her mother, whatever it takes to bring her down) for the general pathology he has inspired. Though an impartial observer would likely suggest that what she needs to do is rewrite the rules of engagement, this is a tall order for someone who by now is losing every round.

Author:
It seems to me that women do eventually find the wherewithal to rewrite the rules of the game, but they do it,as you did, through divorce rather than through reconciliation and this generally isn't purposive for the kids or their next marriage, which generally is shorter than their first.

Woman:
A good discussion of the more diabolical variations on this theme can be found in "Men Who Hate Women and The Women Who Love Them" which you may have come across. Also, the movie "Gaslight" (Ingrid Bergman, Charles Boyer) is a brilliant portrait of a healthy young woman in the downward spiral of marital abuse. (When my lawyer -- a woman -- wanted to know what Harry's modus operandi was in my marriage and I said "gaslighting" she knew immediately what I meant).

Author:
Lawyers are difficult to rely on here I think since they earn a living through divorce. If they know the illness so well why don't they prescribe the medicine for it instead of profiting from it? Lawyers and psychologists and film makers actually have an interest in wallowing in the disease.

9.) A CONVERSATION BETWEEN FRIENDS

Anonymous woman:
Going back to the original question about the female psyche I have to add
that I think its a loaded one (the question not the psyche). What would
you say, for example, if I asked you what you thought it was in the make-
up of the Jews in Nazi Germany that made them such willing victims?
Perhaps (I realize this is an extreme analogy but it works on one level)
there was something wrong with them.... and if Hitler hadn't been so
thorough......and more had survived... we might be hearing more about
whatever it was on Oprah. However, no matter how many holocaust
victims trotted out their horror stories on the talk shows the guest
everyone would most want to hear from is Adolph. What, we all want to
know, was his problem?

Author:
   I don't follow all of that, but it does seem to me the Jews are an
interesting example of victimhood. It seems that enough of them did
survive to form the very militaristic state of Israel. They even destroyed
an American intelligence ship (and killed Americans) in the '73 war so we
wouldn't know how well they were doing in the war even though we were
their major supplier of weapons. They learned very precise and simple
behaviors from their victimhood and are now more secure and less victims
then ever. It didn't takes years of films, psychology, and thought, just a
quick change in behavior.

Anonymous woman:
The point being that we hear too much from women and not enough from
men. The questions I'm interested in run along different lines than yours
seem to. What, for instance, inspires an intelligent, well-educated man to
enter into a marriage and then promptly set about sabotaging the
arrangement?

Author:
   I think you answered that above when you said that they naturally seek
control. Perhaps this is even more so today when

198

control is mostly denied to them in the business world whereas in the past they at least had control of the animal they killed or the land they cultivated.

Anonymous woman:

Why does a husband do so much to destroy the intimacy he worked so long to claim?

Author:

Control wins out because it is thoroughly evolved into him whereas intimacy is relatively new in evolutionary history. Testosterone controls both, and very ambiguously. Perhaps even more than intimacy he was trying to claim control. But you just won't get it will you. Men don't respect the animal or woman they control. They respect and are intimate with the woman who controls them. If she gives up her ability she gives up intimacy.

Anonymous woman:

When does the woman he loves morph into someone he fears and therefore must control?

Author:

I think control starts during courting when he goes from 0 to equality and then goes beyond equality to dominance as the wife allows the progression. It is a normal progression if one party allows it. All people aren't equally dominant or passive. Balance must be managed. The woman, he feels, must always be controlled just like everything else. Every boy knows that the flowers and dinner are for sexual control.

Anonymous woman:

Don't tell me this guy is a romantic innocent, someone who thinks chauvinism is still in style -- ignorant of the rules of modern courtship. He knew the rules well enough, after all, to act the part of an evolved, sensitive, caring and sharing partner when he chose to. Otherwise, she never would have married him in the first place.

Author:

My whole argument is that the man never knew the rules you speak of. He was merely seeking control by doing what was necessary according to the courtship rules the woman established. Men want quick control and sex, and would take it if woman were offering it, while women need a more protracted and broader experience for the benefit of their children. Men go along with the woman's rules (and happily so) as long as she realizes their importance and plays only by them. When she drops the rules so does he. Men will take sex any way it comes. Woman determine how it will come.

Author:
I suppose all this begs the question: What specific strategy would you advise women to employ in order to keep their families off the destructive path you describe? Please help me here one more time. Again I have to thank you for indulging me this way. If you can think of a method of repayment please let me know. You're so articulate that I can't resist learning from you about this horrible but relevant (to me at least) subject. Am I being overly controlling?

Anonymous woman:
My goodness! And I thought all those flowers and dinners were just well -- flowers and dinners!

Author:
Thank you again for the lengthy reply. I honestly do feel honored to be corresponding with someone who knows and writes so well. But, by not responding very specifically to my points I think you have evaded them to a certain extent in favor of general arguments that can't be tested well at that level.

So anyway, about the flowers and dinner. I'm afraid that 13 year old girls do think in terms of flowers and dinner while boys definitely think in terms of sex. This is pure biology; not good or evil and it doesn't preclude the idea that some women can like sex more and some men can like flowers more. My theory is that love requires knowing that it is necessary to make the trade.

Anonymous woman:

WOMAN ARE RESPONSIBLE
FOR RELATIONSHIPS

First, let's get back on track with the Jewish question. I don't care how many Israels were formed after WWII, nothing can compensate for the holocaust. I introduced that subject only to dramatize the point that blaming the victim is a pathetic, possibly immoral, disguise of the real culprit.

Author:
I don't think blame is the subject here or should be the subject at all. Establishing who to blame and to what degree does not directly address the solution to the problem. The subject is: what can realistically be done in the future? And who cares by whom. I think you are a little defensive but please don't hold that against me. I say it as a friend trying to learn from you.

Anonymous woman:
It's not a big leap from this attitude to the suggestion which keeps creeping into these exchanges, namely, that somehow it's up to the victim to solve the problem. (I realize that women are not always the victims but this not being my doctoral thesis let's assume they are, at least in the relationship arena we have staked out.) Anyway, why are women the ones who are supposed to come up with the solutions? Are men so incompetent? Beneath this line of reasoning is the subtle and not too digestible premise that women have to solve the relationship problem because men simply aren't going to change -- when in fact the solution may well be that nothing will really improve unless and until they do (change).

Author:
I think the problem has to be solved and it's not relevant whether its the victim or perpetrator who solves it if even they can be clearly discerned. The person best able to solve it, should. A Jew isn't going to wait around for a Nazi to solve the problem. But here are a few points which argue that women will be the ones to solve the problem:
1) Women buy 90% of the relationship books. No one has a clue how to change this or the mentality behind it.
2) Since the new age of male sensitivity and psychology, divorce, sexual

crimes, and general chauvinism (on daytime television for example) have skyrocketed way beyond what the very gentle Ozzie of Ozzie and Harriet could have imagined. Sensitivity training has made things worse.

3) The nature of man is more complicated since he is motivated toward sex and violence by a single ambiguous chemical called testosterone and so sex and violence are not obviously separated for him. Woman have one chemical too, but it is for two very similar tasks, i.e., sex and childrearing.

4) Relationships tend to be more important for woman whereas men are made, by testosterone, partially for non-relationship activities like hunting.

Anonymous woman:

A while ago I encountered an article in "Woman's Day" titled "Steering Your Marriage Through Mid-Life Crisis" with a picture on the cover of a woman driving a car beside her husband, who was in the passenger seat. Considering the way men regard women and driving this was pretty funny. However, the article was dead serious, and the caption of one photo announced: "If I had known what my husband was going through he would never have committed adultery." I wrote a letter (unmailed) to the editor, something to this effect: "Maybe we should rewrite the Ten Commandments to read-- 'Thou Shalt not Permit Thy husband to Commit Adultery!" The good news is that enough progress has been made since this article appeared 15 or so years back that it wouldn't be printed today (I hope).

Author:

I think a relationship is always the result of what two people do. We put criminals in jail but we know that we create the environment which makes them criminal. We do this because we know how to hold criminals responsible but we don't know, despite out best efforts, how to hold ourselves responsible. We do what is practical regardless of who really is to blame. And, I have seen many recent articles on supermarket magazine covers like: how to keep your man faithful. Every woman wants to do this, and every man too, because they know they must take responsibility for at least the half of the relationship they control.

CONTROL IS AT THE
HEART OF RELATIONSHIPS

Anonymous woman:
It is no longer politically correct to assume that women are responsible for the excesses of men.

Author:
I don't know that it was ever so.

Anonymous woman:
Course correction #2: In your last note, you seem to be assuming that all relationships are a bit testosterone control-freaky, whereas I am focusing only on what I perceive as the pathologically negative fringe of a generally healthy group. I am not assuming in these discussions that all marriages deteriorate into control struggles-- though all marriages have control issues at one time or another. The situations that interest me are ones in which control becomes the governing principle of the relationship, an acute and chronic disorder that cripples and distorts communication enough to subvert the health of those involved. But I by no means think all relationships between men and women are this sticky. Some work quite well.

Author:
I think control is the central issue of all relationships or even the definition of relationships. Without control and dependency there is no relationship. The second you want to be with someone that person has control over you. Love gives control and creates dependency. Men control for sex while woman control for dinner and flowers. There must be a central reason why men and women seek each other out. If this were not deeply evolved into us there would be no human beings. It is a fundamental mistake to think in terms of eliminating control and dependency rather than in terms of a simple methodology with which to balance control so that each party gives and receives love or control.

Anonymous woman:
I can't disagree about the motivations of divorce lawyers but let's face it, the disease is already raging by the time they get involved. They aren't

9.) A CONVERSATION BETWEEN FRIENDS

being hired, after all, to save the marriage, just cut the losses.

Author:
I think the greater lawyers can make the losses the more they get paid for cutting them.

Anonymous woman:
It isn't clear from your response what you mean by women staying with the rules that they (women) made in the first place. "Men go along with the woman's rules [and happily so) as long as she realizes their importance and plays only by them. When she drops the rules so does he." I'm not sure what you are referring to here.

Author:
In the beginning women are in control; their rules prevail. The man knows that unless he is nice she will never marry him. The rule(s) is: flowers and dinner first; then sex. When the woman drops these rules the man does too and the balance that created a loving relationship is lost.

Anonymous woman:
    As far as I'm concerned, the rules are not made by women or men, but are the product of complex factors -- cultural, moral, social, religious -- that are themselves a reflection of some basic human needs. When these rules change it is a signal of some major evolutionary shift, such as the development of reliable birth control in our times, that we all, in one way or another, respond to. Women are not capriciously making these changes any more than are men. We are all, as a human race, responding to forces much greater than ourselves.

Author:
Men want sex and women want flowers; these are very very fundamental rules that have never changed and are an evolved part of us just like our eyes and teeth. The complex factors you speak of are trivial.

Anonymous woman:
I think I should add, as a theological and philosophical footnote here, that

204

I believe we are a civilized society in proportion to our ability and willingness to overcome or in some fashion subdue those biological impulses that would otherwise misgovern our best selves.

Author:
Biological rules are in fact the most perfect rules possible for the survival and prosperity of all. Seeing and hearing are biological rules or functions. We have no reason to think in terms of their evil. They are for survival. They are as purely good as conceivable. We should seek harmony with our biology; not confrontation. We don't want to cut off a leg just because it is biological. If it's there it must be there for a reason, indeed the best possible reason: survival.

Anonymous woman:
Putting it another way, if your thesis is based on biology as a given and unavoidable reality well, that's fine. But you should know you are discussing your thesis with someone who does not hold to that view of man and the universe. In "The African Queen" when Humphrey Bogart (Mr. Aulnutt) contends that his drinking, as well as other excesses, is just his nature as a man, Kate Hepburn replies (as she dumps his booze supply over the side of their boat): "Nature, Mr. Aulnutt, is what we were put on this earth to rise above!"

Author:
Kate Hepburn is very cute and all but I have no idea how you rise above your nature when your nature is all there is. In fact, your nature is what you use to determine that you wish to rise above your nature. A fish in a bowl cannot rise above his nature because it has no tools with which to apprehend the world outside the bowl; so it for us. Trying to do this might require a philosophy Ph.D. from Harvard and it adds 100 times to the complexity of an already complex subject. I cannot see average people profiting from a philosophical experience and I don't see the reason for trying when biology is simple and accessible and solves the specific relationship problems that destroy families.

Anonymous woman:

9.) A CONVERSATION BETWEEN FRIENDS

I can't help but resist, based on all of the above, the suggestion that women have to figure out what to do about all this.

Author:
I don't think they have to figure it out; all they have to do is read this book; besides, regardless of what men do or don't do its better for the female half of the relationship to know the rules than for nobody to know the rules. I have no need to make it a battle between men and women; you should be as peaceful as me.

Anonymous woman:
Divorce may be bad for kids, and maybe more marriages can be saved, but why is it up to women to turn the tide?

Author:
I see no other practical solution. If women lose power after courtship as a relationship progresses then they must reclaim it. If men give power they can just as easily take it back. But again you're hung up on a battle between the sexes.

Anonymous woman:
You have much more data than I on the subject, and I gather from some of what you have shared with me that women initiate most divorces.   I initiated mine.   But why?   What was I responding to?   Sometimes you have to risk ending a relationship in order to save it.

Author:
It is very significant that women are mostly the ones who are willing to take that risk.

Anonymous woman:
Anyway, it isn't necessarily the person who initiates the divorce who wants to end the marriage.

Author:
I'll agree, but it is very significant that woman end 91% of the marriages

that end in divorce..

Anonymous woman:
In answer to "what specific strategy would you advise women to employ in order to keep their families off the destructive path you describe???" I think the answer is implied in much of the above: this question should be directed at men because they need to take more responsibility for the ending of these marriages.

Author:
Taking responsibility for the end doesn't address the problem of relationships in general. If every group that ever killed Jews took responsibility for it, it doesn't mean that the next group won't kill Jews too. It is in the nature of power that isn't given, it has to be taken. I think sadly for you what has happened is that in order to divorce your husband you had to teach yourself to hate him; now though I am asking you look at the situation logically. Divorce psychology is one thing, honest reasoning is another.

Anonymous woman:
(According to another article, divorced women are likely to say "my marriage failed, where divorced men tend to refer to this catastrophe as the marriage -- as in the car broke down -- a mishap that ultimately has nothing to do with them.)

Author:
Yes this was always true. Milton once said something like: for a woman her love is her life and for a man it is a thing apart. Men have testosterone for sex and hunting while women have estrogen for only love.

Anonymous woman:
However, while we are all waiting for this miracle of male accountability to occur,

Author:
There are certain miracles for which we have no reason to wait.

9.) A CONVERSATION BETWEEN FRIENDS

Anonymous woman:
There is much women can do to cut their losses (a tactic more than a strategy). I believe that the more women learn to value themselves despite what society has taught them to believe -- the more grounded they become in fundamental truths about their innate humanity and God-given freedom (a growing awareness that already marks one of the strongest currents of change in the latter half of our century) -- the less likely they will be as a gender to be imposed upon by the childishness of others.

Author:
Wait a minute; who exactly are you calling childish here. You can't just insult biology's most successful creation. And for God's sake, the latter half of the century has been marked by divorce.

Anonymous woman:
Knowing who you are is the best defense against being re-created in someone else's image.

Author:
Knowing who you are takes a Ph.D. in philosophy from Harvard or maybe years of Freudian analysis and perhaps some feminist indoctrination; so let's forget that business altogether and merely think of love as when a man and woman agree that they will always trade sex for flowers.

Anonymous woman:
Though I understand most of what you say about love making being the trade between flowers and sex, there are still some relationships where sex is deferred until marriage. These couples for reasons of religious principles, moral standards, ethnic traditions, and so on, in some cases have established a greater sense of commitment and fewer instances of divorce. But whatever their individual fortunes, I wonder how your theories about sex apply when the trade is not made until later?

LOVE IS OBTAINED THROUGH A CONTRACT

Author

I think the trade is always made later as few women submit on the first date.

Anonymous woman:

Also, how does the idea of trading relate to the concept of unconditional love? Isn't this a higher ideal?

Author:

I have no idea what unconditional love is. That is more a question for philosophers and psychologist to stumble over. In terms of my theory love always has conditions. For example, and most basically, the other persons location must be controlled. That is a condition for love. If love could be unconditional then no amount of absence or , say, abuse could end it.

Anonymous woman:

If I sound defensive on the subject of blame it may be because I have experienced something you have not. Being a victim of abuse is not the - same as hypothecating about it. Assigning blame may not be constructive when dealing with minor power struggles, but in cases of serious abuse the situation is altered. Many abusers are skilled at transferring guilt and anger to their spouses. Often it is not until the victim wakes up to this transference, disavows guilt, and finds the strength to send it back to its source, that the cycle of abuse can be broken.

Author:

I understand that your pain was real but your approach is purely mumbo jumbo psychological. Until psychologists value marriage as much as the rest of us, until they can make their marriages last as long as the rest of us, or until their positions make sense why bother. The Jews were victims who recovered in spades with simple, actionable behavioral changes that provide an easier accurate model to follow. What the hell does "wake up to transference" mean. In the 1950's when your son got knocked down by a bully you told him to get up swinging.(transference as in fist to jaw?)

Anonymous woman:

Your discussions of who should solve the problem are a bit confusing. If men are not participating in the solution and women are doing most of the

9.) A CONVERSATION BETWEEN FRIENDS

work, how good can the solution be?

Author:
If women will merely insist on flowers before sex men will provide the flowers, and women will be happy and not in need of divorce. Male participation is not required. And, all parties don't have to participate in a solution. If you put a murderer in jail, without his cooperation, the problem(to avoid another murder) is still perfectly solved.

Anonymous woman:
In a previous letter you mentioned something about divorce being not the best solution but the one women seem to be choosing. Perhaps, without the participation of men, they don't have much choice.

Author:
Addressed above

Tireless Anonymous woman:
Let's talk about love and control. I do not like the concept of "trading" love since I believe love should be a gift freely given, not something to barter.

Author:
That's what you did in your marriage and that's why you were abused. Love should never be freely given. If this were so it could be given to a tree. It is only given to somebody who can give something back.

Tireless Anonymous woman:
Control as a word has bad and good connotations.

Author:
I think psychology uses it exclusively as a bad word.

Tireless anonymous woman:

In its good sense it expresses self-control, discipline, confidence -- all attractive qualities. When it begins to work at controlling someone else, however, it turns negative.

Author:
Love gives you control over a person. The second you want to be with someone you have given that person a degree of control over you. Being controlled by love is supposed to be the best thing possible.

Tireless anonymous woman:
It implies fear. Fear of loosing control. I find a man who has self-control to be sexy, but a man who starts controlling me a turn off. The difference to me is the distinction between a loving man and a possessive one.

Author:
A man needs to control you if he is going to have sex with you. All men will control you if you let them and no men will control you if you don't. I don't think you can understand love or be a full participant in it until you feel that it is mutual control or mutual possession. Love is the most wonderful feeling of all because the other person possesses us completely and frees us from the responsibility of being alone and unpocessed.

Tireless anonymous woman:
Dependency is another problem for me. My concept of a healthy relationship is a committed friendship, permitting mutual independence. Compromises must be made for any close long-term relationship to function, but compromise does not mean dependency so much as it does cooperation and a dovetailing of needs and interests.

Author:
I think you can cooperate with a store clerk or your boss but that love requires full dependency. I seems that the psychological language you have so thoroughly absorbed is destructive to your ability to understand love. You're dreaming more than thinking.

Anonymous woman:
I can't believe that the only reason men are nice is that otherwise women

9.) A CONVERSATION BETWEEN FRIENDS

won't marry them. Being nice or good or unselfish or honest should be of some value in and of itself regardless of the outcome. I think you are more cynical than I am about your gender and with less reason.

Author:
I see no cynicism in my position. Being nice promotes life more than anything.It is our primary genetic objective. Men understandably are most inclined to be nice to women because it leads to procreation. We are nice so we can procreate. It is better than being nice for nothing.

Tireless anonymous woman:
When you say "when the woman drops these rules the man does too..." are you talking about sex for flowers?

Author:
Yes

Tireless anonymous woman:
Does this mean she stops giving sex or stop wanting flowers? It isn't clear.

Author:
Usually the woman will stop demanding flowers and keep giving sex; this is absolutely destructive to the intended biological pattern of a heterosexual relationship.

Tireless anonymous woman:
Anyway, why are you so sure that she is the one who stops first?

Author:
Men are on automatic pilot; they rarely stop wanting sex.(24 erections per night,while sleeping, well into there 50's, etc.)

Tireless anonymous woman:
Maybe the guy stops whatever his part of the tradeoff is, and she follows suit.

BIOLOGY IS THE
FOUNDATION OF OUR FEELINGS

Author:
This is more the case with illness or advanced age. If men didn't want sex nature wouldn't have created them in the first place. Women bred men for their sexual desire. Creating men who didn't long for woman would have been absolutely contradictory.

Tireless anonymous woman:
Which is the problem with the trade concept in the first place. In unconditional love you don't keep toting up a tally on your lover.

Author:
If you don't tally, any amount of abuse is tolerable. The closer the tally is to 50-50 the more love you feel.

Tireless anonymous woman:
A word about biology. Are you sure that seeing and hearing are innocent in and of themselves?

Author:
Yes very sure.

Tireless anonymous woman:
What good is seeing without perception and comprehension?
A Klu Klux Clansman sees a black man without perceiving him as a human being. An untrained ear hears a Beethoven symphony without understanding its beauty. Biology without education, religion, culture, or morality would have us back in the jungle with the monkeys, and I'm certain we don't wish to be there. I am not advocating cutting off limbs, just resisting the suggestion that biology defines us. It represents only one aspect of our heritage and not necessarily the most important one.

Author:
Biology is our entire heritage or at least the essential foundation of our heritage. We have generally concluded that the Klan is bad because it is inconsistent with biology's desire for abundant life and genetic procreation. Without this biological foundation the Klan would have no

213

moral dimension whatsoever for us. Human culture is not independent of biology, it is a mere objectification of it. We can't decide to eat rocks and kill each other tomorrow. We think and do according to our biology.

Tireless anonymous woman:
Kate Hepburn isn't cute; she plays the role of a courageous missionary in Africa during World War II, and the comment about nature was her statement of a religious truth. "Nature" in this context is that part of man (generic not masculine) which must be overcome to permit any sort of happiness or freedom: pride, envy, hate, malice, lust, etc., are the part of his/her nature which is not to be nurtured but vanquished. This has nothing to do with fish. It's the message of Christianity.

Author
One doesn't argue about religion, but I will agree with you that Christianity became the most successful institution in the history of the world by using negative rather than positive reinforcement. This and psychology may have encouraged you to see men with evil baggage that must be overcome before they can be good lovers. But here's the problem: if envy, hate, and malice are natural characteristics that must be overcome, then all natural characteristics including, love, generosity, and compassion must also be overcome too.

Oddly, even psychologists would agree that it is better to build a religion and raise a child on positive reinforcement. Holding a child in you arms is positive reinforcement. Imagine raising a child with just negative reinforcement. An adult heterosexual relationship is similar. We need to reinforce natural biological characteristics rather than invent non-contextual religious ones.

Tireless anonymous woman:

Of course it is better for the female half of the relationship to know the rules than for nobody to know the rules, but after 20 plus years of marriage I had the distinct feeling that I was playing tennis by myself. One day I stopped and there was no one on the other side of the net returning the ball. Women can only go so far without men in the game.

Author:
I can imagine how it felt-I'm sorry. I notice though how much comfort you take in drawing you ex into the problem. I'll even concede that the problem was 50% his, but I think it should be mostly an irrelevant 50% to you. Even if you were a legitimate, full fledged victim of criminal abuse the real difficulty would be in regaining control of yourself. Control of the perpetrator (putting him in jail for example) would be largely independent of your internal status.

Tireless anonymous female:
I'm not sure that "if women lose power as a relationship progresses then they must reclaim it" makes practical sense when the act of reclaiming is being denied them by the loss of power in the first place.

Author:
The Jews lost power and they took it back. If you are denied a legitimate amount of power in a relationship in the end only you can take it back. Power given, can be taken.

Tireless anonymous woman:
It takes energy and confidence to confront what you perceive as a threatening spouse, especially one who has predicated his very survival on your inability to do this. However, it is doable though the process may have the effect of ending the marriage (as it did in my case). My husband couldn't deal with an empowered woman.

Author:
Without knowing the specifics and without wishing to overstep my bounds and only wishing to be your friend I would argue that he couldn't deal with too much free sex and you couldn't deal with too few flowers. It comforts you to define the problem in feminist terms, but then you do admit that his second wife is a "big, bold, brassy, successful, career woman and that you were a traditional housewife. No man dreams of falling in love with an empty wall flower who just lies there, so to speak

9.) A CONVERSATION BETWEEN FRIENDS

The more empowered she is the more men she will attract. Your feminist, male chauvinist explanation seems perfectly wrong.

Tireless anonymous woman:
"Power isn't given to a woman it has to be taken." I'm not sure where this axiom comes from. There are many sources of power, some bad, some good, some better. Power that is derivative or stolen or bought is not as valuable as power that is discovered within.

Author:
I don't care how well a person knows his vaunted inner child; I only care about simple behaviors and words. Does she trade sex for flowers? I think a paid by the hour head shrinker would love you, as I do (but for different reasons). I think the meaningless adventitious nuance you find in everything is working against your arriving at a conclusion. I guess it's an occupational hazard when you're so intelligent and articulate.

Tireless anonymous woman:
"There are certain miracles for which we should not wait." I didn't mean that we should wait for men to wake up so much as encourage them to, which maybe what the increase in divorce is already doing.

Author:
The increase in divorce is testimony that neither sex has woken up it seems to me.
Tireless anonymous Woman:
Anyway, have you ever watched a woman get a man to change a tire? That is what, I suspect, men have been doing to women on these touchy, messy, issues. The more that women keep changing the tires, the more men just stand around looking pretty and innocent. It reminds me of the Cosby routine when he says men aren't the boss of the house -- women are; men are the geniuses -- because only a genius could manage to look so stupid.

Author:
That was too subtle for me to understand and I suspect not directly

relevant to the subject at hand. I notice though that it is politically correct to put men down these days. Dick Cavett (Mr. New York City old fashioned, ultra compassionate, liberal) did a show on depression the other day; he stopped in the middle after a gender based statistic was read and gratuitously added, "another way women are superior." This is what they did to blacks, and all of the sudden 70% of black babies are illegitimate and 50% of black young men are in jail. Anointing a party to a relationship as the superior one to even things out is perfectly stupid.

Tireless anonymous woman:
I was calling men childish when they behave in patterns of wasteful domination and then rationalize this behavior. Maybe adolescent would be a better word. Anyhow, it's selfish. And wait a minute, who are you calling biology's most successful creation?

Author:
I agree it is childish, but more so are patterns of wasteful submissiveness.

Tireless anonymous woman:
Knowing who you are takes wisdom, experience, humility, patience, honesty, and a willingness to change. It is not an academic pursuit so much as a spiritual quest. It is what life is all about. Trying to separate this fundamental goal from the man/woman thing is impractical. Every relationship challenges our sense of identity and forces us either to reaffirm or to transform once again who we are.

Author:
Socrates advised this centuries ago. We really don't need to hear it again. It is better left in the philosophy dept. at Harvard University. I fear you may be sensing the weakness of your case. Is that why your are turning to such vague arguments?

Tireless anonymous Woman:
"Merely think of love as when a man and woman agree that they will always trade sex for flowers," is a formula for happiness that wouldn't, I

9.) A CONVERSATION BETWEEN FRIENDS

fear, impress the Bard:

> Let me not to the marriage of true minds
> Admit impediment. Love is not love
> Which alters when it alteration finds,
> Or bends with the remover to remove:
> O, no! it is an ever-fixed mark,
> That looks on tempests, and is never shaken;
> It is the star to every wandering bark,
> Whose worth's unknown, although his height be
> taken.
> Love's not Time's fool, though rosy lips and cheeks
> Within his bending sickle's compass come;
> Love alters not with his brief hours and weeks,
> But bears it out even to the edge of doom.
>> If this be error and upon me prov'd,
>> I never writ, nor no man ever lov'd.   (W.S.

1589)

Author:

Yes, yes, Shakespeare is very very beautiful, but the above doesn't purport to be a formula for happiness or love at all. It is merely a description of perfect and imagined love and of no relevance to our subject, but nice try.

Tireless anonymous woman:

I included the Shakespeare sonnet to illustrate what I sense to be unconditional love. I'm sure there are those who would disagree, or would use other examples. Perhaps the man/woman relationship is less appropriate to gauge this kind of love than parent/child or therapist/patient. I wasn't so much refuting your formula as trying to enrich it with the magic love can bring. If we approach a relationship with a sense of what we're going to be getting from it, it isn't as spontaneous as it should be. Unconditional love, in any event, cannot invite abuse because a truly loving person also loves him/herself and would not permit abuse to occur, at least not for any length of time.

9.)A CONVERSATION BETWEEN FRIENDS

Author:
Yes, love can bring magic and so can ballet, but this does not mean that tremendous discipline and knowledge is not required. I think the instant you love someone you concomitantly feel something wonderful that you are getting from it. I think that truly unconditional love is a truly perfect formula for abuse. Moreover, forgive me, it is a stupid, albeit poetic topic. A relationship cannot be unconditional in the real world. A first date does not take place without the condition that both parties agree on when to meet and a million other things. A developing relationship is nothing but a growing web of such conditions. Eventually the web has the strength to endure some broken strands, but if the guy turns out to be a Mafia hit man he has imposed a new condition that presumably is not compatible with love. Love mostly ends in divorce. A relationship then is a contract whose terms must be fulfilled, so please no more Shakespeare.

I certainly agree that the love of a parent for a child does seem unconditional, but I think it is so precisely because the rules are so certain and well defined that each knows exactly what he will get. The gap in age, size, intelligence, strength, and responsibilities is so vast that no one thinks to challenge. Each is free to love from a seemingly fixed and safe natural position. With time the gap narrows and the love becomes more and more problematic.

Tireless anonymous woman:
My question about whether the man withdraws his part of the trade first is still unsatisfied since I didn't realize his side of the trade was sex. I thought his side was flowers. I think I was suggesting that the man withdraws the flowers first, thus upsetting the bargain. Maybe it's a minor point, whether or not he withdraws or she stops expecting.

Author:
I think it is very minor.

Tireless anonymous woman:
I believe there is a trend in popular thought, though I have never read anything specifically on the subject, that morality (assigning blame)

9.) A CONVERSATION BETWEEN FRIENDS

became politically incorrect at about the time psychology replaced religion as the solver of human problems. However, I'm not sure this trend has worked as well as it could. To me, at least, it seems that confusion is created when we pull away from our responsibility to name something wrong when it is. Though there may be explanations for wrong behavior (abuse, criminal action, whatever) our efforts to understand do not condone nor excuse it. Nor does assigning blame mean we can't forgive or take responsibility for our part in the situation, and move on.

Author:
You seem confused. First you talk about unconditional love then you talk about blame and responsibility. You are blaming someone for not meeting conditions. I agree though that it is very important to know who is to blame especially in murders and most things, but in divorce I have some sympathy for "no fault". There was never a model to follow so we threw up our hands and said no one is at fault, but after this book I will blame anyone who initiates a divorce for not knowing and applying the rules.

Tireless anonymous woman:
The confusion that comes from an arbitrary distancing of ourselves from a moral universe leads to odd conclusions, such as equating female submissiveness with male dominance, when in fact the first is most likely a response, and not a pleasant one, to the second.

Author:
I think you're on the wrong track here. A submissive soldier who kills for a dominant general is just as guilty or almost as guilty. This is one of the reasons we burned up 100,000 civilians in Dresden and 80,000 in Hiroshima. If someone responds submissively to a friend who wants to commit a murder he will be just as guilty. A submissive response is not necessarily a justifiable one. But in divorce blame is not the central issue, a solution is. I can see you have a lot invested in blame. The real issue doesn't have to do with who are you going to blame but, what are you going to do differently the next time around t solve the problem?

Tireless anonymous woman:

Or with equating the problem of the victim with the victimizer, leading into dangerous waters in which the rapist and his victim are equally deserving of our sympathies. Whoever said that "silence -- where protest is due -- makes cowards out of men" may have been referring to this sort of distortion.

Author:
I can't see a connection to divorce here, but who would argue that identifying the perpetrator and even killing him is the major solution for the victim?

Tireless anonymous woman:
By the time a marriage has begun, some of this early sex for love stuff should have evolved into something more mature.

Author:
I think if the "something" existed you would have described it. It does not exist. Men always want sex and woman always want flowers. Certainly flowers is more metaphorical than sex but over time woman will constantly want some type or variety of flowers while men will want some type or variety of sex. Short hand approaches can develop over time and often do particularly as a couple ages, but the foundation remains the same.

Tireless anonymous author:
No one disagrees that manipulation is efficient. I recall one episode when I successfully applied the sex withheld ploy in my relationship. But I wasn't proud of doing it and certainly wouldn't recommend it as a modus operandi for an entire marriage. I don't want to be manipulated, and I don't want to manipulate.

Author:
Why not be proud if you both got what you wanted and you both wanted legitimately good things. Any relationship is inherently manipulative. God threatens us: thou shall not kill, this is certainly manipulation and control but it is for good so we accept it and even consider it loving. If

you promised your husband sex for killing someone then that would be a kind of manipulation not to be proud of, but I assume you wanted something legitimate. If you hold a baby to stop her from crying is that manipulation? If a supermarket withholds food until you pay is that bad or does it make a relationship possible?

Tireless anonymous woman:
The implications of a theory such as yours imply, though you may not realize it, that love as a quantity is in short supply, something not to be squandered. It needs to be measured out and carefully orchestrated to avoid imbalances in the relationship. But this concept runs counter to the very nature of love itself, which is a giving, not a taking, attitude. The act of giving it rewards the giver not just the recipient. And by the same token, withholding love deprives the withholder, not just the object of this strategy. When we try to make love obey some formula we are mistaking the nature of love itself, like trying to keep a sunbeam in a box.

Author:
You say love is a giving attitude. I agree; you give sex. If you didn't want equal measure in return you could give it to a dog or tree or yourself and be happy. You give it where you expect it will be returned. Love demands equality from another human being. Of course, withholding sex deprives the withholder too. You want to get in a position where both parties know and accept the ground rules and each can give and take freely and regularly without withholding or a formalized balancing act..

Tireless anonymous woman:
I also think that sex and love are not equal sides in an equation. Love is way more important. You could have a relationship without sex, as people have done when illness or separation or some other misfortune has occurred. But what kind of relationship would you have without love?

Author:
I said sex and flowers; not sex and love. Love is the result of trading sex for flowers. Sorry, but all men will choose a sexual relationship over a non-sexual one. Sex is a necessary condition for love, at least the kind of

LOVE IS JUST A GIVING ATTITUDE

heterosexual love this book is about.

Tireless anonymous woman:
I think men want love too.

Author:
Yes, men want sex and woman want flowers. When they affect a trade they both get what they want most: love.

Tireless anonymous woman:
However, I think the trouble with your theory is that it is an oversimplification of what goes on in a relationship. I am not sure love is the product of the sex-flowers trade, or if it is, it's mostly in the beginning -- in the romantic-love phase. No one disputes that a good marriage is one which is able to maintain romantic feeling over the years, but in most marriages romance changes into something else, -- something tougher. The maturity of a man who can love his wife after a mastectomy, for instance, and reassure her of his love, is perhaps incomprehensible to a teen-age boy picking up his prom date in her strapless gown. Men who love women as people, are not as hung-up on sexuality as men who view women primarily as sexual creatures. Your theory, so far as you have stated it, makes no such distinctions.

Author:
Firstly, if sex weren't of primary importance to men and women the species would have failed instantly. Secondly, the theory does make the distinction. The broad array of behaviors that happily married men are willing to engage in for their families is testimony to their ability to see women as far more than sexual receptacles if they are given the right encouragement, but sex is the reason evolution created the relationship.

Tireless anonymous woman:
I resist the concept of a "one size fits all" remedy to something as complicated as marriage, and which presumes biology as the dominant theme. Marriages are as diverse as people are. Some are based on social status or money. In a relationship where the partners are oriented around

223

financial success, the crisis that breaks them down will be more tied to the stock market than the bedroom. Sometimes people marry because they want change, or want to break away from someone else, -- and tons of people marry without really knowing the character of their partner. Many come into marriage with some form of psychological agenda. These situations create problems that can wreck havoc despite everything else being rather sound -- despite the "rules."

Author:

The sex/flowers trade off starts on the first date, if only symbolically; no marriage should take place if this is not so. If "these situations" do not bend favorably to the "rules" then there should be no relationship in the first place. The "rules" of love determine the meaning of the situation; they make the couple's love greater than external situations.

Tireless anonymous woman:

Marriages break up for a bunch of reasons. I think that even if the sexual dynamics are in good working order, eventually the individuals in a relationship find themselves searching for something more. They want answers to bigger life questions and sooner or later something triggers this need. A parent dies, a child gets seriously ill, money problems create anxiety. Romance (flowers) and sex, however satisfying the trade, may or may not be the best coping mechanisms at times like these. And the love that this mechanism creates may falter if other elements have not been put in place: integrity, consideration, trustworthiness, unselfishness, strength, etc. In other words, character counts too

Author:

Sexual dynamics cannot be in order without character according to the theory. A woman is not going to make love to a man without character. I should think one of the first flowers a woman would ask for would be: character. If after a marriage a woman notices that she overlooked character or that her husband has lost it she must demand that it be created or restored. If he is unwilling or unable to make a trade then she may well consider ending the relationship. Mostly this will not happen though because the promise of sex is designed to be the most important promise you can make to a man. He will develop character for sex.

Tireless anonymous woman:

Most marriages that fail fall apart during or not long following a crisis. Though you may argue that a happy relationship will work this through successfully, I believe that often perfectly happy couples, with the sex-flowers thing cranking along beautifully, fail in the face of adversity. This is because the people involved are not strong, or because one is and one isn't, and the crisis brings out this truth. It is hard, when the crisis has passed, to return to the old patterns and fantasies that made the romance fun. Somehow, reality has intruded too well. Many marriages can't handle change.

Author:
You're describing a marriage that was always adrift because it was never defined by the sex/flowers trade off. In a truly biological marriage change happens around the marriage, but not to the marriage. When a couple sees their sex/flowers relationship as the most central activity to there lives they are united against a crisis; not subject to it. In such a situation the man makes all reasonable efforts to confront the crisis because he doesn't want to confront the most dire crisis of all, namely, losing his wife.

Tireless anonymous woman:
Marriage, after all, is only a part of life, not the other way around. Life is what we are trying to deal with and ultimately the questions mortality forces upon us have to be answered alone, whether or not we are in a relationship ... whether or not that relationship is working.

Author:
I'm sorry to tell you that human beings are simple biological creatures; not philosophers. They are far more concerned with sex than the "questions mortality forces upon us". This is why all couples can agree on sex and get together right away while very few even know of philosophy and far fewer get together on it.

Tireless anonymous woman:
If the dynamics you are describing require us to forfeit integrity or honesty for happiness, then there is something wrong.

9.) A CONVERSATION BETWEEN FRIENDS

Author: This is not remotely implied by the theory.

Tireless anonymous woman:
Manipulation implies some level of dishonesty or a least a lack of candor.

Author:
Only you are talking about manipulation, and then in a pejorative way.
I'm talking about a sex /flowers trade which is like a food/money trade in
a supermarket.

Tireless anonymous woman:
Even if this trade with our conscience works for a time to get us what we
want, sooner or later we are going to be uncomfortable with it and with
ourselves. I believe that a good marriage is one in which both people love
and honor each other in a way that promotes individual growth and
progress.

Author:
That sounds like the Marine Corp theme: "be all you can be." It has
nothing to do with heterosexual relationships. Individual growth within a
marriage ends the marriage. Individual growth for the purpose of having
more to trade within the marriage strengthens it.

Tireless anonymous woman:
Sex is only one aspect of this greater focus. When both partners are
working hard to promote the happiness of the other then problems of
communication or whatever can be overcome, including sex and flowers.

Author:
I'm afraid you're not able to grasp the theory at all. Of course you want
to promote the happiness of the other (did someone say that marriage was
to promote the misery of the other), but couples need a model on which to
proceed and that's what the sex/flowers trade is for. You don't overcome
the sex/flowers trade any more than you overcome your eyesight. It is the
essence of marital communication.

THERE IS NO UNCONDITIONAL LOVE

Tireless anonymous woman:
In this sort of approach, you don't measure how much you are giving or getting, you just do it. It's never equal. Someone always gives more, either because of circumstances or character.

Author:
You must be able to measure. If you don't then when you are being abused, for example, you don't know that balance must be restored. I've explained before that there is no unconditional love.

Tireless anonymous woman:
Your comment that "all men will choose a sexual relationship over a non sexual one" is not responsive to my observation about the importance of sex. I was referring to a sexual relationship which was already established but in which something occurred to interfere with the sex, such as a geographic separation, serious illness, or some sort of dysfunction. Someone with your philosophy would not know how to proceed under such circumstances, but in fact relationships grounded in a mature love will endure just about anything – as distinguished from the self-serving, self-referential type of affection you have described.

Author:
The circumstances you describe are abnormal and therefore not the subject of this book. But you might be interested to know that people in such abnormal circumstances should approximate the sex/flowers trade as best they can, and for exactly the same reasons as any other couple. If an old woman loves an old man who cannot give flowers she is doing it in the loving belief that he would gives flowers if he could.

Tireless anonymous woman:
I don't think the Ten Commandments are manipulative or threatening, though the tone is certainly stern. Later on, in the New Testament, spiritual law evolves into a more loving approach with the Beatitudes. We obey these laws not out of fear so much as from a sense of their innate justice. No one is forcing us to be good (unless you believe in Hell and damnation). Something in us, however, seems to want to be good, or at least fair. We sense that this is who we are. So it is not manipulation that

encourages us to obey these rules, but the recognition of a truth about ourselves.

Author:
Bringing religion in to this is silly, but, suffice it to say that the Catholic Church is the most successful institution in the history of the earth because it manipulatively dictates that hell is the punishment for disobeying the ten commandments. Your oh so sophisticated arguments about the Beatles or Beatitudes or whatever may have a home in more modern and impotent Christian Churches like the United Church of Christ but the major religions are wholeheartedly and thankfully manipulative because this is most consistent with human biological nature. If you want to consider Islam the major religion of the world please do. It is shot through with manipulative references to death and judgement day. Here is a manipulative but loving Quranic verse that tells us what works given the biological nature of human beings:

"Verily, for the Righteous are gardens of Delight, in the Presence of their Lord. Shall We then treat the people of Faith like the people of Sin? What is the matter you? How judge you?"(68:34-36)

Tireless Anonymous woman:
You are mistaken if you believe a mature adult male is as narrow as a teenage boy who will die to fondle a girl's breasts.

Author:
I don't think its a mistake. The captain of the football team gets the prettiest cheerleader for catching a pass; James Bond gets the most beautiful woman for saving the world, and an average guy gets his wife for something less but still something the wife defines and values dearly. A rapist associates sex with nothing, a girl associates sex with football, Bond women associate sex with saving the world, and an average man's wife can teach him to associate sex with family and love. In short, boys and men are the same in that they value sex, and they are different in the level of success or quantity of flowers they offer women.

RELIGION IS CONTROLLING

Tireless anonymous woman:
Let's just face it. Women don't need men anymore because general economic development in the later half of the Twentieth Century has reached the point where AFDC(welfare) or a good job enable women to raise kids without men.

Author:
I'll agree that women need men less in the economic sense, but evolution has many fail safe systems to ensure the creation of the family. The body has two of most everything(eyes for example) so that if one is damaged vision is still possible. Behavior is the same way. If men figure out how to masturbate they are less dependant on woman but they still prefer sex with women. If their real biological inclination was for only sex, i.e., to have sex and run for the hills, then there would be no human race. Family is what they want because family is what makes life possible.

So it is with women, they are not as economically dependant, but they still need men, and perhaps more than ever. If they work they can't actually raise the children they can afford. Rather, they can only pay someone else to do it for them. This is why the vast majority of woman who can afford to stay home with their children, do. Secondly, women know that a child without a father will feel deprived upon awareness of a child with a father. Thirdly, a woman knows that a man can expand a child's psychosexual development in a way she cannot. Fourthly, a woman needs the co-creator father around in order to have someone with whom to share the greatest joy(children) of her life. Lastly, you have to keep in mind that if one reason for women needing men diminishes it does not mean that the other reasons won't become more important to compensate. We see this phenomena everywhere. Today we have all manner of extreme sports in which heroic men risk life and limb just for the thrill of it. This was an evolutionary inclination that enabled men to cope with basic survival requirements. With those requirements largely gone men still choose to live on the edge. The first thrill or the first million dollars in never enough. It is a still a constant battle for them as it always was. Men were designed for battle and they create it when it is missing. For women the desire to be perfect mothers, wives, and, secondarily, breadwinners is a constant and extreme battle that did and still does

9.) A CONVERSATION BETWEEN FRIENDS

require a man. If we watch daytime soap operas we see quite clearly that men are still very critical to women, just not so much for their money.

Tireless anonymous woman:
Women will never accept your idea that sex is so important, let alone controlling sex.

Author:
Have them imagine life without sex, or music without sound. If they don't like control then have them imagine sex without control, or the ocean without the land. It is an impossibility. To see flowers as superior to sex, as women often do, is to be totally anti-biology and invite trouble.

Well, I guess this it for us, at least as regard this conversation; I want to thank you for presenting better than anyone else could have the complex array of misinformation and confusion that modern culture has deployed against us to so thoroughly confuse us about the practical and deliberate behavior necessary for heterosexual relationships.

10.) THE HISTORY OF SEXUAL INTERCOURSE

HOW TO AVOID TOO MUCH SEX

It is not difficult to understand how sex got to be such a foreign part of our lives that we do not deal with in an integrated manner. A wonderful example of the extent to which this can happen is given in Seymour Hersh's recent book The Dark Side Of Camelot. Hersh alleges that President Kennedy would have sex with various women in the bathtub so that just as he was about to have an orgasm he could push their heads underwater and thus induce a panic squeeze that Kennedy apparently enjoyed a great deal. His women probably imagined themselves to be in the hands of a real life Sir Lancelot while Romantic Jack saw women only in mechanical terms.

Going back in history, St. Augustine, for example, taught us that sex was disgusting. Many even believe the concept of a virgin birth stems from the religious view that the rigid behavior and thought demanded by Christianity (at least until recently) was incompatible with the joyous freedom and mayhem of sexual intercourse. At one point in 17th century Spain it was customary to have sex through a hole in a sheet that covered the woman from head to toe. Many couples make love in only one position throughout their entire marriage. When I was 18 I asked a man I happened to work with about his sexual life; he said, " when it rises I use it." These are example of how detached we can be from what ought to be an integrated sex life with a romantic partner with whom we share a full life.

Instead, the greatest joy of our lives has become the greatest shame of our lives. Kids aren't allowed to see the naked women of Playboy, but they're not allowed to see a married, naked, and loving couple either. But in the end they will see more of Playboy than marital love. Marital training is exclusively on the job training. Sexual knowledge is perhaps the most important knowledge and yet it is the knowledge which we have been and are the least able to teach and openly accept. If sex is a biological function that religion sought to control, perhaps it did so because religion itself was controlled by a far more severe force: that created by the death of the last child, the marginal child for whom there was not enough food, clothing or shelter. The Church has always been pro-life. It has been, perhaps, biology's most effective ally. It has always been against death and abortion. Religion was the most important force in preserving and civilizing humankind because it valued humankind the most. It achieved this status, in large part, by giving us rules that seemed obviously necessary to maintain civilization. It invented and promulgated the concepts of right and wrong and good and evil, and applied them to everything, including sex. Extra-marital sex and abortion was strictly forbidden. Marital sex was severely restricted. Offspring were sharply limited to those that were produced within a familial environment which was deemed to provided the best chance for the offspring's survival and development. The Church thus became an important force in civilizing our rampant sexual proclivities.

If we evolved to have as much sex as possible, regardless of how many babies died, it is not difficult to understand that there are side effects from the harsh medicines administered to limit this our most important activity. We desperately want sex but we desperately don't want dead babies. The Church was the primary instructor who taught us how to avoid this biological conflict.

If religion wasn't enough to discourage a woman from focusing on the physical consequences of sex far more than the romantic possibilities, the contradictory force of evolution itself sure was. The male peacock provides an example of this phenomenon that exists throughout nature. Its huge colorful plumage attracts the female even though it has no real value to the female and actually makes the male more vulnerable to attack by predators. The females bred (through natural selection) males to have this goofy plumage by accident. At some point in their evolutionary history some male peacocks probably had an accidental mutation which led to a spot of color on their tail; these males may have also been, by chance, superior hunters. As these males survived and reproduced, they reproduced some females with a sexual sensitivity to a colored tail. Over many generations the sexual attraction to colored tails and hunting skill became alloyed. Perhaps because the colored tail was easier to discern than hunting skills, it became a short hand "turn on" that was easier to transmit across the generations because of its simplicity. But it wasn't a fatal act of genetic suicide because the birds with colored tails were also good hunters.

The above is an example of extinctive sexual behavior. The mutation is significant enough to be a detriment, but not significant enough to lead to quick extinction. Sexual behavior can be related to many things other than love; certainly for animals and almost certainly for humans. Sexual shyness is another of nature's sexual/romantic contradictions, although it is primarily a contradiction between biology and culture that grows out of that biology. Sex is our greatest obsession but we are more likely to talk about how wonderful last night's meal was than about how wonderful last night's sex was. Since the days of Sodom and Gomorrah we have supplemented our genetic understanding of sex by learning to be exceedingly tense and shy about it. We have developed an intuitive sense, apart from a religious one, that the exclusivity of marriage and reproduction is protected by exclusivity of conversation about the intimate aspects of marriage. Casual conversation can lead to casual sex. If someone can hear of your sex life, why can't they then see it or participate in it? The refusal to talk about it is a way to signify that it is private, exclusive, and familial. Some orthodox Jewish sects do not permit an adult male to shake the hand of a female who is not wife or child. They are perhaps overly shy and cautious, but their fear that touching can lead to fucking is a realistic but extreme manifestation of the same attitude found in most familial societies. Sex is exceedingly important. We want to know all about it, but at the same time we are forbidden to know about it because knowing and doing are often closely related. It is no wonder that we have so much trouble with sex and love.

Even today's very modern economy has not been able to change biological roles much from what they were 1000's of years ago. Single mothers find life very difficult without a man. Even married mothers who work find "they can't have it all," at least not without great difficulty. The majority of mothers who work today do it at part time, low wage jobs just as in the past. During much of the period when humankind evolved women were subsistence gathers because their minds and bodies were adapted, most importantly, for child bearing and child rearing. Men were given minds and bodies adapted, most importantly, for hunting and killing. Men brought home meat, natures most complete and prized food. Modern men don't hunt meat very often anymore but they do the modern equivalent. They generally bring home the bigger paycheck that result

10.) THE HISTORY OF SEXUAL INTERCOURSE

from their bigger attraction, preparation and commitment to bigger jobs.

Higher male paychecks are the result of discrimination against the biological nature of women just as more loving relationships with their children are the result of discrimination against the biological nature of men. In the end it is not philosophically possible to determine whether raising a child is more important than raising a bridge or a widget. It is sufficient, though, to realize that there are two sexes because nature had two equally important jobs to do. Men and women evolved for different jobs, with different reproductive strategies, and in a far different physical and cultural environment than today's. It is not surprising that so many have a great deal of trouble integrating all of these conflicting and competing influences.

Throughout history everything was biological. Various cultural overlays were imposed but only those that were somewhat consistent with biology survived. Interpretations of history based on mistaken biology are similarly doomed not to survive. One mistaken interpretation of history holds that marital sex was and is essentially a defensive position that women take in order to avoid rape. Women always competed as best they could to attract the strongest of the strong or the most macho of the macho. It is true enough that the female losers in this competitive struggle were sometimes subject to rape when they had no man to protect them. But, winners competed for the affection of particular males not only to avoid rape but more importantly to attract the man with whom they wanted to mate. The female ape was generally happy to mate with any male who was available while she was in heat. As she evolved and became human she developed into the only female in nature who stayed constantly in heat. She not only was in heat, which made her capable of sex, but it was a controlled heat that could be used as she selectively chose. This gave her more and more power in her selection of mates but also created the concept of rape during the transition period when both sexes were slowly evolving toward monogamy. The mate she selected satisfied her primary need to reproduce as successfully as possible and secondarily was an ally against promiscuous rape. It cannot be said that the female was ever more opposed to rape than the male.

To the forces of evolution the inability to attract a mate was tantamount to death. The more fear of this a woman had the more likely she was to

234

find a way of avoiding it. Nature could no more eliminate this fear than it could eliminate the fear of death. Without these fears and the pressure they bring, life would not be anything that we recognize, if it were possible at all. The fear of death defines life. Without it, it would be easier to put off work, sex, and play until tomorrow. Nothing would ever get done. Our biological clocks would run on meaninglessly and forever. Evolution demands results today because a species may not survive until tomorrow. In general, we can say that a woman without a strong compulsion to mate is a woman whose life serves little evolutionary purpose. The fear and horror of rape evolved in direct proportion to the biological need to more and more selectively mate. Rape didn't cause marriage it was just a reflection of how passionately both sexes desired selective mating.

Twentieth century human culture, which is predominately male culture, has done a great deal to identify and criminalize rape. This is testimony to man's acceptance of the trend toward monogamy. But the more monogamy and love grow the more the fear of rape grows. Today the fear of rape is stronger than ever. Women know to avoid direct eye contact with strangers in public places in order to minimize the possibility of even a misinterpreted glance. Millions of years ago a female came into heat and was compelled to mate with as many of the available males as possible. Rape wasn't an issue, but biology always was.

As human sexuality evolved so did work. Men became more and more efficient and skilled at killing. Two things resulted. Firstly, they became less violent and animalistic as they no longer had to kill with their bare hands or crude weapons, and, secondly, a division of labor became possible so that the most efficient killers could provide for everyone's needs thus freeing more and more men from the need to hunt and kill at all. As men became gentler toward animals, so to speak, they became gentler toward women who concomitantly developed the expectation of gentleness in prospective mates. Women then got three things from men: 1) meat, 2) sex, and 3) gentleness (an asset that seemed to compliment her maternal gentleness).

The mating continuum stretches from monogamous love and sex to general promiscuity and rape. As men became more gentle toward animals and as both sexes came to believe in monogamy, women were able to move down the continuum toward monogamy and love. It is very important to keep in mind that rape and love are modern terms that are not easily applied to pre-modern periods, even though feminists love to do it in order to show man's true violent nature. Today well over 95% of women report that they would abort a child conceived in rape. If most women were routinely raped 5 million years ago, as many feminists claim, and if they killed or were ambivalent toward their children there would be no human race today. If most of the women were raped and then loved their children, then they were not raped, at least by today's standards. It is safe to say that before the human family was formed women came into season and were compelled to mate with any male, and then she evolved to mate with the best male she could attract during that brief period. Finally she evolved to be always in heat so she would have a man around to help her. Nature has given women a larger and larger role in the selection of their mates and presumably this should lead to a larger and larger role in not only who she mates with, but also in the way she mates, and the things she says to her mate before and while she mates that keep the sexual act in its proper evolutionary context.

As the human family began to take its modern form, females moved closer to love on the continuum. It cannot be said that males had a propensity to rape females and therefore resisted this trend. Rather it can be said that they participated equally in its development because it was one way to help insure their specific paternity. Males don't have a propensity to rape, they have a biological propensity to reproduce which is occasionally manifested as rape due to vestigial feelings which remain from an evolutionary period during which generalized promiscuity was desired by both males and females.

It is fine for feminists to talk about rape as the force that drove women to become marital slaves but it should be recognized that they do it merely for political power; to embolden women and to shame men, but not to teach accurate history or to encourage harmony between the sexes.

In nature it often happens that a young, strong male will drive an old weak one from his family or clan. The female will then sometimes kill her offspring and come into season so she can mate with the new male. With the recent rise in divorce among humans from under 5%, as recently as 1960, to over 50% today we see a parallel. An infant's chances of being killed by a parent rise over 2000% when it is raised by at least one non-genetic parent. Where offspring aren't murdered there chances of survival are nevertheless greatly reduced by parents with more immediate genetic concerns. Where human children of divorce aren't killed, which is obviously the majority case, their overall development suffers without the more diligent love of two genetic parents. Children are confronted with a non-genetic parent who insures that both parents will be partially distracted from the child rearing task. The "I'm responsible for my children's lives" attitude slowly gives way to the "it's up to them" attitude. In the case of a genetic family both parents are genetically obligated to do the right thing. In the case of a non-genetic family this is not true and the results are clearly measured by those few biologist who can withstand the criticism from those who wish to rationalize divorce in an effort to make a divorcees happiness more important than the children's.

Love, even human love, is not as poetically transcendent as we often would like to think. We are not really motivated out of love for our own children but out of a chemical requirement to obey the forces of evolution. A mother who kills her own children to carry the genes of another male demonstrates this as does and the human equivalent of this behavior. Until we fully understand the universe we will never know what purpose if any is served by all that we do on earth. But in the mean time we must make do with the limited knowledge we have; that knowledge indicates that we are thoroughly enslaved and defined by our biology and that popular culture offers us little knowledge with which to improve our biological relationships. We exist, despite our most profound efforts, for the benefit of our genes; not for the benefit of a misguided and hasty popular cultural that seeks to race ahead of a biology that is hopelessly slow but infinitely correct.

As an aside on evolutionary purpose and as a fun way to keep us thinking about the totalitarian nature of evolution and biology it is interesting to speculate about how homosexuality evolved given that homosexuals do not reproduce. The obvious theory is that homosexuality is environmentally created without relation to evolution. This is, seemingly, absurd since everything that exists, exists because it evolved. But how can homosexuality exist when homosexuals don't reproduce? Perhaps, despite being reproductively inferior, homosexuals are superior in other ways. This theory is supported by data which shows that despite all the discrimination faced by modern homosexuals they still have a much higher income than heterosexuals. Perhaps they survived evolutionary history because they used their greater skills to help their families survive. Thus their homosexual genes, which were present to some extent in other members of the family, survived and occasionally were manifested as a homosexual offspring.

In addition to rape, war is a particularly masculine business for which men are often criticized. But how do complex wars which seem to be political in nature serve a biological purpose? World War II and the long cold war that followed were examples of wars that were, it seemed, modern and largely political and yet at heart were actually biological. War serves to settle questions about ideas for which men are willing to die. A man who is willing to die for an idea is more likely to see it prevail than a man who is not. A man who is able to enlist allies in his cause is more likely to succeed than a man who is not. Modern war forces men to select ideas; it speeds up the flow of history for the benefit of those who deeply believe their ideas should dominate. Nazi Germany had virtually no allies because it sought none. It saw almost everyone as its enemy. The USSR had fewer and fewer allies because Soviet ideas never produced higher and higher standards of living.

In the end, wars are won by the average men and women who select allegiances to ideas based on the basic biological value those allegiances hold for themselves and their families. Wars do resolve great ideological disputes and accelerate history forward, but they do these things only to the extent that they help the mass of men fulfil nature's most basic purpose, i.e., to survive and reproduce more easily. It is easy to criticize men for their aggressive natures but who can say that human history would have been better without the horror of war? We must remember that evolution is survival of the fittest, and that we are all here only because our ancestors were fit enough to defeat all the enemies who would have destroyed them. We cannot legitimately criticize the struggle when we are the result of the struggle. Death, cruelly, is evolution's best and fastest teacher and in the end the evolution of ideology is about simple biology.

Women initiate divorce 91% of the time because they often get far less than they want from marriage. If family values are important to us, women must be taught how to get what they want from marriage. They must learn what it is that they want from a marriage and then how to get it. They must learn how to participate and shape their marriages so that the families which they claim to value so much will survive. But to do this they must adopt a sensible approach to the problem based on obvious historical precedents.

If this were to result in a sort of female renaissance it would represent a third evolution of the human family. In the first evolution things were very simple. There was no love. Females like other lower animals came into heat at a certain time and were impregnated by almost any geographically available male who then promptly left in search of the next needy female. Women raised and supported offspring/children largely on their own.

In the second stage, female hips became bony and strong enough to enable upright walking. In evolutionary terms you might say that the first women who had these beneficial bony hips survived long enough to reproduce while those who did not have that advantage died off without successfully reproducing. Along with bony hips came a great problem though. Internal space was severely shrunk to the point where offspring could no longer grow and mature internally. They were then born relatively small and immature and consequently in need of constant and long term maternal care. With the adult female partially incapacitated by this need to care for her helpless offspring she needed help to gather food, hunt meat, and to do other domestic chores.

Males were the likely source of that help, but they had little interest in being around after sexual intercourse because the women would soon be out of season and unable to perform sexually. For men sexual intercourse was a testosterone driven thing just like hunting. The problem for the female was to maintain the male's interest when she was no longer in heat or after her period of estrus had passed. It turned out that females who were able to stay in heat the longest were able to keep the helpful males around the longest and thus they and the genes for that behavior survived and were passed on more often than those of women who did not have the same sexual longevity. But women still had to teach men that testosterone driven sex and hunting (violence) were really two very different things, or at least things that she wanted to be different.

The human female eventually became virtually the only female product of evolution with the ability to stay in season and in control constantly. This explains, many believe, the origin of the human family. Another similar but far more dreary theory holds that women entered into a sexual contract with men to avoid constant rape. We may never know the precise or all the precise stimuli that led to the evolution of the human family as we know it today, but we are certain that there was a gradual transition to monogamy that both sexes favored.

In the third phase of the human family land was acquired primarily for the purpose of farming when hunting and gathering could no longer support the human population. This marked a significant demarcation in family structure. Men became even more highly prized because they were far better qualified to work the land than women. Gathering, which previously had given women a large degree of self-sufficiency, was less and less possible as human populations grew. Naturally growing food supplies had to be divided among larger and larger populations. As a large group could no longer be sustained in one area they would wander off in small groups to find more plentiful food supplies. Social groups became far smaller, more isolated, and more familial as each group become more and more acquisitive toward the piece of land on which it gathered, cultivated, and then farmed. A woman had to have a man to clear and work the land. If she failed to attract a man or left a man, her future would be very uncertain at best. If she left her man and took the children their future would be even more uncertain.

Frederick Engels, the famous philosopher who, along with Karl Marx, founded communism, seized upon this private property inequity between men and women as a partial justification for the centralized power of communism. He reasoned that in a communist state this unnatural inequity could be redressed by the state so that both sexes could contribute with equal enthusiasm to the creation of a communist utopia. He was a true economic determinist. Like modern day feminists, he sought to ignore the biological basis for behavior to achieve political ends. From Asia to Eastern Europe and from the Israeli Kibbutz to Central America, communists sought and grandly failed to legislate the equality that biology temporarily forbade. Interestingly for many years after World War II the

USSR made a big point of all the women in important jobs (particularly medicine) that their system had produced. It turned out that these women were only there because of the shortage of men caused by the loss of 25 million of them in World War ll. As time went on the war generation was replaced by a new generation that did not put women in such high positions at a rate any greater than capitalistic countries. Ideology never did replace biology.

As time passed male power in the family was further enhanced as men became aware that the children were genetically theirs as much as their mates. The genetic connection between a man and his children was not obvious during most of evolutionary history. Men simply copulated and departed. The tremendous power of male semen was unknown. It seemed to be no more significant than female vaginal secretions. Sexual intercourse did not transmit genetic material, or so it seemed. In some societies sexual intercourse was seen as a way to open the female up in preparation for child bearing and birth or even to nourish the developing fetus. Any resemblance between father and offspring merely showed that the father was involved but not that the child was genetically half his. This is why human society was originally matrilineal. It traced family lines through the female because she was the significant, if not the only biological parent.

In the fourth stage, which we are now in, the female is again no longer wholly dependant on the male. With greater law and order, rising standards of living, over population concerns, and govt. welfare, males have created a world in which it is again possible for females to raise children without much male participation. This new female freedom comes with a terrible choice though. On the one hand, forth stage feminist / psychological culture tells women that they shouldn't necessarily need a man to be happy; that they have been victims and that they now should concentrate on their own happiness and personal power. Biology, though, has created them with feelings from conflicting periods in their evolutionary history. During one period they needed and loved men for survival and during another they could make do without him. Generally they have emerged favorably disposed toward men although their relationships with men have suffered terribly under the destructive influence of the current feminist / psychological culture. Those women who are married and those who wish to be married must understand the conflicting demands that popular culture and biology make in order to become mature and responsible marital partners. Divorce will continue to be a major problem until this happens.

11.) A DEFINITION OF LOVE AND MARRIAGE

WHY IS CINDY CRAWFORD SO BEAUTIFUL?

At first, love may just seem to appear when in fact both parties worked all their lives to be worthy of the other's love. Neither party thinks much about falling in love; they are more enveloped by it, or so it seems. If you ask people why they fell in love with a particular person, words and logic will mostly fail them. A woman will often say, "he's so sweet and kind; only grudgingly and with embarrassment will she mention money, accomplishments, or appearance. Generally they tell lies because they don't actually know why they fell in love or because they are too embarrassed to mention that they fell in love with his hair, broad shoulders, handsome face, or sexy body when they really know that he is only average in these areas. In reality they fell in love because they found someone who seemingly had achieved the same or a higher evolutionary height. This is why a Harvard boy falls in love with a Harvard girl and why a Harlem boy falls in love with a Harlem girl. We seek out someone who is similar enough so that we are comfortable but superior enough that we feel enhanced.

However, there is more to it. A Harvard girl won't fall in love with just any Harvard boy. Something else is in operation that allows us to focus a generalized and powerful interest in love down to only one person. Sometimes it is a chance occurrence during which important feelings are quickly shared. One person will present a feeling and the other will successfully project an understanding or sympathy for that feeling which then becomes the seed from which love grows. And/or, some suspect that during childhood a sort of imprinting goes on during which a part of the brain is programmed for love by certain qualities, mannerisms or characteristics seen in the people around them, most often parents and siblings. The importance of siblings has been often overlooked by most professionals even though it is with siblings that our first peer to peer relationships develop. When, after puberty, children again see those certain qualities, with their then hormone drenched eyes, in potential mates, the brain reacts by secreting love chemicals. In more common parlance, they acquire experience or baggage during childhood that determines how they we react to the opposite sex during and after puberty.

Still though, some women are partially susceptible to persistent male courting in allegiance to the genes which millions of years age propelled her to passively mate with the male who survived (persisted) to be there when she was in heat. Today we teach that "no" means "no" because persistence doesn't always persuade a modern female. Al Pacino and Michelle Pfeiffer glorify this kind of "no" means "yes' love in their recent movie: Frankie and Johnny. The genetic theory apparently holds that the more persistent a man is the more he has survived as a warrior and that perhaps he will be as persistent, loyal, and successful as a husband and father.

Most men are a little more honest about why they love since there is no way to avoid knowing what they really love about the woman they marry. Their wives simply appear to be sexually beautiful and attractive to them or at least more sexually beautiful and attractive than anyone else who is available to them. I once overhead a single man tell a woman that he was longing for a beautiful woman to marry. The woman he was talking to objected on the ground that he was being shallow and should want a woman who was sweet and caring, etc., etc. The man then objected by saying, "I have seen hundreds of women interact with their children and, as a result, I assume they are all basically sweet and caring." While this man's assumption was generally quite true it failed to recognize that he really wanted a woman who was not only beautiful but, secondarily, someone who was somewhat equal (for comfort) and somewhat superior (for evolutionary growth).

Men's varying perceptions of beauty relate to, at least a little, more than mere physical beauty. To be bullied into believing that sweetness and kindness are the triggers for male love, probably wouldn't be a wise step toward a happy marriage since it would not be biologicially reasonable and it would make almost any woman fully qualified. Women like the kindness and sweetness standard because it allows all of them to be qualified without the competitive element that a beauty hierarchy would engender.

There must be a biological reason to explain why some women appear to be more beautiful than others. After all, it seems to be at the very least something of a basic genetic response. Tests show that even very young children respond to pretty women. In one study a little boy put the best face on his emotional quest for beauty by saying of prospective kindergarten teachers, when asked to choose between a pretty one and a not so pretty one: "if she's pretty you know she's smart." Similarly, Princess Diana's death stopped the world in a very unprecedented way; not because she was royalty; not because she did a little charity work from a Lear jet, not because her personal life was a well accepted tabloid joke, but rather because of her exceptional beauty with which the tabloids had made us so familiar. When her extraordinary beauty was gone we all felt its' loss. Her beauty produced a halo that covered her whole life. It tricked us into believing that all of her life and activities were important to us.

We are too proud to acknowledge this beauty lust; and so we struggled vainly to find loftier explanations for our singular interest in, for example, Diana's death. This struggle arises because we are taught that biological beauty is trivial or skin deep. We are taught this in part because we don't understand beauty and in part because it is soothing to the vast majority of us who are not beautiful, but beauty is always very close to our hearts and to our motivations whether we want it there or not.

To be sure, imprinting, shared emotions, values, activities, and general quality are important to men but beauty is a separate standard which is more central and more essential to them. The question then becomes: Why are women like Cindy Crawford and Princess Diana so beautiful? Male love is in large part genital. We see this when we see that whole societies can love young boys, that masturbation can be central to a single male's energy flow, or that farm animals can be substituted for women, all in harmony with the genital nature of male love. But, it was important for biology to keep men's primary focus on women so they would mate and procreate with women despite the large genital component in their love. Cindy Crawford has emerged as perhaps the most popular or ideal symbol of what a woman is. Without having a "ideal" there is no easy standard to which everyone can aspire; young boys, masturbation, and farm animals could become potential candidates without an obvious and genetic beauty standard. The singular and common desire to mate with the best provides a standard toward which all men can aspire. The more beauty she has relative to the men who pursue her the more attractive she appears to them. This is what Henry James was referring to when he said that difference is the basis for all intimacy. The closer to Cindy Crawford a thing or woman is the more suitable a mate it is, according to biology. Of course, our modern and complex culture provides some variation in the beauty standard but the standard doesn't stray far from Ms. Crawford. If a man prefers a scientist or a mother to a runway model he would not necessarily be taking unfair advantage of the system which inherently recognizes that not everyone can marry Cindy Crawford, and that a variety of standards are necessary in a broad, diverse culture like ours.

On the negative side, because Cindy Crawford is seen through the media by virtually every man in the world, she probably encourages men to believe that the availability of such women is far grater than it really is. During the period when humankind evolved people lived in relatively tiny groups without the media and the possibility of anointing one woman as the prettiest in all the world. In a small village 10,000 years ago no single woman would have been considered far above the others in beauty. And, perhaps men, seeing the total universe of possibilities right outside their door each day, quickly developed realistic expectations about whom they should court and what standard of beauty they should aspire too.

The mechanisms of evolution insure that men and women must always be nothing more than reflections of one another. We are merely the reflection of the person we mate with. The best man who mates with the best woman says to other men, in effect, "if you want to mate with Cindy Crawford you have to try very hard to look and be like me and to accomplish the things I have accomplished which encouraged Cindy Crawford to select me as her mate."

The standard of beauty also creates the standard of behavior in men. If a man isn't in the same league with Cindy Crawford he isn't allowed to give up, he just plays the same game in a different or minor league. Sadly, women have to cope with not looking like Cindy Crawford and men have to cope with not being able to attract her. It is the nature of the process. Women are constantly evaluating men, and men are constantly jockeying for a improved position from which to impress women. Beauty then emerges at the heart of human sexuality as the single most powerful biological force in nature, despite our protestations.

But how did Cindy Crawford get to be the standard of beauty? In part because she is a woman. Men are more sensitive to physical beauty than women; probably because a woman is beautiful (fertile) for a shorter time. A man must know beauty in order to pick out fertile women. This is why a young woman is more beautiful than an old one. Cindy Crawford is beautiful in part because someone had to get the job. Without a standard we have no direction, and sex, of all things, needs direction. Sure, there is beauty in her height (good for hunting and gathering), slimness (implies physical fitness), muscles (hunting and gathering), broad hips (good for delivering babies), big breasts (maternal symbols and aphrodisiacs which took the place of buttocks when women began to walk upright with their chests forward and exposed), and tanned, smooth, consistent skin (implies strength and health from outdoor sunlit activity rather than weakness from being too sickly to leave the shade).

But mostly Cindy Crawford has facial beauty. Much of this beauty comes from symmetry (one side matches the other; one eye matches the other), proportionality (nose to jaw etc.), and smoothness (jaw, nose, skin without harsh or irregular angles). These things are beautiful to us because they imply harmony with an ordered universe. As we are biological creatures our biology is a creature of nature. The sun, the moon, and the stars all have beautiful, powerful, and symmetric features, like Cindy Crawford's. At one time there seemed to be Gods that arbitrarily granted us life and death depending on how much harmony with them we could feel and create. A healthy tree, a strong river, and a steady mountain range all have features that we worshipped into our biology; as these features grow old and die the symmetry, proportionality and smoothness of them die too. A swamp, jungle and wind swept desert don't have these beautiful features and we don't often picture beautiful people in them.

But in the end, even powerful modern computers, which can make thousands of measurements over a woman's face, can't create a new face judged to be prettier than Cindy Crawford's. This is because beauty is also somewhat arbitrary, and also active and controlling. A runway model acts beautiful as much as she looks beautiful. She walks the ultimate walk to give life to her perfect beauty. Without the implication that she would be sexually active and controlling her beauty would have little value. Beauty acquires value only when it becomes sexually actionable.

Beauty exists in nature as a beacon like the north star. It is somewhat

11.) A DEFINITION OF LOVE AND MARRIAGE

arbitrary, it changes its look and even its location over the centuries, but we use it because without it we have no direction. One star is the brightest in the heaven and one woman is the most beautiful on earth. Someone has to emerge to fulfil this need because we need a standard to know our sexual direction, and, indeed, our direction in the universe.

Part of the problem in understanding love publicly is that it is essentially a private matter. A woman can say, "I love my husband because he is so sweet and kind, "but she can't say," I love him because he is filthy rich and successful, why do you love yours?" Most social intercourse sets up the same dilemma. Rita Wilson, for example, recently joked about her husband Tom Hanks by saying, "on Oscar night he so humbly thanks the members of the Academy, but at home he runs around naked with an Oscar in each hand shouting, "I'm king of the Oscars." Public intercourse serves public purposes but often serves to confuse private intercourse. A woman can't talk intelligently and privately to her husband about sex because she learned to speak in public and in public terms, but in this case what seems so particular and private is really very common to most humans.

The thought that a modern marriage could be sustained by the woman's beauty and a man's sweetness and kindness is not realistic. These things may not interfere with getting a couple into bed (nature's pre-eminent concern) but they do not insure a couple's ability to sustain a long term marriage. A couple whose sustenance depends on these illusory qualities is destined to flounder under the weight of what are, ultimately, half-truths. When a man claims to love a woman because of her beauty he is really pretending to himself that she is beautiful when the probability is that she is average. Even if she does have beauty, beauty fades by morning or, if not, by several mornings or years. A wife is common but beauty cannot be. Soon enough this will become obvious to someone who has married a beautiful woman. When a woman claims to love a man because he is especially sweet and kind she too is pretending that he is above average when he is really average too. We all do this because we all need the illusion that there is something special about the one we love. Without illusion we would be left to love ordinary people and wouldn't we seem like fools to invest so heavily in something so ordinary? Love is everyone's best chance to rise, if only in spirit, above the ordinary.

THE WILL TO LOVE OR THE FEELING OF LOVE

In the end, though, our public dialogue harms our private lives. Beauty can fade, a man's taste can change, and a woman's perception of her man's kindness can change as he has affairs with his job, hobbies, friends, kids, or another woman. A marriage can never stay what it was the first day or the first year. And even if both parties did maintain their original view of one another there is nothing to stop them from eventually getting bored with that view and each other, and then moving on to a newer, fresher romantic illusion. If a marriage doesn't endure naturally a couple must have the will for love to survive and a realistic and meaningful basis on which to sustain that will.

Will comes from broad principles that define a family in general rather than specific sexual terms. Accepting the concept of sexual balance between a husband and wife goes a long way for most couples. It leaves both parties free to say, "this is what I want" when they engage in the most unique and intimate activity of their marriage, and in the more trivial aspects of their relationship too. When someone can say "this is what I want" and they know how to get it, it becomes geometrically harder to say I've fallen out of love because:............ But, nevertheless a significant percentage will require a more conceptual basis on which to sustain a long term marriage.

An adventurous person, for example, might effectively strike up a sexual bargain within a marriage, but then decide that he/she would like to feel the more intense pleasure of a new love. If the kids are raised or there never were any; what's the problem here? Let's recall that two sexes were created for the purpose of reproduction. Once reproduction has taken place a family is necessary to finish the process. Children, after all, need to be raised. Nothing is apt to be more satisfying or rewarding for a couple than working together to accomplish this. While biology is apt to be relatively silent about a man who abandons his family (as opposed to biology's very loud noise about the importance of having sex), no culture is apt to bestow esteem on a man who is a poor father or one who elects to abandon his paternal responsibilities altogether. A man who prefers to whore around or go fishing instead of raising his children is not apt to find many rewards either internal or external for his choices. A woman who is a good mother is universally respected both biologically and culturally because we implicitly understand how necessary a function motherhood is. A couple and a culture that accepts these realities has the most complete basis possible on which to build a long term marital/sexual relationship.

But, in the case of women, the will to love is, to a large degree, genetically induced; in the case of men, will must often be culturally induced because it did not evolve directly. In this situation culture leads and compliments biology until biology has time to catch up. Women are the obvious primary purveyors of the cultural inducement men need.

If a balanced and harmonious sex life does not naturally extend itself over the decades of a changing life a couple must rely on their will or volition to provide the incentive or rationale for marriage. If they see a larger value and purpose in maintaining a harmonious marriage they can achieve long term love with the least difficulty, or the most joy possible. This behavior is not purely sexual. Sex is important to men, sure, and the kindness women expect in return is important to them too but what is to stop either party from eventually getting bored; from wondering if it might somehow might be better, fresher and reinvigorating with a new person. What is to stop them from thinking as the great anthropologist Margaret Mead did that it is ok to view each marriage in a string of marriages as successful while they lasted? Sex and illusion are helpful to marriage but in the end they do not provide a broad enough context to satisfy most people. Sex does not completely address the issue of from where the will for long term marital happiness comes.

The concept of love and will is clarified when we compare our relationship to our spouse with our relationship to our children. We can divorce our spouse and often do but we can't divorce our children. In one sense this appears unusual since, theoretically, we should be more happy with our spouses than our children. Not only do we get to pick the sex of our spouse but we get to pick everything else right down to hair color if we choose. With kids we get no choice and as a result we get a very wide variety. But judging from the high rate of divorce, we seem to love our children far more than our spouses. This happens mostly because we have the will to love our children. We love them unequivocally and without ambivalence because biology and culture have defined this as our highest responsibility, and concomitantly, as our greatest source of happiness. This gives us the will to have flexible expectations; to make whatever adjustments and accommodations to our perceptions are necessary in order to keep loving our children without the need to judge them harshly or in a

11.) A DEFINITION OF LOVE AND MARRIAGE

way that kills our love.

In our current environment where the divorce rate is 50% and where marital "will" has so little value, a modern mother is more likely to love a son in jail than a husband who watches too much football. Shouldn't it be easier to induce compliance out of a husband with the promise of sex tonight than to induce hours of homework out of a child with the promise of a good job in 10 years? We have divorce to the extent that we lack the will to define it as something of which we will not approve. We legalized abortion and we caused millions of new abortions that otherwise would not have been needed. We legalized divorce and we caused millions of them too. Feminism and psychology pushed in this direction. And so did Hugh Hefner's sexual revolution and the pornography industry that burgeoned in his wake. The Homo-sexual movement with its emphasis on male ephemeral love helped as did the birth control industry. The excessive spread of democracy indirectly encouraged an egalitarian androgyny that made us incompetent at sex with the opposite sex. In the end the divorce revolution was just a clash of two cultures. There was the humanitarian wisdom of the 2000 year old "till death do you part" culture that created civilization versus the narrow political and economic wisdom of the "till divorce do you part culture" which has contributed nothing to civilized values and certainly even less to our children.